# THE CONSENSUAL DEMOCRACIES?

# The Consensual Democracies?

The Government and Politics of the Scandinavian States

Neil Elder
Alastair H. Thomas
David Arter

Martin Robertson · Oxford

© Neil Elder, Alastair H. Thomas and David Arter, 1982

First published in 1982 by Martin Robertson & Company Ltd.,
108 Cowley Road, Oxford OX4 1JF.

Reprinted 1983

All rights reserved. No part of this publication
may be reproduced, stored in a retrieval system,
or transmitted, in any form or by any means,
electronic, mechanical, photocopying, recording
or otherwise, without the prior written permission
of the copyright holders.

**British Library Cataloguing in Publication Data**

Elder, Neil
   The consensual democracies?: the
   government and politics of the Scandinavian
   states
   1. Scandinavia – Politics and government
   I. Title   II. Thomas, Alastair H.
   320'.948   JN7011
   ISBN 0-85520-423-0

Typeset by Cambrian Typesetters
in 10 on 12pt Press Roman

Printed and bound in Great Britain at
The Camelot Press Ltd, Southampton

# Contents

| | |
|---|---|
| *List of Tables* | vii |
| *Map of the Scandinavian states and the North Atlantic* | ix |
| *Preface* | xi |
| Introduction: Scandinavia as a Region | 1 |
| **1 The Scandinavian States: the Consensual Democracies?** | 9 |
| Defining the three dimensions of consensual democracy | 10 |
| Regulating the resolution of political conflict | 11 |
| The nature of political conflict | 16 |
| The obviation of conflict | 25 |
| **2 The Structuring of Mass Politics, 1870–1945** | 29 |
| The Scandinavian parties and party systems in developmental perspective | 29 |
| The initial era of two-party politics: 1870–1900 | 34 |
| The rise of mass-based parties, 1900–21: the Social Democrats and the Agrarians | 35 |
| The completion of the five-party Scandinavian model: 1920–30 | 43 |
| The 1930s: the Scandinavian party systems and the challenge of economic recession | 51 |

## vi Contents

3 *Social Cleavages and Partisan Conflict after the Second World War*    58

    Structural alterations to the five-party system prior to 1970    58
    The Scandinavian party systems in the 1970s: declining consensus?    85

4 *Political Structures in Scandinavia*    100

    Constitutions    100
    Executives    105
    Unicameralism in Scandinavia    119
    Parliaments: plenary sessions    122
    Parliamentary committees    130
    Administrative control    138
    Electoral systems    143
    Political recruitment    151

5 *Consensualism and Policy-Making in Scandinavia*    159
    Denmark    161
    Finland    166
    Iceland    172
    Norway and Sweden    180

6 *Regional Co-operation and International Roles*    192

    Regional co-operation in social and economic policy    195
    Scandinavia as an international actor    206

Epilogue: Some Trends and Prospects    215

*Select Bibliography*    220

*Index*    232

# List of Tables

0.1 Population size and density of the Scandinavian countries   1

2.1 The five-party Scandinavian model in the late 1960s   31

2.2 The percentage of the labour force employed in the non-primary sectors, 1890–1920   36

2.3 Levels of urbanization in the Scandinavian states, 1800–1920   38

2.4 The percentage of the population engaged in agriculture and allied occupations, 1890–1910   39

3.1 The occupational structure of support for the four largest Finnish parties in 1975   60

3.2 Regional variation in support for the four largest Finnish parties at the general election of 1975   61

3.3 The decline in the population engaged in farming, fishing and forestry in three Scandinavian states, 1950–70   69

3.4 The occupational structure of the Swedish Centre Party vote in 1968   75

3.5 The political cohesion of the working-class electorate in four Scandinavian states in the mid-1960s   77

3.6 The size of the economically active population engaged in mining, manufacturing and electricity in Scandinavia, 1960–70   78

3.7 The percentage of the economically active population in service industries in Scandinavia, 1960–70   78

viii  *List of Tables*

| | | |
|---|---|---|
| 3.8 | The fall in the Social Democratic vote in Denmark, Norway and Sweden in the first half of the 1970s | 80 |
| 3.9 | Election results in Scandinavia since 1969 | 86–8 |
| 4.1 | Public expenditure as percentage of GNP, selected countries, 1950–76 | 109 |
| 4.2 | Cabinet composition in the Nordic countries, 1980, in order of precedence | 111 |
| 4.3 | Selected statistics for levels of activity in the Scandinavian Parliaments | 124 |
| 4.4 | Standing committees in the Scandinavian Parliaments | 132–3 |
| 4.5 | Denmark: occupational composition of the *Folketing* by party, 1968 and 1977 | 153 |
| 4.6 | Norway: occupational composition of the *Storting* by party, 1969 and 1977 | 154 |
| 4.7 | Sweden: class composition of Second Chamber representatives, 1968–9, by own occupation and parents' occupation | 155 |
| 4.8 | Sweden: class composition of Second Chamber representatives, 1968–9, by party | 157 |
| 5.1 | Average number of working days lost through industrial disputes, selected countries, 1969–78 | 162 |
| 5.2 | Nordic governments 1945–82: Prime Ministers and party composition | 174–7 |
| 6.1 | Regional co-operation and active neutrality: a chronology of post-war events | 196–7 |

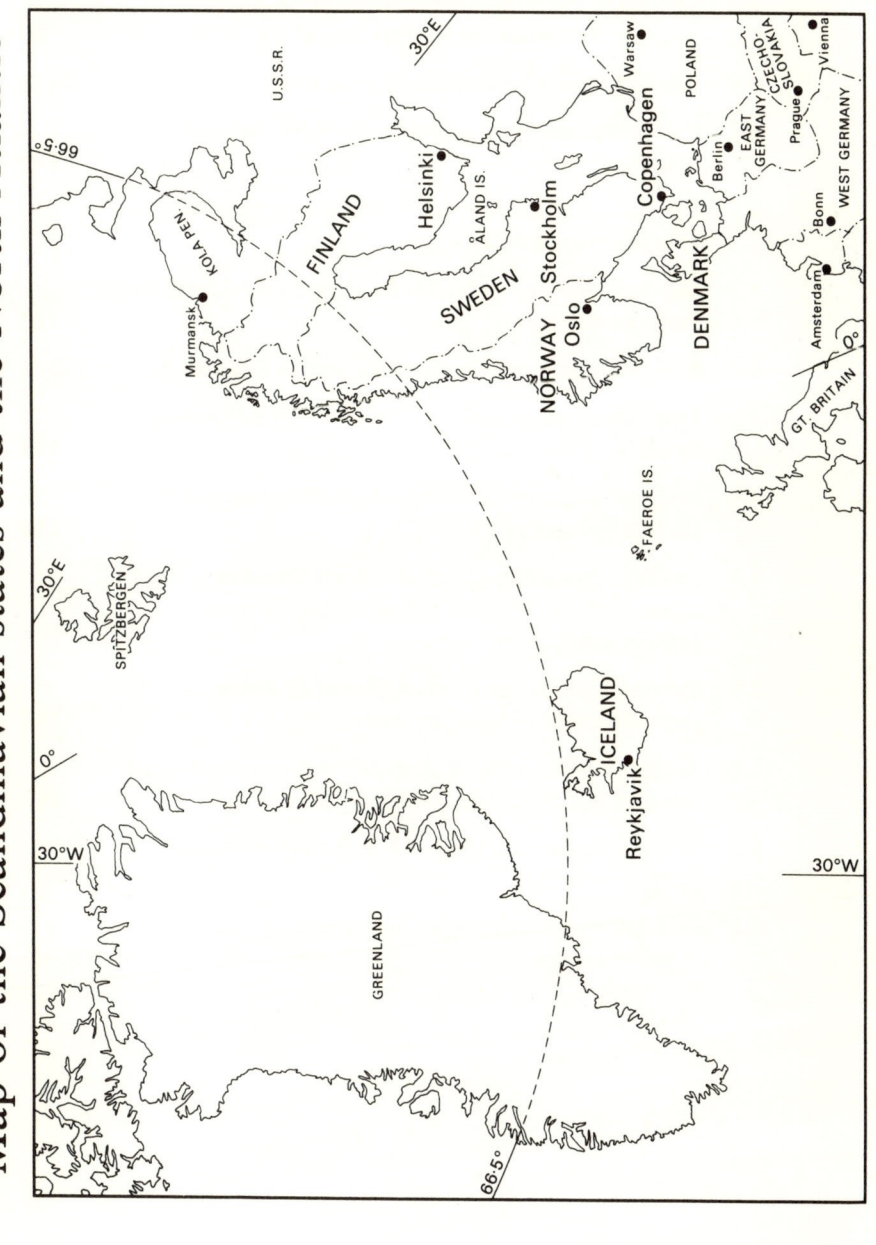

Map of the Scandinavian states and the North Atlantic

# Preface

This book stems from Neil Elder's comment at the Political Studies Association's conference at Liverpool University in 1977 that his students lacked a modern and serviceable study of Scandinavian politics in English. The idea was taken up in conversation by Alastair Thomas, and it is hoped that the present volume goes some way towards remedying the deficiency. David Arter agreed subsequently to join in, and so the project was launched. From the outset we would also like to acknowledge a special debt of gratitude to Mr Rolf Gooderham, a specialist writer on Norwegian economic and political affairs.

Neil Elder is grateful to Ove Svensson, formerly Cultural Attaché at the Swedish Embassy in London, for arranging a visit to carry out interviews in Stockholm, and to the Swedish Institute for subsequent help with the details. In consequence his thanks go to the following: Professor Olof Ruin, University of Stockholm; Professor Assar Lindbeck, Director of the Institute of International Economics, University of Stockholm; Dr Daniel Tarschys, Cabinet Secretary, 1978–9; Professor Birger Hagård, University of Linköping; Professor Nils Elvander, Olof Petersson and docent Evert Vedung, all of the Department of Government, University of Uppsala; Per Lindhagen of the Social Democratic Party's research bureau; Riksdagman Per Unckel; Bertil Lund, Director for International Affairs, Ministry of Foreign Affairs, Stockholm; Jan Bröms, Head of Economic Policy Department, Federation of Swedish Industries; Dr Dietrich Timm, Federation of Swedish Industries. Thanks are also due to Professor Bo Särlvik of the University of Essex for help with Swedish material and to Mr Martin Kaan for help with Icelandic material. Thanks go also to Mrs Anne Martin of Melrose, and to Mr and Mrs Eddie Hunter, of Newton St Boswells, for use of the bothy.

David Arter wishes to express his gratitude to Professor Tatu Vanhanen, Esko Almgren, MP, and the 'koti-lauma'.

Alastair Thomas gratefully acknowledges the inspiration of the late Fru Lisbeth Krøyer of Nakskov, Denmark.

Ms Catherine Jackson typed the manuscript with patience and accuracy, and Mrs Avril Griffiths of Preston Polytechnic drew the map of Scandinavia. Mrs Evelyn Whyte took on the tedious task of typing the index, and did so with great accuracy. Last, but far from least, a good deal of the enjoyment during the working out of the project derived from the hospitality provided by our wives, Eeva-Kaisa Arter, Enid Elder and Janet Thomas.

The book developed through many lengthy and stimulating discussions between the authors, and the responsibility for its merits and defects is solely theirs.

Neil Elder
Alastair H. Thomas
David Arter
1981

# INTRODUCTION

## Scandinavia as a Region

The five states of Denmark, Finland, Iceland, Norway and Sweden can be characterized as a family of nations at the north-western corner of Europe. Together with their home-rule territories — Greenland and the Faeroes, belonging to Denmark, and the Åland Islands, belonging to Finland — they occupy between them a space stretching from the borders of the Soviet Union, in the cases of Finland and Norway, across the north Atlantic, to within close range of the north Atlantic mainland. In terms of demographic strength, if not always of size of territory, they belong to the category of the smaller democracies. Geographically they are diverse, as table 0.1 reflects. Thus Iceland, the outlier, has large expanses of desert terrain, uncultivable but scenically magnificent; Denmark is an extension of the continental European plains, closer to Holland than to her northern neighbours in degree of population

TABLE 0.1: POPULATION SIZE AND DENSITY OF THE SCANDINAVIAN COUNTRIES

|         | *Population, 1979–80 (million)* | *Density per sq. km* |
|---------|---------------------------------|----------------------|
| Denmark | 5.1                             | 118                  |
| Finland | 4.77                            | 14                   |
| Iceland | 0.23                            | 2                    |
| Norway  | 4.08                            | 12                   |
| Sweden  | 8.30                            | 19                   |

*Note*: UK density figure, 229; USA, 23
*Source: Yearbook of Nordic Statistics 1980* (1981), chart 1, pp.22–4 and table, p.38.

concentration; Norway, Sweden and Finland have common regional problems in their Arctic zones and the main centres of settlement in their central and southern areas.

All five states are bound together by a strong sense of regional affinity, which finds its chief institutional expression in the Nordic Council, an agency founded in 1952 partly to co-ordinate the work of existing sectoral specialist bodies and partly to stimulate fresh cooperative initiatives by acting as a pressure group on governments. The terms 'Nordic' and 'Scandinavian', it may be mentioned in passing, are interchangeable for all practical purposes: it would be as pedantic to limit the latter to the geographical core-area concept (Denmark, Norway, Sweden) as to interpret the former in a strict anthropological sense as referring to the tall, blond, dolicephalic race whose representatives are in a clear minority in the region anyway.

The fact that such a politically low-key agency as the Nordic Council was approved by the Norwegian Parliament (*Storting*) only on a vote of 74 to 39 bears witness to the tensions and touchiness that, as in a family, surface from time to time within the group. Fears about possible Swedish predominance help to explain this particular instance, as also they explain past reluctance to pool economic resources. If the Nordic region could be isolated from the rest of Europe by a 'magic circle', as one commentator has put it, 'Sweden would undoubtedly form a natural core.' But then, 'As a core, Sweden is too small, its leadership attraction too weak' (Ørvik, 1967, p.57). Nevertheless, the sense of regional affinity is in some respects stronger among the Scandinavian states than among the Benelux countries, which furnish the closest European parallel. Even in January 1943, when wartime circumstances had driven them unusually far apart and when Iceland was on the verge of a declaration of full independence from Denmark, Churchill considered a 'Scandinavian Bloc' an obvious candidate for membership of the post-war United Nations organization as one of a number of confederations of smaller states alongside the Great Powers (Churchill, 1951, p.656).

Historically the region has been at times sharply divided by conflict, not least between the two metropolitan powers of Denmark and Sweden. But historical interrelationships, cultural similarities and cultural diffusion have between them produced a strong regional consciousness, tending ultimately towards the maintenance of national identities within a stable but unconstricting framework of regional co-operation, chiefly at the micro-level. The Viking age will be ignored for present purposes, despite the occasional political science hypothesis and the tributes paid to it, in more or less romantic vein, at Scandinavian dinners. Its relevance to the contemporary political scene appears roughly analogous to that of the Witanagemot and Anglo-Saxon judicial and administrative practice to contemporary British politics. The Kalmar Union (1397–c.1523) is invoked at times as a period when the whole of the region was one political unit under a common (Danish) monarchy. But it was formed for purposes of interest solely to the medieval historian, and its chief abiding significance, apart from its symbolism for advocates of Scandinavian unity, is probably that by paving the way for the perpetuation of Danish rule, it helped to imprint a strong Danish cultural influence on Norway, particularly in respect of the language.

Danish rule over Norway ended in 1814, as a result of Denmark's alignment with the Napoleonic side in the wars of that epoch. In the few months' interregnum before Norway was forced into union with Sweden as a consequence of the same larger conflict, she managed to enact her own constitution. This document remained essentially intact under the terms of the union, so that the Norwegians were able to enjoy a large degree of autonomy in domestic matters. It is still in force, amended more in spirit than in letter. More will be said of it later, but meanwhile the point is worth making that it gave scope for nationalist sentiments effectively to sharpen the struggle for parliamentary government in Norway (1880–4), so that the Norwegians, despite the union, were the first in Scandinavia to achieve a modernized parliamentary system with a government responsible to the legislature rather than to the monarch. Had they continued under Danish rule, it seems unlikely that this would have been the case – partly because of the greater identity of outlook between Norwegian and Danish elites, partly because of the course of Danish political history in the latter half of the nineteenth century. In the event, Norway did not win full independence from Sweden until 1905. She thus moved formally to equal status within the Scandinavian group but, as mentioned earlier, came to feel unease at the greater economic power of her neighbour. This contributed more than anything else to the prolongation of the negotiations on a proposed Nordic Common Market in the 1950s until they ceased to be relevant because of the creation of the European Free Trade Area (EFTA) in 1959–60. However, marked economic growth in the 1960s and the exploitation of North Sea oil from the 1970s – when recession hit the rest of the domestic economy – have powerfully consolidated her position within the group.

Finland was ruled by Sweden for some six centuries before falling under Russian jurisdiction in 1809 as a result of the Swedish king's suffering defeat in a war against the tsar — the last war, in fact, in which the Swedes were engaged. Swedish continued to be the language of the governing and educated classes throughout the nineteenth century, and Finnish political institutions retained a Swedish cast throughout this period. In the latter half of the nineteenth century the nationalist revival involved the rapid growth of competition for Swedish as the official language from the totally unrelated Finnish tongue, and national consciousness was intensified by the policies of repression adopted by the tsar in the years before the Revolution of 1905. So here, as in Norway, nationalism reinforced the drive towards the modernization and liberalization of the political system. In the Finnish case that movement bore its first fruits with the radical constitutional reform of 1906, which set up a unicameral legislature and granted equal voting rights to women and men. Had the country remained under Swedish rule, it seems unlikely that political progress would have been as rapid. Here there would have been a similarity of outlook between the Swedish-speaking Finnish elite and the governing power, and the course of political advance in the metropolitan state was not as speedy. When the Finns seized full independence in December 1917, as a consequence of the Bolshevik Revolution, they evolved an eclectic but distinctive constitution in which it seemed natural to retain many elements, especially in the judicial and administrative sectors, deriving from the long Swedish connection. Historical factors have also left Finland with a politically significant, if steadily dwindling, Swedish-speaking minority, settled mainly in the west and south-west of the country and on the Åland Islands (which are entirely Swedish-speaking). This minority has its own representation in the Finnish Parliament in the shape of the Swedish People's Party (and Åland Union), the only sizable party in Scandinavia with an ethnic basis: it polled 4.3 per cent of the vote in the 1979 elections and obtained ten seats out of 200. The position of the Swedish minority is safeguarded by the provision of equal rights for the Swedish language at the official level.

Iceland was the third of the Scandinavian nations to experience a politically dependent status for many centuries. She obtained domestic autonomy from Denmark as a result of the Act of Union of 1918 but did not acquire full independence until 1944. This last was by unilateral declaration, but amounted to the exercise of an option open to her after 1940 under the terms of the 1918 Act. Her constitution, like that of Finland, can be described as an original amalgam, in this case with strong Norwegian influences (e.g. the type of legislature) and Danish influences (e.g. the electoral system). Her small population, with its high degree of concentration in the Reykjavik area (53 per cent of the total in 1978–9), has helped to develop to an extreme degree the mutual interaction and acquaintance of her political elites — for a long time, indeed, to the point of a concentration of many roles in few hands (Grimsson, 1976). With independence and equality of status within the region, the Icelanders have come to place a high value on Scandinavian co-operation. It both provides compensation for geographical isolation and helps buttress Iceland's modest national resources. Thus in the Cod Wars over fishing rights in the surrounding waters it seemed natural for Iceland to seek diplomatic support from Norway and, more generally, through the agency of the Nordic Council. Again, Iceland has not the material or human basis for development into an advanced industrial society, but she has turned to her Scandinavian neighbours for aid in capitalizing modest projects for economic diversification. Linguistically she belongs, unlike Finland, to the Scandinavian group. But though the man in the street in Denmark, Norway and Sweden can usually understand the gist of what is written and, if not always as readily, spoken in the other two languages, Icelandic is a different proposition: to the average Swede, for example, German would be roughly as intelligible. Icelandic, it may be added, is the language of the region closest to the Old Norse of the Sagas, and a strong continuing literary tradition is a major component of the country's national pride.

The fading of the distinction between the metropolitan and peripheral nations has been the precondition for the growth of a strong sense of regional affinity. The Scandinavianist movement which had its origins in Denmark in the 1840s, when Orla Lehmann evoked the potential strength of a revived Kalmar Union against Prussian power and the mistrusted motives of Russia, was too closely connected with a forlorn Danish political interest to have much practical effect. The loss by Denmark of a third of her territory and population in consequence of the (second) Prussian war of 1864 dealt her a severe blow as a serious political force. Nevertheless, attachment to a Scandinavianist ideal lingered on in university circles and among trade unionists and educationalists generally — in this last instance greatly fostered by the spread northwards of the Danish Folk High Schools founded by Bishop Grundtvig in the 1840s — until focused more sharply by the voluntary

Norden Associations which began to come into existence (again spreading outwards from Denmark) shortly after the end of the First World War. The successive achievement of independence this century by Norway, Finland and Iceland has enabled the ideal — or, indeed, the ideology — of Scandinavian co-operation to spread more widely among both masses and political elites.

In the key integrative sector of defence and security policy, however, the Scandinavian states are much further apart than are the Benelux countries. This aspect of the region will be looked at in more detail later, but meantime a few general points should be made. Norway, facing westward and with a strong mercantile marine, has an Atlanticist orientation; Finland is bound to pay particular regard to the requirements of Soviet security policy in the region; Denmark has particularly close economic ties both with Britain and with the German Federal Republic; Sweden follows steadily her traditional policy of freedom from alliances in time of peace, designed to secure neutrality in time of war.

The Swedish proposal for a Scandinavian Defence Pact in 1948—9 was an attempt to include Norway and Denmark in a neutral but armed alliance. It reflected the hope that those in the north-western corner of Europe would be able to stay on the sidelines in any Great Power conflict. For a time it struck a responsive chord, and during this period the prospects for a Scandinavian bloc were probably at their brightest. Norway was interested enough to take part in the negotiations: the desire for neutrality had dominated her foreign policy before the Second World War. Thus even in 1902, while the union with Sweden was still in force, the Storting had unanimously supported the concept of permanent neutrality, with Great Power backing, for Norway/Sweden. Two years after independence, in 1907, Norway obtained Great Power guarantees (from Britain, France, Germany and Russia) for her territorial integrity, but failed to achieve the recognition which she sought as a permanent neutral. During the First World War she was successful, together with Denmark and Sweden, in keeping out of the conflict. In the 1930s, unlike Sweden, she rejected a rearmament programme.

But when the opportunity to join the North Atlantic Treaty Organization (NATO) alliance arose in 1949, the Norwegians quickly drew the lesson from their wartime experience that membership in this new and wider grouping would be the better insurance against war. A certain disillusion with the United Nations as a force for peace at a time of increasing tension between the Great Powers helped to impel them. The Danes pursued for a brief space the notion of a bilateral pact with

Sweden, but this had not the same attraction for the Swedes. Thereupon Denmark followed the Norwegian lead and entered NATO. The negotiations on the pact could not in any case have included Finland at the time because Stalin was then making the last of his own security demands on that country and viewed the project with suspicion. Only *after* the formation of NATO did an arrangement of that kind come to appear desirable to the Soviet Union.

The collapse of the Scandinavian Defence Pact scheme prompted Hans Hedtoft of Denmark to propose the creation of the Nordic Council to systematize and strengthen regional ties. Because defence and security questions are not in principle subjects for Nordic Council debate, Finland was enabled to join that organization in 1955. So it may be argued that the chief agency for intra-regional co-operation came into being as the reflection of a recognized diversity in security and defence policy, and that, having come into being, it provides something of a refuge from pressures on the members from outside the region. Indeed, proposals for the intensification of intra-regional co-operation often have the character of compensation for developments on a wider front which, it is feared, may prove divisive. Thus, for example, the strengthening of Nordic Council institutions that followed upon the accession of Denmark, along with Britain and Eire, to the European Economic Community (EEC) in 1973 conformed to this pattern. This in turn owed something to the desire of the Danes to maintain their own Scandinavian identity to the full while being compelled by economic circumstances to strengthen their links with continental Western Europe.

Although the Scandinavian states pursue differing security and defence policies, the consciousness of a regional affinity is apparent even in these spheres. Decisions concerning these matters are regularly taken with an eye to their likely impact on neighbours within the region, and the emergence of the concept of a 'Nordic Balance' — of which more later — is in itself a reflection of this. Again, although it is quite conceivable that a Norseman might, if asked, express a preference for, say, Dutchmen over Swedes, much of the strength of the sense of regional consciousness springs from an awareness of similarities and parallelisms in the political landscapes and the political cultures of the neighbouring states within the region. Each state has evolved along its own particular path, so that, for example, Denmark, Norway and Sweden are constitutional monarchies, Iceland and Finland two very distinct types of republic. At the same time, there has long been a ready interchange of ideas and political impulses across the intra-regional frontiers. In consequence, among the states there is a sense of having more in common with their neighbours than with those outside the circle. It will be part of the aim of the present study to trace some significant similarities and parallelisms while not doing injustice to the separate political profiles, so to speak, of the individual states. This aim links with another, and wider, question: are the Scandinavian states distinguishable as a separate species of the West European genus of parliamentary democracies? Finally, there is the question posed in the title of this work, suggested by a number of books and articles on the government and politics of the region, beginning with Marquis W. Childs's celebrated piece published first in 1937, *Sweden: the Middle Way:* can the Scandinavian states be described as consensual democracies? To an examination of this issue we now turn.

CHAPTER ONE

# The Scandinavian States: the Consensual Democracies?

All liberal democratic states must be consensual democracies in some degree: there must at least be some measure of agreement on fundamentals. But some are more consensual than others. Rules of thumb for evaluation can be extracted by reference to three dimensions: first, the framework of rules and regulations for the resolution of political conflict; next, the nature of the conflicts arising within that framework; and, finally, the manner in which the resolution of those conflicts is attempted. But preliminarily it can be said that the more consensual the democracy, the more it tends towards depoliticization; the more dissensual, the more towards destabilization.

Arend Lijphart (1969), in his typology of European political systems, assigned Sweden to the sub-category of 'consensus systems' – briefly, countries with a homogeneous political culture and 'coalescent' elite behaviour. Norway, following Eckstein (1966), was put in the separate sub-category of 'community systems' – countries where social divisions are largely neutralized by 'overarching sentiments of solidarity'. Torgersen (1962) had already noted a steady trend towards the growth of political consensus in Norway, interrupted only by two periods of stress – 1884, the year in which the modern parliamentary system finally broke through, and 1919–20, when the Labour Party, alone among its parallels elsewhere in Western Europe, linked itself to the Comintern in the Third International. This was written in the now far-off days of the 'end of ideology' debate. Just recently, Marquis W. Childs, forty-three years after the appearance of his pioneering work, has brought out some new reflections under the title *Sweden: the Middle Way on Trial* (1980). The 'Middle Way', in its original formulation in the 1930s, was asserted to lie between Fascism and Communism. The meaning has now shifted: it is now taken to lie between capitalism and socialism, so that the argument is that consensus about the mixed economy is now 'on trial'. To what extent, then, can the separate states within the region be classified as consensual? Is consensualism on the wane within the area? What follows is designed to draw attention to some of the salient distinguishing features of political life in the Scandinavian region in a comparative context.

First, however, some amplification is needed of the three dimensions of consensual democracy briefly sketched at the outset of this chapter, together with some suggested guidelines for assessing the extent to which a state may be thus categorized. The blunt but trenchant question 'So what?' will be dealt with later.

DEFINING THE THREE DIMENSIONS OF CONSENSUAL DEMOCRACY

With respect to the first dimension, a consensual democracy is here taken to be *a liberal democratic state characterized by a low level of opposition to the framework of rules and regulations for the resolution of political conflict within that state.* This is the most important dimension of the three, for without a working consensus about the rules and regulations of the system, the state is threatened at its foundations: all else is secondary. Clearly, however, not all such rules and regulations are of equal importance: constitutions may be amended, updated and superseded – and have been so in Scandinavia as elsewhere, as is shown in chapter 4 – provided that the essential rules of the parliamentary game are maintained. So for the purposes of evolving rules of thumb for assessing the degree of consensualism prevailing on this first dimension, one point of relevance is the presence, strength or absence of anti-system parties. Another is the presence or absence of alienated sub-groups within the national community and, again, whether or not recourse is had to violence as a method of protest. More positively, there is the question of evidence of popular support for the rules of the game, minimally reflected in voter-participation levels in both elections and referenda.

The first dimension focuses upon regime legitimacy; the second is concerned with the nature of the political conflict occurring within the framework of the basic rules and regulations. On this dimension, a consensual democracy is taken to be *a liberal democratic state characterized by a low level of conflict about the actual exercise of power within that state.* The concern here is with the character and *intensity* of political cleavages. Rules of thumb for assessment can be obtained by considering such questions as: is there a wide or a narrow ideological gap between the parties over a significant period of time? Is there a tendency towards convergence or the reverse? Are conflicts frequently or seldom perceived in zero-sum terms? These questions are not readily susceptible to quantitative analysis, although some research has been done on the measurement of distances between political parties: it does not necessarily follow that the questions are meaningless, nor that an attempt to arrive at some determination of them is valueless. At the same time this dimension of inquiry is of secondary importance compared with the first. Sharp cleavages about policy can readily be accommodated, together with zero-sum conflicts, provided the antagonists are prepared to give their opponents their turn if the electorate so decides.

The third dimension is concerned with the manner in which the resolution of political conflict is attempted — including the extent to which the obviation of political conflict is pursued. On this dimension, a consensual democracy is taken to be *a liberal democratic state characterized by a high degree of concertation in the gestation of public policy*. Rules of thumb for assessment would include a consideration of the extent of coalition-building based on the parliamentary channel of representation and the extent to which conflict-obviation mechanisms exist in the corporate channel of representation. Clearly, this dimension has a close connection with the second, but analytically it seems reasonable to make the distinction.

Limitations of space preclude a leisurely survey of each of the countries of the region from the point of view of each of these several dimensions, so attention must be focused on the salient points. 'A week', as Sir Harold Wilson put it, 'is a long time in politics' — but not in the analysis of politics. For present purposes the time-span of a generation is the minimum.

## REGULATING THE RESOLUTION OF POLITICAL CONFLICT

In connection with this first dimension of consensual democracy, it would seem reasonable to take the period since the first arrival upon the scene of modern parliamentary government. For Norway this can be dated to 1884; Denmark, 1901; Finland, 1917; Sweden, 1917–21, and Iceland, 1918 — the year in which Copenhagen finally granted home rule.

With the important exception of Finland, electorally significant anti-system parties, to begin with, have been and are generally conspicuous by their absence in Scandinavia. Since this characteristic is shared with many other liberal democratic states, it merits only a brief mention here. The Norwegian Labour Party, with the most radical tradition of any Scandinavian Social Democratic party, could be reckoned an anti-system party during its brief flirtation with Moscow (1920–3). A combination of factors accounted for this: an infusion of revolutionary fervour under the leadership of Martin Tranmael; the rugged militancy of the strong backwoods component from the peripheral North; bitterness at wartime inflation and profiteering; and disenchantment with the operation of the parliamentary system (though the grounds for this began to be removed with the introduction of proportional representation (PR) in 1920). However, Labour was sufficiently reformist by 1928 to form a brief minority Cabinet. Denmark, Iceland and Sweden have lacked anti-system parties other than tiny fringe groups, such as the handful of Nazis in their day in Denmark and Sweden (and, of course, Norway — Vidkun Quisling). There is the phenomenon of the Danish Progress Party, which sprang from nowhere in 1973 to become the second largest party in the *Folketing* but by 1981 had declined to fifth in size. But this is probably best categorized as a protest party rather than as an anti-system party: it enters at times into the parliamentary arithmetic of other parties as an ingredient in majority-building for particular measures, and it seeks a reorientation of public policy rather than changes in the rules of the game. It tends to behave as a comet of eccentric orbit — and, in the process, to confound the arithmetic.

Parties challenging the fundamentals of the parliamentary system have played a much more significant role in Finland. The 1918 Civil War both polarized the nation for a whole generation and sharply divided Social Democrats from Communists within the left. The radical Socialist Workers' Party was banned in 1923, and the Communists were proscribed in 1930. This last measure came about as the result of pressure from the Lapua movement, representing anti-system forces on the far right of the political spectrum. In 1932 an attempted coup by these same forces was headed off with ease by the republican authorities. Although shortly afterwards a Fascist-inspired Patriotic People's Movement, *Isänmaallinen Kansan Liike* (IKL) was formed, and although this polled almost a tenth of the total vote in the 1936 elections, the strength of the democratic constitutionalist tradition helped to fend off the threat. The defence of the system was promoted by the 'red soil' Cabinet of 1937–9, a coalition between the Centre Party and the Social

Democrats. In this the Centre provided the Prime Minister (Cajander) and the Social Democrats were very much the junior partner, but the alliance marked a stage in the reintegration of the moderate left into Finnish political life.

The reincorporation of the radical left was a by-product of the Russian victory in the Continuation War in 1944, and the Communists under Pekkala took part in the first post-war coalition. Simultaneously the IKL movement on the extreme right was put under interdict. But the power of the presidency was a crucial factor in keeping the Communists out of office for two decades after the break-up of the post-war coalition, while their loyalty to the system was under suspicion. Similarly, the power of the presidency has been equally crucial in bringing them back into coalition Cabinets for most of the period since 1966. Communist co-operation in government has helped to ensure a measure of union co-operation in the passage of package deals in the field of incomes policy. It has also split the Communist Party into a majority and a minority (anti-system) wing. During the past decade the balance within the divided Finnish left at the macro-level, so to speak, has shifted markedly in favour of the Social Democrats, who now have a quarter of the electorate in their support, while the *total* Communist vote has fallen away from just below that same level to less than 18 per cent. At the 1981 Finnish Communist Party Congress dissatisfaction at this development reached such a pitch that the leader of the majority wing, Saarinen, had his mandate provisionally renewed for one year only. Summing up, therefore, in Finland it can be said that social cleavages along ideological lines have run far deeper than elsewhere in Scandinavia and that only since the Second World War has the country moved markedly from the dissensual towards the consensual end of the spectrum — to the point at which only half an anti-system party can be discerned. The number of parties represented in Parliament is still large enough to fall under the Sartori heading of 'extreme multi-partism', but intransigeant oppositionism has significantly declined (Sartori, 1976, p.285). Although the art of governing has long remained more difficult to practise than elsewhere within the region, it could be argued that since 1976 the political situation in Finland has been more stable than that, for example, in Sweden. The anomalous position of the Finnish Conservative (Coalition) Party is best considered under the second dimension because this cannot be classified as an anti-system grouping.

Alienated sub-groups, and the resort to violence in the pursuit of political objectives, are both almost completely absent in Scandinavia.

## 14  The Scandinavian States: the Consensual Democracies?

Neither ethnic nor religious minorities pose any threat to system stability. The largest of the ethnic minorities, the Swedish minority in Finland, has accommodated itself to the transition from dominant to dwindling minority group, its cultural and linguistic rights safeguarded under the Constitution. The Swedish People's Party, its main vehicle for political expression, plays a significant centre-ground role in Finnish political life as well as defending the interests of the minority group. Meanwhile, the Finnish minority in Sweden has been steadily increasing during the past two decades, to the point at which in 1981 every tenth child born to Finnish parents was born in Sweden. The explanation lies, of course, in the Nordic labour market and the significantly higher wage rates prevailing in the Swedish economy. This last factor has also been responsible for an influx of Yugoslavs, Turks and others. Some minor friction has occurred between 'aggro' groups in the local population and immigrants, but public policy makes generous provision for language instruction and also grants enfranchisement at local government elections after a short residential period. (Denmark, in 1981, has followed suit here.)

The Faeroe Islands (population 40,000) obtained home rule from Denmark in 1948, and their Parliament, the *Lagting*, unanimously voted against entry into the EEC when Denmark decided to go in. A special agreement concluded with the EEC preserves fisheries rights. Since 1970 Denmark has reserved two places in her Nordic Council delegation for members of the *Lagting*: she is now promoting the cause of independent representation on the Council both for the Faeroes and for Greenland (population 50,000) – Greenland having been granted home rule in May 1979. Greenland, it may be added, is currently allotted one of the sixteen Danish seats in the European Parliament, although the larger of her two main parties, *Siumut*, favours withdrawal from the EEC and the negotiation of a Faeroese-type arrangement. This line won at the February 1982 election. The Swedish-speaking Åland Islands (population 20,000) have home rule within the Finnish political system and rights entrenched under the Constitution. All of these outlying areas have their own distinctive political parties, some of which, in the Faeroes, are pleasantly styled 'flocks'. All have their own particular political problems – youth emigration in Greenland, for example – but none can be terned an alienated community, and all practise the principles of democratic self-government.

Otherwise the only ethnic minorities within the region are the small German population of Slesvig in Denmark and the Lapps (population

35,000). The Germans had an arrangement until recently with the Centre Democrats in Denmark under which they were allotted one place on the Party list for parliamentary elections, but this broke down, at least for the time being, when their nominee turned out to have had a Nazi background. The Lapps, still to some extent migratory, together with their reindeer herds, across the borders of Norway, Sweden and Finland, have for a couple of years been engaged with some success in trying to obstruct the Alta/Kautokeino hydro scheme in Finnmark because of the threat to their fishing rights in the district. Despite a highly publicized picket of the Norwegian Prime Minister's office, they now appear, however, to be losing the fight.

Broadening the perspective, and looking at the positive side of the first dimension, widespread support for the principle of parliamentary government can be discovered throughout Scandinavia. The way was paved for it by a number of underpinning factors. These, briefly, included the early introduction of compulsory primary education, beginning in Denmark in 1814; the spreading throughout the region of the Folk High School movement, beginning in Denmark in 1844; and the training in the processes of democratic self-government afforded by pre-reform voluntary societies and organizations. These included the Free Churches, whose membership grew apace in the last quarter of the nineteenth century; temperance societies, which, like the Free Churches, received a powerful impulse during this same period from transatlantic sources via the emigré connection; the rapidly spreading agricultural co-operatives, again beginning in Denmark after the switch from cereal to stock-farming in consequence of the expansion of American and Russian grain exports in the 1870s; and, of course, the growth of the labour movement, which everywhere except in Norway predated the arrival of parliamentarism on the scene. Of this last more will be said later.

To these generalizations Finland has been something of an exception. The point has been made elsewhere (Kirby, 1979, p.51) that the frustration of aspirations to democratic self-government under tsarist rule engendered a climate of political violence in the period before independence and the outbreak of the Civil War. Again, but on another level, the Finns adopted a hybrid semi-parliamentary system with strong powers vested in the presidency. However, violence and the threat of violence have disappeared from the Finnish political scene in the years since the ending of the Second World War. Elsewhere in Scandinavia the last appearance of domestic political violence was probably the

16    *The Scandinavian States: the Consensual Democracies?*

shooting of strikers in the course of a labour dispute at Ådalen in Sweden in 1931: violence has otherwise only occurred as a backwash from extra-regional conflicts and has been committed by Croat terrorists, participants in the Arab–Israeli conflict and the like. On the subject of the character of the Finnish political system, the strong presidency exercises power within the admittedly broad limits set by the parliamentary situation. The extent of the authority possessed by the recent incumbent, Urho Kekkonen, was reflected in the fact that throughout the 1970s *all* the main parties united in supporting successive extensions of his mandate to 1984. The root of that authority sprang from the special relationship which he enjoyed with the leaders of the Soviet Union.

Voter participation in general elections throughout Scandinavia showed a secular tendency to increase until levelling off in the 1970s at a range between 80 and 92 per cent – and this in the absence of any provision for compulsory voting. Finland, with the sharpest political cleavages, interestingly remains at the lower levels of this range, but even so participation is high by British and American standards. Participation in referenda – about whose incidence more is said in the section on constitutions in chapter 4 – is generally between 5 and 15 per cent lower. (It was, however, *higher* in the Danish EEC referendum, at 90.19 per cent: Fitzmaurice, 1981, p.65.) The principle of state funding for political parties in proportion to their strengths in the national legislature was introduced in Sweden in 1967, chiefly in order to buttress the ailing position of party-affiliated newspapers, and has since spread elsewhere within the region. (Finland has a separate support law for party newspapers.) Similarly, the mass media are notably impartial in the allocation of time to the parties – for example, during electoral campaign periods in Sweden equal allocations are made to the five parties with representation in Parliament.

THE NATURE OF POLITICAL CONFLICT

Turning now to our second dimension, the Scandinavian states are like the majority of continental West European states in having multi-party systems and in conducting their elections under one form or another of PR. Class, as many analysts of Scandinavian voting behaviour have pointed out, is the chief determinant of how people cast their ballots in the region. The basic regularity in the party systems, which will be examined more closely in the ensuing two chapters, is a fivefold structure arranged on a left/right continuum: radical left – Social Democrats/

Labour – Agrarian/Centre parties – Liberals – Conservatives. In the Icelandic case this is reduced to four, the last two categories combining in the shape of the Independence Party. Although, as has been seen, ethnic minorities can be found within the region, and although the political landscape has been changed by the appearance on the scene of religiously based parties in the period since the Second World War, there is nothing to parallel the sub-cultural blocs following these lines in the Dutch and Belgian political systems, for example. So it is reasonable to focus upon the nature of class divisions in Scandinavia when looking at the second dimension of consensus. Three singularities are worth drawing out in this connection: the role played by farmers, and more specifically by farmers' parties, in the political life of the region; the high degree of loyalty shown by blue-collar workers to the parties of the left; the relative weakness of Conservatism as a political force within the region.

The first of these salient characteristics is interconnected with the third: the twentieth century cleavage between urban and rural property-holders has contributed to the narrowing of the base for Conservative recruitment and, until the past decade, has helped to make Conservative parties in the region predominantly urban-centred. So in Finland, for example, the Agrarian Party emerged in 1906 as the second party of functional representation in response to the growth of the Social Democrats; and the defence of rural interests has everywhere in the region been the *raison d'être* of the growing farmers' parties within the PR voting systems. Characteristically, these parties began life as vehicles of political expression for independent family farmers, whether concentrated regionally (Finland, Norway, to some extent Sweden) or more widely spread (Denmark, Iceland). Agricultural rationalization and the drift from the land that has occurred in Scandinavia, as elsewhere in Western Europe, since the Second World War have threatened them at their foundations. In response, they have in some cases called themselves 'Centre Parties' (Sweden 1957, Norway 1959 and Finland 1965) and have attempted, with varying degrees of energy and success, to broaden their appeal. But they remain farmers' parties in the sense that a majority of farmers continue to support them (Worre, 1980).

Englishmen, remarked Walter Bagehot (following Newman), are 'hard to be worked up to the dogmatic level' (Bagehot, 1949, p.122): that was in 1867. The same could be said of the farmers of the Agrarian parties, who carried little or nothing in the way of ideological baggage and who, under the pressure of economic adversity in the 1930s, entered into various kinds of horse-trading deals with the Social Democratic and Labour parties of the region. The result was, broadly speaking, reform programmes in the spirit of social liberalism — a rapid extension of social welfare programmes in exchange for support for primary producers. Under more normal economic circumstances this Red—Green combination does not come about naturally, as the experience of the 1951—7 Swedish coalition goes to show. Individualism comes more readily than collectivism to the farmer, except in respect of marketing arrangements; and the gap between producer and consumer interests is often wide enough to produce zero-sum conflicts; in Finland it has led to the collapse of a number of coalitions.

In Finland the Centre Party occupies a strategic position at approximately the equilibrium point of the political see-saw, continues to rank as one of the four large parties in the political system and is an ever-present member of coalition governments. The Icelandic Progressive Party, also an agrarian grouping by origin, is likewise one of four major parties: it is at present approaching the position, held by the Social Democrats, of the party most often in a governmental coalition since national independence was achieved in 1944. In Sweden the Centre Party has provided the Prime Minister (Fälldin) in three of the four non-socialist governments that have been in power since the Social Democrats lost office in 1976. It has travelled farther than any other Scandinavian farmers' party in broadening its appeal to articulate new-style 'Green' questions — environmental protection in general and opposition to nuclear power in particular, together with the improvement of the quality of life in backward regions of the country. In the process it became at one time a competitor of the Social Democrats for votes and set out, with some success, to become the dominant force of the centre ground on the non-socialist side. However, it has been losing steam lately, the nuclear power issue having been defused by the 1980 referendum. In Norway the less enterprising Centre Party took part in non-socialist coalitions for much of the decade after 1965 and enjoyed temporary prominence as one of the main driving forces behind the Norwegian rejection of Common Market membership in 1972. Finally, in Denmark the Agrarian Liberals (Venstre), one of the more right-of-centre members of the Liberal International, provided a new combination for that country by joining the Social Democrats in government in 1978—9. This was a temporary alignment, unlikely to herald a new trend, and it came about on what might be called a *faute de mieux* basis.

To summarize the political role played by farmers and farmers' parties within the region, it can be said that their general grain runs in a non-socialist direction, despite the fact that farmers' parties like to consider themselves 'neither socialist nor bourgeois'. At the same time there is force in the argument that they have on the whole helped to shift the centre of gravity of their political systems to the left of Britain's and, as far as the agricultural sector is concerned, to the left also of, for example, those of the German Federal Republic and Switzerland. The modest size of the average landholding disposes them to be sympathetic towards low-income groups in society and towards blue-collar workers viewed as individuals rather than as members of a class — hence, for instance, the general tenor of Centre Party co-partnership schemes for industry. A sort of instinctive egalitarianism can be traced here: where the farmsteads are so marginal as to require the farmer to eke out a livelihood by part-time or seasonal work in the local forests or sawmill or factory — as in the harsher parts of Finland and Norway — agrarian radicalism is prominent, and the parties of the left do well. Where the farmsteads are more prosperous — as in those areas of Norway where the Centre Party is strong and in most of Denmark — a spirit of individualistic liberal capitalism prevails. It is not perhaps too fanciful to detect an affinity here with the spirit of the American farmer as depicted in Hartz's scintillating study (Hartz, 1955) — even though Denmark, for example, emerged from a state of feudalism only in the eighteenth century, while Norway and Sweden were untouched by this development. At all events, no mention of a deference vote will be found in any of the numerous and thoroughgoing studies of Scandinavian voting behaviour.

The second salient feature of Scandinavian political life proposed for consideration earlier under the general heading of the nature of class divisions within the region is the high degree of loyalty shown by blue-collar workers to the parties of the left. Everywhere except in Iceland, where there is significant union affiliation to the liberal—conservative Independence Party, the percentage of blue-collar workers voting for moderate and radical left-wing parties combined was, in the mid-1960s, closer to three-quarters than to the two-thirds usually voting for the Labour Party in a British general election (see table 3.5). Although the Scandinavian countries are less heavily urbanized than other advanced industrial societies — only the capital cities (excluding Reykjavik), Gothenburg and Malmö could be classified as sizable in a comparative European context — they are on the whole comprehensively unionized. The percentage of organized wage-earners ranges from about half in

Finland to 90 per cent in Sweden. Formal structural links between unions and party are fewer than in Britain — there is, for example, no union block vote at party congresses — but both are closely linked as parts of a labour movement in which historically the unions have provided extensive welfare, educational and even recreational facilities for their members.

In the 1970s the vote for parties of the moderate left fell away sharply in both Denmark and Norway because of the impact of the taxation issue and the Common Market question. Since the nadir of 1973, however, the trend was until the 1981 elections towards recovery of underlying strength, with signs of another trough in the Norwegian case before the arrival of Dr Brundtland as the Labour Party Prime Minister in February 1981. At the same time the past decade has been one of increasing voter mobility throughout the region, with, for example, evidence that net Social Democratic losses have slightly exceeded Social Democratic gains in the Swedish case (Särlvik in Cerny, 1977, *passim*). It may be said in parenthesis that one explanation offered for this phenomenon in Sweden is the break-up of settled Social Democratic communities through the operation of labour market policy — voter mobility in a physical sense. In the present context, that of looking at the extent of consensualism on the second dimension, one central question is the extent to which Social Democratic and Labour parties have held power through pursuing class-based policies or through attempting to turn themselves into catch-all parties of greatly diluted ideological appeal (Smith, 1976, p.46).

In order to hold power, the Social Democratic and Labour parties in Denmark, Norway and Sweden have had to seek support outside their natural class base, narrowly defined. In their early days the path to power was opened, in Denmark and Sweden, by co-operation with the Radical Liberals and Liberals respectively in pursuit of franchise reform. The period of Red—Green combinations has already been mentioned: in Denmark the Radical Liberals, who were in part representative of rural smallholders, formed with the Social Democrats a government that lasted from 1929 to 1940. With the rise of the white-collar salaried workers and the increase in the tertiary sector, support from this quarter was necessary and was enlisted with a large measure of success. The record for longevity of tenure belongs to the Swedish party, whose loss of office in 1976 was one of the rare occasions when Scandinavian domestic politics made the headlines elsewhere in Western Europe: a virtually unbroken span of forty-four years of Social Democratic government meant that a large slice of the electorate in 1976 could not recall a time when the Social Democrats were not in government, whether solo (1932–6, 1945–51, 1957–76) or in coalition. In Norway the war divided a spell of Labour rule that otherwise lasted from 1935 to 1965, except for a month in 1963; and Labour held office on a minority basis, but with a narrow overall left-wing majority, from 1973 to 1981. Of these three, the Danish Social Democrats have been in the weakest position, never having been able to muster a majority on their own: small-scale industrial units and the strength and impermeability of the agrarian sector go towards explaining this. Even so, they have been in government for more than two-thirds of the period since the end of the Second World War.

So what has been the strategy of the ruling Social Democratic and Labour parties? Has there been a wide gap between themselves and other parties in the system? Has there been a tendency towards convergence or the reverse? The submission here is that two broad phases can be distinguished, with the second half of the 1960s as the watershed. In the first of these phases the main thrust of the appeal of the parties of the moderate left was their articulation of a cross-class national interest, taking the kind of position which the Conservative Party in Britain used to be so adept at getting across; in the second phase there has been a marked trend towards radicalization, hence towards increasing polarization.

In the first phase, starting in the 1930s, Social Democratic/Labour policy can be summarized thus. There was no evident desire to change economic structures, which were overwhelmingly those of the mixed economy with a dominant private sector. More specifically, there was little desire to push ahead with nationalization programmes: such nationalization as existed had almost all been carried out by non-socialist administrations with an eye to securing revenues (e.g. tobacco and spirits monopolies, Danish pawnshops – possibly), defending national assets from foreign encroachment (a common reason in the Norwegian case) and so on. Collective bargaining thus took place in a climate in which industrial relations were seen in positive-sum terms both by elites and by the great majority of the mass union memberships. More specifically, hard bargaining was encouraged at the expiry of agreements to secure the maximum share of the available resources: but wage restraint was sought in exchange for legislation in the interests of the mass membership (Panitch, 1976). This kind of understanding was always hardest to implement in Denmark, and continues to be so, because of the weaker position of the Social Democrats in the system.

Was the legislation provided by Social Democratic and Labour governments, then, legislation in a class interest? Yes, as Castles argues (1978, *passim*) – but not obviously nor narrowly so over the great majority of the ground covered. The extensive welfare legislation drew much upon industrial wealth for its finances, but was not radically redistributive in its effects. Legislation on the industrial front was largely directed towards increasing the size of the cake available for distribution and, ultimately, improving efficiency: this could be seen at its most sophisticated in Swedish labour market enactments. Thus, for example, firms were given tax concessions for voluntarily putting some of their profits in central reserve for release to counter cyclical downturns in the economy when the central authorities so decided. The introduction of a comprehensive state educational system, beginning in Sweden in 1962, aroused no strong political passions, as in Britain, because it replaced municipal rather than private provision. A more far-reaching reform was the introduction of a compulsory supplementary pensions scheme in Sweden at the end of the 1950s. This originated from within the union movement (Heclo, 1974) and was designed to iron out differentials of advantage between blue- and white-collar workers. Certainly, it aroused fierce party controversy, but it won much white-collar support. It also marked a large step towards the realization of the Swedish Trade Union Confederation's (*Landsorganisationen*, LO) demand for an increasing state share in the capital market: the creation of a State Investment Bank in 1967 was another move in the same direction. But although the Swedish Social Democrats were the most radical of the three during this first phase, possibly excepting the Norwegian Labour Party's five-year spell of physical controls over the economy in the interests of national reconstruction immediately after the war, the main thrust of the policies of moderate Left governments in this period conformed with diffusely egalitarian norms: hence the cogency of the slogan 'Sweden – the People's Home'. The growth of welfare provisions, in fact, became almost a facet of nationalism in these countries.

To the extent that Conservative parties opposed the extension of welfare programmes – as was the case, for instance, in connection with the Swedish supplementary pensions reform – they appeared as parties of reaction. Here the third salient feature of the region under the heading of the nature of class impact on politics may be interwoven with the second. For Conservative parties, in this first phase, predominantly represented the wealthier sections of Scandinavian society

— big business, higher-level civil servants, the most prosperous landowners of south-west Finland and southern Sweden, top professional people. They have, not surprisingly, attracted virtually no support from the workforce. The exception to this general rule is the case of Iceland, where Conservatism had a cross-class appeal because it so clearly articulated nationalist sentiment when Denmark still held sovereignty and where a merger with the Liberals was effected in 1929 to form the Independence Party. This has the support of many farmers, white-collar workers and employers and, as mentioned earlier, a part of the blue-collar workforce also (Kristjánsson, 1979). But elsewhere Conservative parties began life as establishment parties *par excellence*; and in Sweden, where they are most dependent on the co-operation of the 'mid-parties' (Centre and Liberals), they found it prudent to change their name in 1969 to the Moderate Alliance Party. In Denmark they are the Conservative People's Party; in Finland they go under the title of the Coalition Party; in Norway alone they are uncompromisingly 'the Right' (*Høyre*).

In Finland the blue-collar vote has always, since independence, been split between the parties of the left. In addition, the Social Democrats were themselves split in the 1950s and early 1960s: latterly, as has been said, it has been the turn of the Communists, and the Social Democrats have become the largest party in the system once more. Nevertheless, neither separately nor in combination have the parties of the left been able to win a parliamentary majority save in 1958 and 1966. So the clear-cut ideological appeals (e.g. for nationalization programmes) have to date had little chance of realization, given the degree of disunity within the left. A loss of ground by the left in the last elections (1979) was marked by the replacement by the President of Sorsa, a more leftward-leaning Social Democrat, by Koivisto in the premiership. Koivisto is much more the centre-ground politician, acceptable to the non-socialist parties.

It will be clear from what was said above that the argument is that during the first of our two periods politics on the second dimension in Denmark, Norway and Sweden were predominantly consensual in character and that since then they have become less so. A high degree of consensualism is incompatible with a Marxist approach to political conflict, except as a tactical interlude. It has thus been argued that what the Swedish Social Democrats were really doing was to promote the 'maturation of capitalism' (Korpi, 1978, ch. 4). It has also been argued that depoliticization during this period was spurious on the

Social Democratic side because ideology, while not manifest, informed practical politics (Himmelstrand, 1962). Large parties exhibit a spectrum of opinion, and then the prevailing political style was incrementalist. In any event, an increasing tendency towards political polarization became evident in the mid-1960s which, although it was interrupted in Denmark and Norway by the turbulent issues surfacing at the 1973 elections, can be said still to be in evidence.

The causes of radicalization may be summed up as the influence of New Left attitudes, generational change and, beginning in Sweden, sharpened awareness of continuing income inequalities through a 1968 Commission report. From the union side came demands for a drive for 'economic democracy' to supplement the arrival of political and the growth of social democracy — this throughout the region. This demand was designed to appeal to white- as well as to blue-collar workers, and it has had the advantage of not costing much to execute in times of economic stringency. Least progress has been made in Denmark, where at the same time the Social Democratic programme for economic democracy has been the least radical (Elvander, 1979a, pp.25–35). In Sweden the Social Democrats enacted a series of measures before leaving office in 1976, including putting workers on company boards and culminating in a Co-Determination Law which ended the unilateral right of employers to hire and fire labour and made the allocation of work within firms subject to collective bargaining (1976). Most of these measures, it is fair to say, received a wide measure of cross-party support on grounds of the extension of democratic principle: they managed to be both radical and consensual. But it is scarcely possible that the same can hold true of proposals for a radical shift of power on the industrial and economic front through the setting up of union-controlled worker funds financed from company profits and carrying with them increasing shareholders' rights.

This piece of policy formulation will be looked at again in chapter 5. Meanwhile, it may be mentioned that the Danish Social Democratic government was seeking support in 1981 for a Bill to promote company profit-sharing. The Norwegian Labour administration, with radical left assistance, put through a Bill in 1978 nationalizing the boards of commercial banks. After that a spell of ideological quiescence set in, paralleled by evidence of falling support for the party. This quiescence appeared likely to be disturbed by the new Prime Minister and party leader, Dr Brundtland, with plans for equal worker representation on company boards and the withdrawal of subsidies from industrial firms unless half their employees were women. Finland, too, has seen the passage of a modest package of economic democracy.

All these developments have been accompanied by an increase of support for, and a broadening of the base of, the Conservative parties of the region. These share a common desire to lower rates of direct taxation in order to provide incentives to work (at one job, it ought perhaps to be added – there has been a growth, at least in Sweden, of a 'grey' working sector of the economy). They also wish to reduce the scale of the public sector, which has been steadily expanding to proportions well above the Western European average.

Finally, on the second dimension of consensus, the 1970s have seen the emergence of other new issues which often have the character of sharply defined conflicts involving a question of principle. Prominent among these have been ecological issues, particularly sensitive in Scandinavia where many city-dwellers, irrespective of class affiliation, are country-lovers at heart (where else would a Social Democrat leader urge that summer cottages should be made more generally available?). The evolution of Swedish Centre Party policy on nuclear power furnishes an interesting study in this connection which will be looked at later. Then there have been questions of public morality, commonly left to free votes in a British environment as questions of conscience. In Scandinavia these are taken up as questions of principle by the religiously based Christian People's parties. The stance of the Norwegian party in opposition to abortion, for example, foreclosed in 1981 the possibilities of non-socialist coalition-building in that country.

## THE OBVIATION OF CONFLICT

The third dimension for assessing the degree of consensus, that of the manner in which conflict obviation is attempted, requires only a few introductory remarks here, since it will be covered more adequately in chapter 5. Perhaps the central question to be asked in this general context is: to what extent is the maximization of agreement sought *before* political decisions are taken? This involves devoting some attention to the question of coalition-building in multi-party systems. It also raises the issue of whether a predominant policy style can be said to exist. Clearly, it has interconnections with the second dimension: the transition from the first to the second phase outlined above can be expected to be accompanied by a lessening of effort to secure the maximization of agreement in advance of decisions. Four out of the five Scandinavian states can be classified as advanced industrial societies. The fifth, Iceland, certainly ranks as a modern society with a modern political system; but the degree of her economic dependence upon a single primary product, fish, has led to her being categorized as a Third World country. However, in the present context the point at issue is the range and scope of the rules for the settlement of labour market problems, with their great significance for the management of state economic policy, and here Iceland is also a relevant case.

Turning now to the corporate channel of representation, the Scandinavian countries have developed in varying degrees relatively sophisticated mechanisms for the containment of industrial strife which contribute to the efficient management of economic policy. Broadly speaking, they originated in agreements voluntarily concluded between both sides of industry, starting as far back as 1899 in the Danish case (Elvander, 1974b, p.373): the best-known example is probably the Saltsjöbaden Agreement of 1938, which contained rules designed to head off state legislation about disputes damaging to public safety or to third parties. At least equally important are the arrangements arrived at throughout the region for periodic negotiations on wage levels leading up to contractually binding agreements valid for one or two years at a stretch. These negotiations are usually conducted on a centralized basis: the prototype dates back to the 1930s (Denmark). Even making allowance for wage drift, the existence of agreements of this kind eases the problem for firms making investment decisions.

Law is used as a *supplement* to voluntary agreement: there is thus not the same degree of mistrust of legal regulation in the field of industrial relations as that which historical evolution has ensured, for example, in Britain. So disputes about the interpretation of agreements go in the last resort for settlement to a Labour Court: the first of these courts was once again a Danish creation, in 1910 (Elvander, 1974b, p.375). State mediation in labour disputes is extensively used in Norway and Denmark, less frequently elsewhere — although economic hard times have led to its more frequent use in Sweden of late. Settlements enforced by the state have also occurred in Norway and Denmark, commonly through compulsory arbitration (especially in Norway), to defend vital public interests. The splintered union organization of salaried employees in Norway and the predominance of craft unionization in Denmark help to explain this circumstance.

The general picture which emerges on the corporate front in Scandinavia is one of a comparatively comprehensive and orderly framework for the regulation of industrial conflict, some of it — notably in the Danish case — of remarkable early vintage. Various factors help to explain the phenomenon. Trade union acceptance of centralization, especially in Norway and Sweden, has been made easier by union pursuit of a general policy of levelling up wages. The early predominance of small-scale units of industry in Denmark promoted harmonious relations between both sides and, when conflict did occur, sharpened awareness of its costs. The injection of expert economic surveys as background factors helped to create a climate in which both sides tended to start negotiations from the assumption that a cake of a certain size was available for distribution — even though there was usually disagreement about the precise size of the cake. The heavy dependence of all Nordic economies upon exports, and their consequent vulnerability to international competition, accentuated this tendency. The crucial point in this connection is their awareness of being comparatively small-scale and exposed economies. Last but by no means least, there has been the predominance in government of the Social Democratic and Labour parties for long periods of time in Denmark, Norway and Sweden, and particularly in Norway and Sweden.

The severe industrial conflict which broke out in Sweden early in 1980 in the wake of the second steep rise in oil prices within a decade occurred under a non-socialist administration. It might appear to bear out the contention that the existence of rules and regulations for containing industrial strife comes near to guaranteeing results only when the government is a Social Democratic one. The point has some force, although the established framework worked well under non-socialist administrations at periods of economic difficulty in 1977, 1978 and again (but only for LO/SAF *Svenska arbetsgivareföreningen*, the Swedish Employers' Federation) in 1981. In Finland, however, the powerful Communist hold within the union movement has made it a matter of peculiar difficulty to formulate and work a system of rules for conflict resolution. Something of the same problem exists in Iceland, compounded here by an endemic inflationary trend with rates in the 30—60 per cent range in the past five years. In the Finnish case such rules as there are have been largely adapted from Swedish models, though the success rate in their application has scarcely been growing since the formation of the first of a series of centre-left coalitions in 1966. In both Iceland and Finland the consensus ranking in the corporate sector is comparatively low by Scandinavian standards, although both countries attempt to operate a system of contractual wage agreements.

The Swedish style of policy-making, it has been suggested, has been predominantly consultative and radical in temper, the British predominantly consultative and non-radical (i.e. incremental) (Gustafsson and Richardson, 1980). The foregoing analysis suggests the qualification of the word 'radical' in the Swedish case, but the categorization draws attention to the point that the British system is much more consultative than the superficialities of adversary politics might suggest. The maximization of agreement before decisions are taken is the essence of the system of most departmental committees concerned with the gestation of legislative proposals, for example. So the wide use of Commissions of Inquiry for this purpose in the Scandinavian countries is not as distinctive in itself. Indeed, just as the conventions of adversary politics in Britain (or the USA) serve to conceal the less spectacular but often more significant business of legislative activity within Whitehall and indeed Westminster (or within the US Departments and Congress), so the convention that 'politics is work' serves to conceal the impact of party political considerations upon the work of commissions of inquiry and the like in Scandinavia. It may be noted parenthetically that while lawyers fit well with adversary systems, unlike in the US and, to a lesser extent, in Britain lawyers do not feature prominently in Scandinavian legislatures. When they do appear there, it is usually as administrators, and then not as practitioners of a forensic tradition.

The chief significance of this dimension in the Scandinavian context lies in the fact that in the prevailing multi-party conditions parties have a choice between seeking to maximize their influence over the shaping of decisions or making oppositional gestures. Equally, in the corporate sector some attention needs to be paid to the modes and extent of the concertation of policy — in particular, the formulation of incomes policy as part of wider economic package deals. These issues will be taken up in chapter 5.

CHAPTER TWO

# The Structuring of Mass Politics, 1870-1945

## THE SCANDINAVIAN PARTIES AND PARTY SYSTEMS IN DEVELOPMENTAL PERSPECTIVE

The formative era of party-building in the Scandinavian states comprised three distinct, albeit overlapping, stages. First, there was an initial phase of bipartism between 1870 and 1900 when, prompted by a surge of parliamentary and electoral reform, the power-seekers based mainly in the countryside (the Left) challenged the holders of power in the towns and capital cities (the Right).

Next came a twenty-year period after 1900, when, with the impact of rapid economic modernization transforming predominately rural societies into increasingly urban-industralized ones, mass-based parties emerged. The Social Democratic and Labour parties were rooted in the industrial working class and farm labouring population, while the Agrarian parties articulated the class interests of landowners at various stages of integration into the capitalist economy.

Finally, there was the decade of the 1920s, which saw the completion of a basic five-party Scandinavian model. This was achieved when ideological divisions in the socialist camp in the wake of the Russian Revolution produced a radical left at about the same time as the 'old' nineteenth-century Left and Right transformed themselves into Liberal and Conservative groups respectively.

The present chapter is concerned to trace the formative era of party-building in Scandinavia from 1870 to the late 1920s; chapter 3 analyses the mutations in the basic structure after 1945. In the context of our focus on the Scandinavian states as consensual democracies, of course, it is imperative also to consider how successful the nascent party systems were in integrating the electorate. Were they instruments in the maintenance of high levels of popular consent or, alternatively, agencies for expressing declining legitimacy? In the latter connection the implications of economic recession in the 1930s are studied. However, before examining the nature and development of the Scandinavian party systems, a note on the main electoral characteristics of the region is in order.

*The electoral contours of the Scandinavian party systems*

The radical left – Social Democratic – Liberal – Agrarian – Conservative five-party model typifying the Scandinavian states by 1930 remained fundamentally unaltered until the 1960s. Thereafter a period of electoral instability saw the rise of protest parties, like Mogens Glistrup's Progress Party in Denmark and Veikko Vennamo's Rural Party in Finland, and extended the political spectrum on the radical right. Earlier, a significant radical right had been confined to Finland, where, as we have noted, the Fascist-inclined Patriotic People's Movement polled close to 10 per cent of the valid vote in the 1930s.

The electoral dominance of the five main parties is most clearly seen in Sweden, where no other party has ever gained as much as 2 per cent of the national vote and where, unlike Denmark, Norway and Finland, the protest mood of the 1970s was contained within the established party framework. In Denmark the share of the five main parties rose from 96.6 per cent in 1932 to 97.3 per cent in 1968, although, in fairness, the radical left had split into three distinct groups by the latter date. The only other durable fixture on the Danish political spectrum until the 1970s was the Justice Party, based on the ideas of the American economic theorist, Henry George, which at its peak in 1950 gained 8.2 per cent of the poll.

There have been two minor modifications to the basic five-channel model: in Norway, the emergence at the national level after 1945 of a Christian People'e Party, the only sizable religious party in the five Scandinavian states, and in Finland the existence of a fourth non-socialist party, the Swedish People's Party, based on the one major ethnic minority in the region. Iceland represents the most deviant case, for there liberalism and conservatism joined forces to found the Independence Party – a unique phenomenon in the region in being a catch-all party of the Right comparable with the West German Christian Democratic Union or British Conservative Party. The configuration of parties in Scandinavia between 1930 and the 1960s is presented in table 2.1. The Agrarian parties of Norway, Sweden and Finland became Centre parties in the 1950s and 1960s, while the Liberal parties, along

# The Structuring of Mass Politics, 1870–1945

with the Norwegian Christian People's Party and Swedish People's Party in Finland have generally regarded themselves as members of the political centre.

TABLE 2.1: THE FIVE-PARTY SCANDINAVIAN MODEL IN THE LATE 1960s

| Country | Socialists | | Non-socialists | | | |
|---|---|---|---|---|---|---|
| | Radical left | Left | Centre — Liberal | Centre — Agrarian | Centre — Others | Right |
| Denmark | Communists; Socialist People's Party; Left Socialists | Social Democrats | Radical Liberals | Liberals (*Venstre*) | – | Conservative People's Party |
| Finland | Finnish People's Democratic League | Social Democrats | Liberals | Centre | Swedish People's Party | Coalition Party |
| Iceland | People's Alliance | Social Democrats | – | Progressive Party | – | Independence Party |
| Norway | Communists; Socialist People's Party | Labour Party | Left (*Venstre*) | Centre Party | Christian People's Party | Right |
| Sweden | Left Party Communists | Social Democrats | Liberals | Centre Party | – | Moderate Unity Party |

Even a cursory look at the relative electoral strengths of the parties and the balance between socialist and non-socialist groupings in the Scandinavian states reveals some interesting geographical contrasts. In two of them, Finland and Iceland, a sizable party of the radical left has, paradoxically, coexisted with regular non-socialist majorities at the polls. Thus while support for the Finnish People's Democratic League, comprising mainly (though not exclusively) Communists, has ranged from one-sixth to one-quarter of the electorate since the party was legalized in 1944, the socialist parties in Finland have gained a majority of the vote in only one of the twenty elections since Independence. In Iceland, too, although the radical leftist People's Alliance has averaged between 15 and 16 per cent of the poll since replacing the United Socialist Party in 1956, the two socialist parties have never exceeded a combined vote of 38 per cent and in 1974 obtained less than one-third of the valid poll. In contrast, in Sweden and Norway, where the radical left has been weak and fragmented, the strength of social democracy has enabled the parties of the left to claim an overall majority of the vote on numerous occasions. In Sweden the combined left has managed to obtain an absolute majority in over half the eighteen general elections since 1921, and in Norway the socialist parties have done likewise four times since the last war.

Indeed, outside Iceland, where social democracy has been unusually weak, the Social Democratic and Labour parties have been the dominant electoral force in Scandinavian politics this century. By 1930 they were regularly polling 40 per cent or more of the active electorate in Denmark, Norway and Sweden; on two occasions, in 1940 and 1968, the Swedish party obtained an absolute majority of votes; and even in Finland the Social Democratic Party has invariably been the largest party, with about a quarter of the popular poll. The exception of the two patterns identified above is Denmark, where a strong Social Democratic party has almost claimed an overall majority on several occasions – within 64,000 votes of it in 1935 – but the parties of the left have achieved a parliamentary majority only in 1966–8 and 1971–3.

Holding the balance of electoral power in Scandinavia *as a whole* since 1930, the non-socialist parties have nonetheless displayed an historic lack of unity which – in Denmark, Norway and Sweden at least – has had not a little to do with the predominant governing role played by the Social Democratic parties. Thus the emergence by 1921 of interest-specific agrarian parties, supplementing the more familiar division of the bourgeois camp into liberalism and conservatism, prompted a three-way competition for the non-socialist vote which has produced variable outcomes in each of the Scandinavian states. In Sweden the Conservatives were the leading non-socialist party during the inter-war period, the Liberals between 1948 and 1968 and the Centre Party until 1979. In Norway the Conservatives have been consistently the largest bourgeois party, whereas in Finland this position was occupied continuously by the Agrarian–Centre from 1919–70, when it was overtaken by the Conservatives. In Denmark in 1905 liberalism split into a smallholders' and intellectuals' wing, the Radical Liberals, and a larger farmers' wing, the Agrarian Liberals, the latter remaining easily the largest non-socialist party until 1968, when it was overhauled by the Conservatives, who in turn were sensationally surpassed by the Progress Party in 1973. The merger of conservatism and liberalism in Iceland in 1929 has meant that the Independence Party has been not only the largest single party (ahead of the agrarian Progressive Party) but also overwhelmingly the strongest non-socialist party in Scandinavia, comparable in relative electoral strength with the Social Democratic vote in Sweden.

## Economic change and party formation

The initial generation of cleavage lines, and hence the particular form of Scandinavian multi-partism, owed much to the rate of economic modernization which transformed overwhelmingly rural societies in the mid-nineteenth century into significantly industralized ones by the time of the completion of mass democracy in 1920. Indeed, from being among the poorest nations in Europe in 1850, the Scandinavian states reached a level of occupational differentiation – a balance between primary and non-primary sectors – which was doubtless an important structural prop to multi-partism. No class could lay claim to the mastery of political society by dint of sheer weight of numbers, but rather the emergent party system reflected the real extent of socio-economic pluralism.

The mechanics of change, which was marked by the steady incorporation of the Scandinavian economies into the international commercial order, need not detain us; suffice it to note that rapid growth was predicated on a marked expansion of overseas trade in proportion to GNP, and this in turn on a heightened foreign demand for Scandinavian export goods – agricultural products in the case of Denmark, timber from Norway and Finland and manufacturing commodities from Sweden. At the same time, the employment base in the region altered: the size of the economically active population engaged in agriculture and related occupations fell by 7–13 per cent from 1890 to 1910, while well over half the labour force in Norway and Sweden and nearly two-thirds in Denmark were employed in the non-primary sectors by 1920. Diversification took place most rapidly in Sweden, where the pace of industrial development probably exceeded that of any other contemporary European nation, and most slowly in Finland which remained the most agrarian of the four independent states in 1920. Throughout Scandinavia, however, the nascent party systems reflected in large measure the conflict lines produced by economic modernization.

THE INITIAL ERA OF TWO-PARTY POLITICS: 1870–1900

The decisive stimulus for the emergence of a period of two-party politics common to all the Scandinavian states (except Iceland) by the 1890s came from a thrust of parliamentary and electoral reform which provided for the enrolment of new political actors and the creation of fresh arenas for elite confrontation. Bicameral legislatures were established in Denmark (1850) and Sweden (1866) – the single chamber Norwegian *Storting* dated back to the 1814 Constitution – while in 1863 in the Grand Duchy of Finland, Tsar Alexander II saw fit to convene the quadricameral Diet of Estates after a 'recess' of over fifty years! Roughly contemporaneous franchise reforms in every state but Finland meant that the propertied classes in the countryside formed the bulk of the electorate by the last years of the century.

Scandinavian bipartism pivoted on an essentially rural–urban axis. Indeed, this first era of political mobilization aligned the *power-seekers* – broad and subsequently unstable alliances of enfranchised groups (mainly farmers) and non-incorporated groups (tenants and industrial workers) in the countryside, along with a number of radical intellectuals – against the *power-holders*, high-status and mainly town-based groups of aristocrats, bureaucrats and commercants. Restated, the left emerged as the spokesman of the predominantly agrarian *nation* – its economic interests, language and lifestyle – whereas the right defended the urban *state* and the administrative and financial elites controlling it.

In Denmark and Sweden the early two-party system had a largely functional or economic character, with the United Left (*Det forenede Venstre*) in Denmark and Rural Party (*Lantmannapartiet*) in Sweden mainly concerned with 'bread-and-butter' issues – support for technological improvements in farming, for example, and, in the Swedish case, legislation to protect domestic production, inspired by the *Bund der Landwirte*'s successful lobby for a grain tariff in Germany.

In Norway, by contrast, the Left (*Venstre*) was a cultural nationalist party championing the rural language, *landsmål* (a composite of several peasant dialects) against the Danish-impregnated *riksmål* spoken by the

Establishment in Oslo. The national question was also at the heart of Finnish politics in the late nineteenth century, with the peasant-centred Finnish Party (*Suomalainen Puolue*), based on the majority Finnish language, opposing the political and economic power exercised by the (mainly urban) elite speaking the minority Swedish language. Indeed, the issues connected with the national question in the three *dependent* states, Norway, Finland and Iceland, played an important role in the emergence of the first political parties as well as having something of a lag effect on the transformation of the party system along predominantly economic lines.

Throughout Scandinavia, however, the initial period of two-party politics proved short-lived, and by the turn of the century the Socialist—Liberal—Conservative tripartism which Duverger (1964, p.236) has observed as widespread in Europe obtained in general form in the region.

## THE RISE OF MASS-BASED PARTIES, 1900–21: THE SOCIAL DEMOCRATS AND THE AGRARIANS

### Social Democratic and Labour parties

With the exception of the Icelandic party, which was a relative latecomer, all the Scandinavian Social Democratic and Labour parties were in existence by 1900. The Danish Social Democratic Party was formed in 1876, the Norwegian Labour Party in 1887, the Swedish Social Democratic (Workers') Party in 1889 and the Finnish Workers' Party in 1899. The Finnish party became the Social Democratic Party in 1903 but did not participate in elections until 1907, following the abolition of the Diet of Estates, when it became the largest parliamentary party of its kind in Europe, with 40 per cent of the seats in the single-chamber *Eduskunta*. The Social Democratic/Labour parties became the largest popular parties in Sweden, Norway and Denmark by 1917, 1918 and 1924 respectively, making the rise of Scandinavian socialism as rapid as its support was appreciable. A fundamental condition of its initial breakthrough was the existence of a significant industrial working class during the decisive period of parliamentary and electoral reform.

The scope of the changes occurring in the occupational structure of the Scandinavian states between 1890 and 1920 can be seen from table 2.2. Thus in Denmark close to two-thirds and in Norway and Sweden almost three-fifths of the labour force was employed in the non-primary

TABLE 2.2: THE PERCENTAGE OF THE LABOUR FORCE
EMPLOYED IN THE NON-PRIMARY SECTORS, 1890–1920

| Year | Denmark | Norway | Sweden | Finland |
|------|---------|--------|--------|---------|
| 1890 | 53.1 | 44.7 | 32.8 | 24.0 |
| 1900 | 56.9 | 53.4 | 39.3 | 28.0 |
| 1910 | 60.0 | 53.1 | 49.3 | 30.0 |
| 1920 | 62.3 | 57.9 | 56.3 | 37.0 |

*Source:* Kuhnle, 1975, p.45.

sectors by 1920, and in the Swedish case this figure had almost doubled since 1890. The crucial waves of political mobilization, in short, coincided with a period of accelerated industrialization and meant that electoral support could be activated by a conventional appeal to class interests. In this context, two other factors were vital: the secondary importance of cross-cutting cleavages, and the organizational superiority of the social democratic parties over their bourgeois opponents. Admittedly, elements of the Christian (and particularly revivalist) working class adhered to the 'old' Left in Denmark and Norway, various liberal groups in Sweden or the non-socialist Christian Workers' Party, which contested elections from 1907 to 1919 in Finland. But in the main the 'natural' loyalties of the nascent working class were not strained by membership of subcultural groups based on language or religion. Furthermore, the incidence of cross-class voting was minimized by a network of local party branches, working men's clubs, unions and so on, which enabled the social democratic parties to perform an effective mobilizing as well as an aggregating role. This was especially the case in Finland, where the Social Democratic Party's success stemmed in large part from the fact that it was really the only mass party in 1907.

In consequence, the lion's share of the industrial working class supported the Social Democratic and Labour parties by the start of the First World War. They then polled more than 50 per cent of the vote in Copenhagen, Nakskov, Randers and Rønne (on the island of Bornholm) in Denmark, Oslo in Norway, Gothenburg and Stockholm in Sweden and the new industrial centres of Kotka and Tampere in Finland. At the same time, the Social Democratic parties recruited much of the blue-collar population in the countryside. Indeed, the development of a wide range of rural industries — steel, timber, manufacturing — attracted large concentrations of migrant labour which were particularly susceptible to radical, collectivist ideas (Bull, 1967, pp.86–106). It was not by chance that in Norway the first unions grew up around the large steam-operated saw mills as early as the 1860s or that Sweden's first full-scale strike occurred in the timber-producing district of Sundsvall in 1879. It was no surprise either that the Social Democrats polled well in rural industrial districts like Lolland-Falster (Denmark) and Kymenlaakso (Finland).

Despite the rapid advances made by industrialization, the Scandinavian states still possessed relatively large primary sectors by the completion of enfranchisement – a fact persuading the urban leadership of the Social Democratic parties to attempt political alliances with the smallholders, tenants, hillsiders, labourers and (in Norway) 'marsh men' (*Myrmandsvaesenet*) making up the rural proletariat. Their task was considerably facilitated by the deterioration in rural class relations under the conditions of encroaching capitalism. Friction was generated partly as a result of growing pressure from the larger market-orientated farmers to evict unproductive tenants and reduce the numbers of farmworkers in their employ and partly because the boom in timber exports emphasized the differences between the larger owners with plenty of wood to sell and the smallholders and tenants with little or none (Alapuro, 1976). The result was unequivocal. In the province of Häme, in central southern Finland, an area of commercial landowners and a dense landless population, the Social Democrats polled over 60 per cent of the vote in 1907; in the outlying provinces of Norrland, where the extensive purchase of forest land by timber companies swelled the ranks of the rural proletariat, the Swedish Social Democrats had begun to displace the Liberals by 1914; and in Norway the Labour Party's initial success came less in the more industrialized east than among the farmer-fishermen (*småbruker*) in the far north (Heidar, 1977, p.295). Only in Denmark, where the national economy rested heavily on a highly integrated network of co-operative small farming were rural conditions less conducive to the advance of social democracy.

Indeed, the high level of farm *proprietorship*, coupled with the proportion of the population living in the towns, which was much higher than elsewhere in the region (see table 2.3), meant that social democracy in Denmark emerged as far more a purely urban phenomenon than in the other Scandinavian states. Its electoral constituency also reflected the relatively earlier impact of industrialization on that country, for the Danish Social Democratic Party drew upon a labour

TABLE 2.3: LEVELS OF URBANIZATION IN THE
SCANDINAVIAN STATES, 1800–1920

| Year | Denmark | Norway | Sweden | Finland |
|------|---------|--------|--------|---------|
| 1800 | 20.9 | 7.4  | 9.8  | 5.0  |
| 1850 | 20.8 | 12.8 | 10.1 | 6.4  |
| 1900 | 38.3 | 28.2 | 21.5 | 12.9 |
| 1920 | 43.2 | 39.8 | 29.5 | 17.3 |

*Source:* Jörberg, 1973, p.385.

movement which developed in the context of small independent unions rather than in that of the larger-scale factory production of Norway and Sweden. A significant element of its support, therefore, comprised urban craftworkers, a group which, in fact, had been instrumental in bringing socialism to Scandinavia in the first place.

In the latter context it should be noted that Scandinavian socialism owed much to the ideological debates taking place elsewhere in Europe and to the German Sozialdemokratische Partei Deutschlands' *Erfurt* programme of 1891 in particular (Tilton, 1979, pp.505–20). However, while Marxist and revolutionary in theory, the young Scandinavian socialist parties were essentially gradualist in practice, contributing, in alliance with liberal elements of the bourgeoisie, to the establishment of universal suffrage under conditions of capitalism. Only in Finland could the Social Democrats be described (albeit briefly) as an anti-system party, and even then, their leadership, dominated by Kautskyite centrists, initiated revolution in 1917–18 with the utmost reluctance (Kirby, 1979, pp.40–8). The pragmatic line of 'ministerial socialism' ultimately favoured by the Scandinavian Social Democratic parties during the inter-war period may well have been a factor in the consolidation of their support. Certainly, by the 1930s they were polling about 40 per cent of the vote in Denmark, Norway and Sweden, and this included, especially in Denmark, elements of the white-collar population. This is less surprising perhaps when it is remembered that the Social Democrats did not in the main present themselves as narrowly class-based parties and aspired to the support of the whole working population (Thomas, 1977, p.254).

*Agrarian parties*

The emergence of Agrarian parties, following hard on the heels of social democracy, reflected the size of the agricultural population and, in particular, the regional density of family-sized farms during the vital period of political and economic modernization. Agrarian parties were not peculiar to Scandinavia: in addition to the 'Green rising' in central and eastern Europe, there were farmers' parties in France, Ireland, Switzerland and Bavaria between the wars. But in terms of their voter strength and durability, the Scandinavian parties remain unsurpassed. In Finland, the most agrarian but least developed farming nation (see table 2.4), the Agrarian Party, formed in 1906, consistently polled on average one-quarter of the vote; in the more industrialized Sweden and Norway support for the Agrarians, founded in 1910 and 1915 respectively, while somewhat smaller, ranged from one-seventh to just under one-tenth of the vote; and though in Denmark, with the smallest but most highly developed agricultural sector, an Agrarian party as such never appeared, *Venstre*, often translated as 'Agrarian Liberals' and enjoying more than half the vote in rural Jutland in 1920, may be considered essentially a farmers' party. It is considered at the end of this section as something of a special case. Reference throughout is also made to the Progressive Party in Iceland, which explicitly defined itself as a farmers' party.

TABLE 2.4: THE PERCENTAGE OF THE POPULATION ENGAGED IN AGRICULTURE AND ALLIED OCCUPATIONS, 1890–1910

| Country | 1890 | Year 1900 | 1910 |
|---|---|---|---|
| Denmark (agriculture and fishing) | 49 | 44 | 36 |
| Norway (agriculture, forestry and fishing) | 51 | 44 | 43 |
| Sweden (agriculture, forestry and fishing) | 62 | 55 | 49 |
| Finland (agriculture) | 73 | 68 | 66 |

*Source:* Jörberg, 1973, p.392.

In terms of their initial support, the Scandinavian Agrarian parties possessed much in common. Thus, excluding the Norwegian party (*Bondeparti*), the impetus for which came in 1906 from the larger farmers in the East and Trøndelag, who were members of the pressure group *Norsk Landmansforbund*, the Scandinavian Agrarian parties originally comprised mainly small farmers or peasants (Aasland, 1974). The Finnish Agrarian Party (*Maalaisliitto*) had its strongholds in the only two provinces — Oulu in the north-west and Viipuri in the south-east — to boast a preponderance of independent peasants, so lending support, at the regional level at least, to Lipset and Rokkan's contention that a large family-sized farming population is a *sine qua non* for the growth of strong agrarian parties (Lipset and Rokkan, 1967, p.45). At the general elections of October 1917, on the eve of Finnish independence, the Agrarians' 12.4 per cent of the popular vote was almost exclusively derived from these two provinces (Arter, 1978a, pp.66—74). In Sweden, too, the Agrarians (*Bondeförbund*) emerged at the regional level in 1910 as the spokesmen of the small and medium-sized landowners in the south-west (Carlsson, 1956). The party organized itself on a national basis in 1914, replacing the Rural Party which had been devastated at the polls two years earlier. Following the achievement of domestic sovereignty in 1918, the Icelandic Progressive Party (*Framsóknarflokkur*) established itself as the leading non-socialist party in the small farming territories in the north and east of the country where the co-operative movement was most firmly rooted (Kristjánsson, 1978, pp.17—18).

Despite their initial small-farming support base, the Scandinavian Agrarian parties were not peasant parties in the fundamentalist sense that they were striving towards a completely 'New Deal' for the entire countryside; rather, they were essentially farmers' or interest-group parties promoting the class interests of agricultural producers at varying stages of integration into the capitalist economy. Indeed, in recruiting support really only from farmers, they were even more evidently class parties than were the Scandinavian Social Democratic and Labour parties. In large part, the Agrarian parties reflected a reaction to industrialization and the threat posed to the role of farming in an increasingly urban economy. Indirectly, of course, industrialization was an important factor in raising the economic level of the farming population, for while its absolute size declined, agricultural productivity rose to meet the growth in consumer demand for foodstuffs. At the same time, there was a tendency for the political representatives of the urban-industrial interests to conspire to keep domestic prices down. Consequently, the dominant logic of the Scandinavian Agrarian parties was the urge to achieve measures of protection: for the home market against an influx of cheaper foreign grains, as in Norway in the 1920s, and for the farming sector in general through land reform and the provision of credit facilities, as in Sweden and Finland.

Though unqestionably class parties in practice, the Agrarians strenuously rejected left-wing accusations that they merely served the economic interests of bourgeois farmers. Indeed, it must be allowed that in Sweden and Finland in particular, the Agrarians initially espoused a radical and romantic rhetoric which urged the *moral* as well as the economic case for small farming and defended a vision of rural society based on the spirit of co-operative *gemeinschaft* against the contamination of urban *gesellschaft* (Torstendahl, 1969). The writings of P.J. Rösiö in Sweden were influential in extolling a type of society based on peasant thrift and hard work, while the leading ideologue of the Finnish Agrarians, Santeri Alkio, even spoke of the feasibility of *autarkie* and the need to avoid the ethically corrosive large-scale capitalist route to the modern world (Alanen, 1976). However, by the 1920s both parties had tended to become more conservative as well as more structurally diverse following the affiliation of elements of the larger farming population.

In Sweden a dissident Agrarian faction had joined forces with a separate agrarian movement in the Skåne region in 1915 to form a second farmers' party, *Jordbrukarnas Riksförbund*, which contained many larger landowners and landless 'gentlemen' and was rather rightist in complexion (Jonnergård, 1950). When this in turn merged in 1921 with the original Agrarian Party (whose name, *Bondeförbund*, was retained), the result was an initial loss of support, and it was not until the 1930s that the party achieved its best electoral successes, with over 14 per cent of the vote. After the resolution of the national question in Finland in 1919, the Agrarians, who had played a central role, first on the White side in the Civil War in 1918 and then in advocating a republican Constitution during the form-of-government crisis later the same year, attracted some of the larger farmers in the south and west, becoming, like the Swedish party, less radical in the process (Arter, 1978a, pp.91–123). Unlike the latter, however, it grew rapidly, achieving a record vote for a Scandinavian agrarian party in 1930 when it obtained 27.3 per cent of the poll.

Unlike its sister parties in Sweden and Finland, the Norwegian Agrarian Party's support base was relatively diverse from the outset. At the general elections of 1921, running slates of candidates everywhere except Oslo, Bergen and Finnmark, it achieved 13.1 per cent of the valid poll — its vote drawn fairly evenly from the small and medium-sized farmers in the south and west, most of them former supporters of the Left (*Venstre*), and the larger producers in the east who had previously backed the Right. By 1924 the Agrarians' popularity had declined in the south-west, while increasing in the east. As in Finland, the party gained its optimal vote of 15.9 per cent in 1930 (Greenhill, 1965).

It was largely because the economy was so unquestionably dependent upon agriculture and protection was therefore less needed, that a durable interest-specific farmers' party never emerged in Denmark. As early as the 1850s co-operative credit associations, similar to the German *Landschaften*, were organized in Denmark, and they provided capital for the transformation of agriculture from grain to dairy produce in the 1870s — significantly, the decade of the emergence of the left–right two-party system (Jensen, 1937, p.319). Indeed, the continuity of the 'old' Left in Denmark (*Venstre* gained 34.5 per cent of the vote and was the largest party in 1920) remained essentially unbroken — notwithstanding the formation in 1905 of a splinter Radical Liberal party, *Det radikale Venstre*, around the issue of pacifism — precisely because *Venstre* had traditionally been the party of a modern, well integrated farming sector heavily reliant upon exports to Britain (Rasmussen, 1955). As long as the British market held, the need for an agrarian party *per se* did not exist, nor was there a case for membership of the Green International, which, based in Prague and boasting the membership of the other Scandinavian agrarian parties, was basically a multinational farm-export syndicate aspiring to compete in the same British market! However, Britain's adoption of an Imperial Preference in 1933 changed matters and led the Agrarian Liberals to do a deal with the Social Democrats and the Radical Liberals whereby they promised to support social reforms in return for guarantees for agriculture. This proved widely unpopular among the farmers, and at the general elections of 1935 the Agrarian Liberals sank to their lowest pre-war ebb, gaining only 17.8 per cent of the valid poll, while a lobby of disenchanted agriculturalists formed a Farmer's Party (*Bondepartiet*) which attracted from 3.4 to 1.4 per cent of the vote between 1935 and 1943 (Monrad, 1970). Interestingly, co-operation involving the Progressive Party and the Social Democrats against the background of Depression was a factor in the split in the Icelandic farmers' movement in the 1930s and the creation, as in Denmark, of a Farmers' Party (*Baendaflokkur*) which polled over 6 per cent of the vote at the general elections of 1934 and 1937. In the second half of the 1930s, in other words, all five Scandinavian states boasted Agrarian parties, albeit briefly.

## THE COMPLETION OF THE FIVE-PARTY SCANDINAVIAN MODEL: 1920–30

*The emergence of a radical left*

The radicalization of the working-class political movements in Scandinavia after the First World War enhanced the identity of social democracy while depriving it of a section of its natural working-class constituency. Only in Finland, however, where the Communists, masquerading as the Socialist Workers' Party (*Suomen sosialistinen Työväenpuolue*) polled approximately 15 per cent of the valid vote at their initial attempt in 1922, did the new parties of the radical left achieve much electoral success in the inter-war period. The optimal vote for the second largest such party in the region, the Icelandic Communist Party, founded as late as 1930, was only a little over half that of the Finnish Socialist Workers' Party, and it managed to claim a modest 3.0 per cent of the active electorate when it first contested general elections in 1931. Indeed, the radical left in Iceland was only briefly, in the early 1930s, 'anti-system' in the conventional sense, and in 1938 it became more explicitly reformist in adopting the designation United Socialist Party.

The distinctive strength of the radical left in Finland in the 1920s was indebted in at least three ways to the nation's geopolitical location. First, Finland's former status as a Grand Duchy of the Russian Empire had enabled the tsar as head of state repeatedly to veto working-class demands for social reform, as well as to impose tariff laws binding the Finnish and Russian economies together (Rasila, 1966, pp.278–98). Finland's dependence upon Russian grain became critical when the Imperial harvest failed in 1916 (foreign supplies were not forthcoming, owing to a war-time blockade), for it was in conditions of domestic famine that the Finnish labour movement, encouraged by Lenin, attempted revolution. Secondly, the comparative brevity of the journey from Helsinki to Leningrad was significant because after the Whites' victory in the Finnish Civil War of winter 1918, a radical elite and thousands of refugees found a sympathetic exile in the Soviet Union, where in September 1918 they founded the Finnish Communist Party. Using the agency of the Finnish Socialist Workers Party, established in June 1920, the Communists targeted an electoral base in Finland and by 1922 had achieved a membership of about 70 per cent of the Social Democrats (London, 1975, pp.4–5). Last, Finland's geographical position enabled illegal Communist literature to be smuggled in easily and quickly: the network of social contacts formed by widows and orphans seeking information from the peripatetic Red agitators was also important in the diffusion of Communism.

The Finnish Socialist Workers' Party was outlawed in 1930, but before that it had laid an organizational infrastructure in the industrial areas of Turku, Vaasa and Western Kuopio which was to serve as a springboard for the Communist Party when it was legalized in 1944. True, the Social Democrats' support in central southern Finland between the wars remained largely unaffected by the emergence of the radical left, though, as Pertti Laulajainen has suggested, had it not been for the loyalty of leaders on the left wing of the Social Democratic Party in key towns like Viipuri, the Communists might have been in a majority on the left in 1922 (Laulajainen, 1979, p.139). As it was, the Socialist Workers' Party polled 13.5 per cent of the valid vote on the eve of its suppression in 1929, while the Communist Party (and Radical Democrats) managed to claim nearly 24.0 per cent the year after its appearance in 1944.

The ban on the Finnish Socialist Workers' Party left the way clear for the Icelandic Communist Party to become the largest single party of the radical left in the region in the course of the 1930s. It was the only party of its type in Scandinavia to show significant gains over the years of the Great Depression, achieving 8.5 per cent of the valid poll in 1937 and, in the process, winning three of the forty-nine seats in the *Althing*. A Communist group had been formed within the Social Democratic Party in 1921 but, on the advice of the Comintern, had remained where it was until 1930, when, in the conducive conditions of recession, it seceded. The year after it won 3.0 per cent of the vote, a proportion that grew to 7.5 per cent in 1933, following well orchestrated agitation during the worst of the slump and reaching its pre-war peak in 1937. In part, this was the result of the Social Democrats' rejection of the Communists' demand for a Popular Front coalition, which prompted a left-wing faction in the Social Democrats to break away and join forces with the Communists. In order to accommodate the new splinter elements, the Communist Party changed its name in 1938 to the United Socialist Party and also left the Comintern. As the United Socialist Party, the party became increasingly reformist. Geographically remote from the centre of revolutionary socialism in Moscow, the influence of the Comintern and its hardline ideology had never been strong, and its directives were followed only when it was tactically convenient for the Icelandic party to do so. Indeed, the influence of the radical left in Iceland before 1939 should not be overestimated: only once, in 1937, did it boast parliamentary representation, and only really in the early 1930s did it preach revolution.

Compared with Finland or even Iceland, the inter-war Communist parties of Denmark, Norway and Sweden were small and their national role marginal (Sparring, 1973, p.61). This is not to suggest that conditions were particularly unfavourable to the emergence of a strong radical left. On the contrary, all three states were situated close enough to the USSR to feel its influence, and in Norway, as in Finland, there were serious food shortages which led to the spontaneous formation of workers' councils (Rohde, 1973, pp.38–9). Indeed, in 1918 the Labour Party was captured by Tranmael and the following year became only the second party outside the Soviet Union to join the Comintern. As in France after the Congress of Tours at Christmas 1920, in other words, the *majority* of the Norwegian labour movement was in the hands of the radical left, though in the form of the Labour and not of the Communist Party. That this did not prove to be a lasting state of affairs was probably the result less of any marked deradicalization of the working class consequent, among other things, upon improvements in living standards – though there was an upturn in the economy – than of the unwillingness of the Labour Party leadership to condone interference from Moscow with regard to implementing the notorious Twenty-One Theses (insisting on the adoption of the name Communist Party) and, above all, its refusal to regard the instigation of civil war as an appropriate strategy in the Norwegian case. It was perhaps to be expected that in 1921 a right-wing group left the Labour Party to found the Norwegian Social Democratic Party, while two years later, despite Bukharin's mediations on behalf of the Comintern, the Labour Party itself broke with Moscow, leaving the pro-Soviet minority to found the Norwegian Communist Party. The latter gained 6.0 per cent of the vote at the general elections in 1924, but after the Social Democratic Party merged with the Labour Party in 1927 the radical party left in Norway steadily declined.

The essential unity of the labour movements in Denmark and Sweden and, conversely, their low propensity for radicalization compared with that of Norway and Finland may well have been linked to the differential completion of full democratization. In Norway manhood suffrage had been effectively achieved in 1897, but the labour movement had succeeded in little by 1918, not least because of an electoral system (introduced in 1905) which, in employing single-member constituencies, discriminated heavily against it. Similarly, in Finland, though mass democracy had been enacted in 1906, the aims of the labour movement were frustrated by the Russian tsar's repeated dissolution of the Finnish Diet. In both cases the electoral means to working-class reforms had been secured but their attainment thwarted by existing political arrangements. Moreover, the consequent tendency to radicalization was compounded by domestic famine and the events of 1917 in Russia. In Denmark, and particularly in Sweden, where suffrage extension was a rather more gradual process, the completion of mass democracy remained a primary objective of the labour movement that much longer. Furthermore, its realization involved the working class in arrangements with progressive elements of the bourgeoisie which had a markedly integrative effect and led subsequently to Social Democratic–Radical Liberal or Liberal coalitions in both countries (Castles, 1978, pp.19–22). Clearly, the contrast must not be overdrawn, for the radical left in Sweden, the Left Social Democratic Party (*Sveriges socialdemokratiska vänsterparti*), founded in 1917, brought together a heterogeneous group of persons all doubting the wisdom of the Social Democratic Party's proposed democratic and parliamentary route to socialism. The Left Social Democratic Party affiliated to the Comintern in 1919 – the majority accepting the Twenty-One Theses – and, as the Swedish Communist Party (*Sveriges kommunistiska Parti*), polled 5.1 per cent in elections to the Second Chamber in 1924. But the vital point is that in both Denmark and Sweden the Social Democrats maintained the fundamental solidarity of the labour movement and so prevented the rise of substantial parties of the radical left. Indeed, racked by internal dissension, the Danish Communist Party (*Danmarks kommunistiske Parti*) managed to poll only 0.4 per cent of the vote in 1926.

*The transformation of the nineteenth-century Right and Left*

The 'old' parties of Right and Left which had characterized the initial period of Scandinavian bipartism had transformed themselves into Conservative and Liberal groups by the 1920s. In some cases the nineteenth-century labels were retained: the Right in Sweden and Norway, for example, and the Left in Denmark and Norway. In others, new parties or new names came into being: the Conservative People's Party in Denmark and the Liberal Party in Sweden; the conservative National Coalition and the liberal Progressive Party in Finland; and the Independence Party formed by a merger of conservatism and liberalism in Iceland. In every case the modernization and reorganization of conservative and liberal groups in the 1920s took place against the backdrop of the organizational strength and tactical skill of the Social Democratic and Agrarian parties, which served to restrict their electoral progress.

During the era of two-party politics, the Right had been essentially defensive, resisting the Left's campaign for franchise reform and representative government and, in the dependent nations, favouring a conciliatory approach towards the colonial power. In Norway, for example, the Right had represented the continuities with the Danish culture of the educated classes and had defended the Swedish king and his officials in the constitutional struggle of the 1880s. Soon after the First World War came a distinct change in orientation. The Danish Right changed its name in 1915 to the Conservative People's Party (*Det konservative Folkeparti*), partly to turn its back on the negativism of the nineteenth-century party, which had opposed parliamentarism and the liberalization of the upper house, *Landstinget*, but also with a view to broadening its support beyond the wealthy and propertied classes that had traditionally backed it. The Swedish party's willingness to support the Liberal–Social Democratic suffrage reforms of 1919–21 was similarly motivated, although it did not change its name.

Yet by contrast with their counterpart in Britain, the Scandinavian Conservatives did not take the initiative in extending the franchise to the working classes and consequently failed to profit from the incorporation of the new blue-collar electors. Moreover, as Stein Rokkan has observed, 'in contrast to the British Conservative Party, the Right in Norway, as in the other Scandinavian countries, was not able to bring about an alliance of urban and rural elites and to create the basis for a broad national movement' (Lipset and Rokkan, 1967, p.395). Consequently, as in Imperial Germany, where the Free Conservatives and Conservatives reflected the division of the non-socialists along a town–country axis, Scandinavian conservatism, denied significant rural support by the emergence of interest-specific agrarian parties, drew mainly on the power-holders: the civil servants, professional and business people in the towns and capital cities in particular.

This is not to say the right lacked any rural allegiance. In Finland the National Coalition drew votes in the south-west from both landowners and tenants, partly as a result of its staunch defence of the Evangelical Lutheran Church against threats from the other parties to separate Church and State and also as traditional champion of the Finnish language against the minority Swedish. In Sweden some of the larger farmers in the central districts mistrusted the small-farming bias of the Agrarians and voted for the Right, while in Norway opposition to prohibition (1919–26) indirectly explains much of the Conservatives' breakthrough among the *småbruker* in the far north in the 1920s. When the Liberal government imposed a ban on foreign wines, and the exporting countries of southern Europe retaliated by forbidding the importation of Norwegian fish, the hardships experienced in the fishing districts of northern Norway prompted a defection from the Liberals to the Conservatives. The Conservatives have retained this area of rural support to this day.

Yet with most of their support drawn from the towns, the Scandinavian Conservatives were relatively weak electorally. In Denmark, for example, although the Conservative People's Party drew on about two-fifths of the vote in Copenhagen in the inter-war period, only once, in 1926, did it achieve over one-fifth of the *national* vote. In Denmark and Finland the Agrarians were consistently larger than the Conservatives, and though the reverse was the case in Norway and Sweden, Scandinavia has lacked a broadly based party of the right, comparable with the British Conservative Party, which has at the same time played a key role in determining the outcome of events. In fact the right emerged as something of a champion of lost causes: it failed to prevent the acceptance of parliamentarism, to thwart the process of electoral reform or, in Finland, to prevent the enactment of a republican Constitution in June 1919. Indeed, the National Coalition, formed in November 1918, was an alliance of those who had favoured a constitutional monarchy. The one exception to the rule of predominantly urban middle-class Conservative parties in Scandinavia has been the Independence Party in Iceland.

Founded in 1929, at a time when the Conservatives and Liberals were in opposition to a Progressive Party government backed by the Social Democrats, the Icelandic Independence Party became the largest single party at the first general election it contested in 1931 and achieved its greatest ever success at the polls two years later with 48 per cent of the vote. From the outset it eschewed its opponents' functionalist view of representation, claiming to possess free and independent agents acting in the national interest and not delegates mandated narrowly to serve the needs of the main economic groups in society. Indeed, as it emerged, the Independence Party constituted a unique alliance between the urban bourgeoisie – public officials, merchants, owners of fishing vessels — the farmers and manual workers, united beneath the banner of nationalism. Thus Kristjánsson has described how the party developed close ties with Óðinn, a society of workers and sailors founded in 1938, making it plain that the Independence Party's distinctive character as a catch-all party of the right was evident *before* it presided over the completion of national autonomy in 1944 (Kristjánsson, 1978, pp.23—8).

Twentieth-century Scandinavian liberalism was a linear descendant of the parties of the 'old' non-socialist Left. However, from a position as leading parliamentary force before 1914, these parties lost significant electoral ground by 1930. In Norway the Liberals' vote dropped from one-third of the electorate in 1915 to well below one-fifth by the 1930s. In Finland the Progressive Party's poll disintegrated from 12.8 per cent in 1919 to no more than 5.6 per cent ten years later. In Sweden the Liberal Party vote fell nearly 8 per cent over the same period, and in 1932 the party hit an inter-war low, with only 11.7 per cent of the active electorate. Even in Denmark the Agrarian Liberals were surpassed by the Social Democrats as the largest single party in 1924. There appear to be two general explanations of the declining popularity of Scandinavian liberalism at the time of the completion of the basic five-party Scandinavian model in the 1920s. First, there were the difficulties of reconciling a wide variety of interests with which, as the leading anti-establishment party of the late nineteenth-century, the 'old' Left had become identified. Secondly, there was its tardiness in adapting to the needs of an electorate increasingly differentiated along sectoral economic lines.

As the principal anti-establishment party during the era of two-party politics — champions of the nation against the state — the Left had attracted a heterogeneous clientele ranging from small-farm proprietors and tenants to journalists and urban intellectuals. More particularly, it became identified with a wide variety of opposition causes which liberalism subsequently found difficult to embrace. The question of reforming Church—State relations, for example, divided the Low Church and active Christian adherents from the more nominal members of the Evangelical Lutheran Church, while the issue of prohibition in Norway, Sweden and Finland divided 'moral' Liberals from the more secularized, individualistic elements in the parties. The Swedish party split over this latter issue, with the majority prohibitionist wing forming a splinter group, the Free Liberals (*Frisinnade Folkpartiet*), in 1922 following a consultative referendum which narrowly failed to produce a favourable result (49 per cent voted for prohibition). It was 1934 before the two wings of the party reunited. In Norway the sequence was replicated in reverse: a referendum on prohibition held in October 1919 produced a majority of 61.6 per cent in support, and two years later a minority broke with the Liberal leadership, opposing what it saw as undue public interference in the realm of private morality. The Liberals split again in 1933, with the emergence of a Christian People's Party (*Kristelig Folkeparti*) in the 'Bible Belt' areas of western Norway. This remained a very small regional affair before 1945 but was nonetheless an important reminder that even in the relatively homogeneous political cultures of the Scandinavian states parties based on non-functional cleavages and issues were possible. Indeed, the question of prohibition – the Christian People's Party wanted to reverse the repeal of 1926 – aroused extra-parliamentary movements and internal party factionalization on a scale unsurpassed in the region until the EEC and nuclear energy issues came on to the agenda of politics in the 1970s.

Other issues dividing the Scandinavian Liberals included the question of reducing defence expenditure, which ranged pacifists against those committed to orthodox defence spending, and this, coupled with the growing tension between the smallholders traditionally aligning with the 'old' Left and the urban leadership of the Liberal parties, led to the formation of a permanent splinter party, the Radicals (*Det radikale Venstre*) in Denmark as early as 1905. Initially, the party's success was modest, but a financial scandal in 1908 sullied the Liberal name and the Radicals proceeded to form a minority government the following year, relying on the support of the Social Democrats. Ironically, the Radicals themselves lost support to the Justice Party (*Danmarks Retsforbund*) formed in 1919, which, by advocating Henry George's theories for a single tax on land values, attracted a small-farmer following. In Finland, too, the vast majority of small farmers backing the liberal Progressive Party (*Kansallinen Edistyspuolue*) defected to the Agrarians over the course of the 1920s.

Indeed, though the Liberal parties of the region had pioneered such vital *political* causes as full democratization, constitutionalism and responsible government, they tended to neglect (outside Denmark at least) the *social* and *economic* aspects of liberalism. In consequence, the parties which had been historically the instrument of the power-seekers appeared to have little more to seek when they achieved power. The Swedish case illustrates the point. Founded in 1900, the Liberals (*Folkpartiet*), under the leadership of Nils Edén, joined forces with the Social Democrats in a coalition administration between 1917 and 1920 which effected such important constitutional changes as votes for women and electoral reform for the upper house. With their main aims achieved, however, the Liberals seemed exhausted, and their poll of 19.1 per cent at the general elections of 1921 compared badly with a high point of 40.2 per cent ten years earlier. Above all, at a time of accelerated industrialization and urbanization, the Liberals' lack of a cohesive social reform programme enabled the Social Democrats to consolidate control over the growing blue-collar constituency. True, by the 1930s social liberalism was imposing curbs on the unbridled interplay of marked forces and stressing the need for public spending in the social policy area, but by then the initiative had been largely surrendered to the socialist left.

## THE 1930s: THE SCANDINAVIAN PARTY SYSTEMS AND THE CHALLENGE OF ECONOMIC RECESSION

### Denmark, Norway and Sweden

Although the Social Democrats had established themselves as dominant parties in Denmark, Norway and Sweden by the 1930s, none of these three countries escaped the relatively high levels of government instability common among regimes first experiencing the conditions of mass democracy. In Sweden, for example, there were eight administrations between the completion of universal suffrage in 1920 and the start of the Social Democrats' almost unbroken forty-four year rule in 1932. In Norway a series of short-lived administrations culminated in a first Labour minority government in 1927 which lasted only eighteen days! Indeed, with left—right differences sharply demarcated, there was a tendency for governing responsibility to devolve upon centre-based (and usually liberal) parties. Even so, not only were the party systems of Denmark, Norway and Sweden, unlike several of their counterparts elsewhere in Europe, able to withstand the main systemic challenge of the inter-war period, the Great Depression, but they also contrived a growing consensus in support of state involvement in the field of social and economic policy. Their task was, of course, facilitated by the absence of significant parties of the radical left, which meant there was little ballast for reactionary radical rightist movements of the Fascist type. However, the basic argument advanced here is that with the Danish and especially the Norwegian and Swedish economies still very much at a transitional stage and still containing sizable small-farming sectors, there existed a *potential* susceptibility to millenial movements. The fact that they did not emerge on any scale should be attributed in no small measure to the capacity for elite accommodation demonstrated by the party representatives of the main sectoral interests. In particular, the Social Democratic–Agrarian, Red–Green coalitions of the 1930s constituted the 'historic compromises' of inter-war Scandinavian politics.

On the Social Democratic side, the prelude to Red–Green co-operation was a perception that although the Depression constituted a crisis of capitalism which could be remedied only by far-reaching changes in the productive fabric of society, these could best be achieved by participation in government, not by standing in the wings waiting for inevitable revolution. Obviously, there was more to it than that. The joint legislative programme of the Social Democrats and the Radicals in Denmark in 1929 – the foundation of their post-election coalition – reflected the *long-term* reformism of the Danish party and not a sudden change of tack. Moreover, the Social Democrats' participationist strategy in Sweden must be seen in the context of their electoral defeat in 1928, when the party lost ground as a result of being presented as an anti-system threat by its opponents. Nonetheless, the governing orientation of the moderate left during a period of acute economic recession needs emphasis. Particularly in Norway, the Labour Party's adoption of a gradualist approach by the mid-1930s acquires fundamentalist significance when it is noted that it was 1927 before references in its programme to 'the dictatorship of the proletariat' were removed. Once ensconced in power (with over 40 per cent of the popular vote in Denmark, Norway and Sweden by the Second World War), the Social Democrats promoted Keynesian-style reflationary measures, attacking unemployment through a programme of public investment and social policies. The basis of the welfare state was laid.

On the Agrarian side, the background to Red–Green co-operation was the devastating impact of the Depression in the agricultural sector. Thus in Sweden the collapse of farm prices led the Social Democrats and the Agrarians (the latter abandoning their traditional co-operation with the Conservatives) to make an alliance in 1933; there was a similar alliance between the Agrarian Liberals and Social Democrats in Denmark in 1934, following Britain's decision to establish Imperial Preferences; and in Norway the Nygaardsvold Social Democratic–Agrarian alliance formed in 1935 combined deficit budgeting with agricultural subsidies. Prompted by the conditions of Depression and the need for recovery, the co-operation of industrial workers and farm producers in the Red–

Green arrangements of the 1930s had a twofold significance. First, they were a timely reminder that although the class contours of the party systems of Denmark, Norway and Sweden were clearly enough delineated, bridges at the elite level were by no means impossible to build. Secondly, the Red—Green agreements represented a significant bulwark against extremism of left and right. In all three states the Communist parties remained electorally insignificant before 1945 and the Fascist parties failed to make headway either. The optimal vote for the Danish National Socialists was a mere 2.2 per cent — and that in 1943! — and its Swedish counterpart could manage a maximum of only 1.6 per cent in 1936. Furthermore, despite the Nazi collaborationist Quisling's international notoriety, his National Unity Movement, *Nasjonal Samling*, in Norway attracted little durable support.

## Iceland

The formative Icelandic party system of the 1930s reflected overwhelming support for the achievement of complete independence when the twenty-five-year treaty of union with Denmark expired in 1944. All four main parties, the Communists, the Social Democrats and the Progressives and Independence parties, were, in a real sense, nationalist parties. To be sure, there were inter-elite differences over ultimate goals — the nature of political society in the post-independence period — and also, to some extent, over the means of achieving them. For example, the Independence Party, which participated only once in government between 1932 and 1934, employed the election slogan 'Iceland for the Icelanders', claiming that class co-operation was a fundamental precondition of national solidarity. The agrarian Progressive Party, the smaller of the two non-socialist parties but a regular governing party during the inter-war period, held that the countryside was the home of the national *volksgeist* and that for Iceland the way ahead lay in her being a modernized but essentially rurally orientated nation. The Social Democrats, much the strongest of the left-wing parties *before* 1939, believed that social justice was vital to the consolidation of a sense of Icelandic identity and that when nobody was deprived, commitment to the attainment and subsequent preservation of national independence was greatest. The Communists too, founded in 1930 and renamed the United Socialist Party in 1938, presented their socialist crusade against imperialism and capitalism as an independence struggle — albeit a battle to liberate Iceland from the stultifying embrace of the bourgeois classes.

Indeed, as Svanur Kristjánsson has noted, Iceland illustrated 'the divisive impact nationalism can have within the same nation' (Kristjánsson, 1978, p.12).

But too much must not be made of these broad-guage differences, for at the pragmatic level the party system was united on a number of counts: first, on the completion of mass democracy, which was effectively achieved in 1934, when the voting age was lowered from 25 to 21 and those in receipt of welfare benefits were enfranchised; and, secondly, on measures to deal with the Great Depression. Indeed, as the Icelandic version of the Red—Green arrangements common to all the Scandinavian states at this time, the Progressive—Social Democratic Party coalition government of 1934—9 introduced a state-sponsored system of social security benefits, in addition to providing public backing to farmers and fishing-vessel owners hard-hit by the recession. In this context it was significant that from its position in opposition the Independence Party pressed hard for support for the trawler industry — admittedly, an important source of its votes. It is, in fact, arguable that the only dissenting voice during the slump was the Communists', who, by actively exploiting unrest, claimed over 7 per cent of the poll in 1933.

All in all, however, the Icelandic party system acquitted itself well in the face of this main challenge of the inter-war period. The slump did precipitate a *permanent* split on the left, while, as in the case of the agrarian Liberals in Denmark, Red—Green co-operation in government led a small minority of disenchanted farmers to leave the Progressive Party. But concern for the ultimate attainment of national independence so dominated the party system that it was not until 1942, on the eve of its achievement, that the radical left acquired really significant electoral and parliamentary strength. The relative smallness of the radical left over the critical decade of the 1930s plainly minimized the scope for a corresponding movement of the radical right.

*Finland*

The party system of inter-war Finland appears to have been the most deviant of all the Scandinavian cases. Indeed, with four parties (the Social Democrats, the Agrarians, the Progressives and the National Coalition) possessing governing potential and a relatively large party of the radical left, the Socialist Workers' Party, with considerable blackmail potential, it was clearly located in Sartori's class of 'extreme multipartism' (Sartori, 1976, p.285). Not only that, but during the initial years of independence Finland may be said to have possessed at least some of the characteristics of polarized pluralism. Thus the Agrarian–Progressive Party centre minority governments of 1919–22 were cast very much in a system defence role. They faced claims for regional self-government from a small but vociferous section of the Swedish-speaking population; a Social Democratic Party returning to Parliament (following a post-civil war proscription) with precisely the same two-fifths of the legislative seats that it had obtained in 1917, which promptly demanded an amnesty for political prisoners; suspicion from the (formerly monarchist) National Coalition, now electorally subordinate to the Agrarians; and the emergence of a Socialist Workers' Party, apparently so menacing that its entire parliamentary delegation was imprisoned in 1923. Furthermore, a measure of the overall government instability in the first decade of the new regime is the fact that there were no fewer than fourteen governments between 1919 and 1929, precisely half containing non-party experts and two others that were no more than caretaker administrations of officials. Yet Finland in the 1920s must not be dismissed as simply extremist and immobilistic: on the contrary, the party system manifested a notable degree of elite co-operation, in view of the cleavages generated during the resolution of state-building from 1917 to 1919. The 'losing' monarchists in the National Coalition, for example, participated in government as early as November 1918 – and thereafter several times during the 1920s – while under the moderating influence of Väinö Tanner the former Reds in the Social Democratic Party pursued a gradualist line and formed a single-party minority government in 1926. Moreover, a period of marked economic growth between 1919 and 1928 meant that governments functioned less as predominantly negative agencies – bulwarks against extremism – and instead inaugurated an era of public expenditure on health, education and communication.

The onset of the Depression, however, which first hit the farmers over the winter of 1929 and gave rise to the radical rightest *Lapua* movement, demonstrated the continuing fragility of the Finnish political system. Based on the predominantly medium-sized landowners in the north-western province of Vaasa and espousing a fervently anti-Communist rhetoric, the *Lapua* movement grew into a broadly based bourgeois protest movement opposing the power of organized labour and, at the same time, critical of the weakness of the parliamentary system and the high levels of government instability accompanying it. Between 1929 and 1932, in fact, liberal democracy appeared genuinely at risk as the party system surrendered control of events to an extra-parliamentary movement which forced a ban on the Socialist Workers' Party in 1930, installed Svinhufvud as the President of its own choosing and proceeded to attempt an unsuccessful coup. Indeed, class contours were more starkly etched and the centre of gravity in Finnish politics shifted further to the right than at any time before or since, notwithstanding the immediate aftermath of the Civil War. Ironically, the Communist threat was at its most feeble by the time of the foundation of the *Lapua* movement, for in 1929 its underground organization had been smashed, and the following year it had lost control of the central labour organization *Suomen Ammattijärjestö* (SAJ). Yet the Labour movement had gained in strength over the boom years; many strikes had ended in notable victories for the workers; and memories of conflicts between workers and organized blacklegs haunted the bourgeoisie (Kalela, 1976, pp.111–12).

The failure of the *Lapua* rebellion in March 1932 marked the resumption of control over events by the party system. Svinhufvud's disavowal of the movement on the radio, the upturn in the economy and, not least, ultimate consensus among the bourgeoisie about the legitimacy of the system were the main factors in its growing isolation. The *Lapua* movement was banned in 1932, while the establishment of Red–Green governmental co-operation in 1937 brought Finland more into line with developments elsewhere in Scandinavia. Yet although the extent of political consensus grew throughout the second half of the 1930s, it was a consensus born of a distinctly restricted form of political pluralism: the *Lapua* movement's successor, the Patriotic People's Movement (IKL) was allowed to contest elections, but the ban on the Socialist Workers' Party, its radical leftist counterpart, remained very definitely in force.

In conclusion, the Scandinavian party systems on the threshold of the Second World War can be divided into three types. The metropolitan states of Denmark, Norway and Sweden may be said to have possessed *convergent party systems*: their legitimacy was not challenged by significant extremism on either right or left, while heightened inter-elite co-operation was reflected in the Red–Green 'historic compromises' of the 1930s. The principal actors moved closer together – the Social Democrats in deferring revolution in favour of the participationist line of 'ministerial socialism' and the bourgeois parties in accepting the need for state intervention to protect citizens over the economic crisis. Iceland boasted perhaps the closest thing to a *consensual party system*: there was broad agreement among the parties over the need for national independence, the issue dominating Icelandic politics; and, unlike the other Scandinavian countries, Red—Green coalitions characterized the whole inter-war period. True, the radical left was stronger than in the metropolitan states, but in actively seeking entry into government in the mid-1930s, it was hardly behaving as an anti-system party in the conventional sense. Finally, Finland remained a *cleavage-dominant party system*. Indeed, though the long-standing suspicion surrounding Social Democratic—Agrarian relationships was ultimately subordinated to the end of governmental co-operation, the two came together in 1937 in very much a system-defence role, with the legitimacy of the republic challenged at both ends of the spectrum. The price of regime continuity, moreover, remained the proscription of the radical left.

CHAPTER THREE

# Social Cleavages and Partisan Conflict after the Second World War

## STRUCTURAL ALTERATIONS TO THE FIVE-PARTY SYSTEM PRIOR TO 1970

In a seminal article in 1967 Stein Rokkan observed that, with only a few exceptions, the European party systems 'froze' during the 1920s and forty years later still tended to reflect the cleavage structure of the initial era of mass politics (Lipset and Rokkan, 1967, p.50). Even a decade after the Second World War, a superficial glance at the Scandinavian region would have suggested that this view was still broadly valid. After all, the party systems had all proved consonant with regime stability, and, despite the Nazi occupation of Denmark and Norway, the discontinuities of the Weimar and Third French Republics were avoided. Social democracy, moreover, had retained its electoral and governmental supremacy across much of the region; interest-specific agrarian parties continued; and the balance of power between socialists and non-socialists varied relatively little.

On the other hand, the Scandinavian party systems were compelled to respond to the macro-changes of the post-war period. The structural rationalization of farming, for instance, occurring first in Denmark and last in Finland, led to rural depopulation and a marked decline in the size of the economically active population engaged in the primary sector. Accelerated industrialization brought about concentrations of capital in a few highly developed areas, problems of regional imbalance and the generation of a centre—periphery cleavage. Most recently there has been a gradual decline in the numbers employed in secondary blue-collar production and a corresponding increase in the size of the service industries. The development of the tertiary sector has swelled the ranks of the class of salaried employees or salariat.

Indeed, it is our view that Rokkan's orthodoxy does less than justice to important mutations in all five-party systems of the region *before* the decade of electoral volatility and party proliferation in the 1970s. Posited chronologically, four major changes can be identified: the re-emergence in Finland and the consolidation in Iceland of a powerful radical left; the amendment of the basic five-party model in Norway necessitated by the rise of Christian democracy as a national electoral factor; the decline, first in Sweden, of agrarianism as an independent political movement; fissures in social democracy producing and/or consolidating new parties of the radical left in Finland and particularly in Denmark. This chapter analyses each of these development in turn and concludes with an examination of the extent to which the present Scandinavian party systems indicate high, medium or low levels of political consensus.

## The re-emergence in Finland and the consolidation in Iceland of a powerful radical left

Despite the apparently conducive conditions of the Great Depression, the strength of the radical left in Scandinavia in the 1930s had been variable and generally weak. The onset of the Second World War appreciably changed things, however, and in Denmark and Norway the notable part the Communists played in the resistance movements during Nazi occupations provided a springboard for significant post-war electoral success. Indeed, the Communists in Denmark, Norway and (neutral) Sweden all polled over 10 per cent, and in the Danish case as much as 12.5 per cent, of the vote at the general elections of 1944–5. Dwarfing these achievements was the resurgence of radical leftism in Iceland and Finland at this time. In Iceland the United Socialist Party polled 18.5 per cent of the vote in October 1942, more than twice its poll five years earlier, and by 1946 it had gained the support of one in five voters. In Finland the armistice with the Soviet Union in September 1944 brought with it the legalization of the Communist Party, and this became the leading member of an electoral alliance known as the Finnish People's Democratic League, *Suomen Kansan Demokraattinen Liitto* (SKDL), which polled 23.5 per cent of the vote in March 1945. Moreover, while the Communist coup in Czechoslovakia in 1948 marked, and possibly contributed to, a sharp decline in the popularity of Communism in central Scandinavia, the radical left in the two peripheral nations of the region maintained its position. Thus in 1962 the Finnish People's Democratic League emulated the regular post-war achievement of its Icelandic counterpart by exceeding the Social Democratic share of the poll, and both parties have participated on several occasions in centre–left coalitions. As early as March 1945, in fact, Mauno Pekkala was installed as the first, and so far only, radical leftist Prime Minister of Finland, although a contemporary Agrarian Cabinet Minister commented dryly that Pekkala, a former Social Democrat, was 'a patriot and far too indolent to effect a revolution!' (Virolainen, 1965, p.21). This section analyses the main bases of support for radical leftism in Finland and Iceland and the reason for its post-war growth in the two least urbanized and industralized nations of the region.

The electoral following of the radical left in post-war Finland has comprised predominantly the poorer strata of society across the entire national territory. In a survey in 1975 it was shown that nearly two-thirds of the supporters of the SKDL were employed in working-class occupations, and at the general elections held in the same year the variation in the party's vote between the five main Finnish regions was under 4 per cent (Pesonen and Sänkiaho, 1979, p.121).

In comparative perspective, the post-war *political* cohesion of the Finnish working class has not been particularly high: in the aforementioned survey, 44 per cent of the skilled workforce and 39 per cent of the semi-skilled did not, in fact, vote for either of the two main parties of the left. Yet as table 3.1 demonstrates, with 61 per cent of

TABLE 3.1: THE OCCUPATIONAL STRUCTURE OF SUPPORT FOR THE FOUR LARGEST FINNISH PARTIES IN 1975

| Occupation | SKDL | Social Democrats | Centre | Conservatives |
|---|---|---|---|---|
| Middle class | 18 | 24 | 16 | 53 |
| Working class | 61 | 54 | 24 | 17 |
| Farmers | 5 | 1 | 42 | 4 |
| Students | 5 | 5 | 4 | 12 |
| Others | 11 | 14 | 14 | 14 |
| Totals | 100 | 98 | 100 | 100 |
| n= | 133 | 366 | 201 | 138 |

Source: Pesonen and Sänkiaho, 1979, p.121.

its support recruited from industrial workers, agricultural labourers and lumberjacks (the latter often owning a small amount of land), SKDL emerged as the most *socially* cohesive and class-based of the Finnish parties.

Furthermore, although the median *individual* income of supporters of the two left-wing parties has not differed significantly, the evidence suggests that the economic status of Communist *households* (i.e. their total family income) has been somewhat lower than that of their Social Democratic counterparts (Pesonen, 1974, p.311).

TABLE 3.2: VARIATION IN SUPPORT FOR THE FOUR LARGEST FINNISH PARTIES AT THE GENERAL ELECTION OF 1975

| Party | Region (%) | | | | |
|---|---|---|---|---|---|
| | 1 | 2 | 3 | 4 | 5 |
| SKDL | 21.3 | 17.6 | 20.1 | 20.2 | 20.8 |
| Social Democrats | 26.4 | 14.3 | 28.1 | 20.4 | 10.8 |
| Centre | 6.5 | 13.6 | 16.2 | 35.4 | 28.3 |
| Conservatives | 26.7 | 16.8 | 27.0 | 18.9 | 10.6 |

Region 1 = the south (Helsinki and Uusimaa); Region 2 = the southwest (Turku-Pori); Region 3 = central south-east (Häme and Kymi); Region 4 = intermediary belt (Mikkeli, Kuopio, Keski-Suomi and Vaasa); Region 5 = northern and eastern Finland (Pohjois-Karjala, Oulu and Lapland).

*Source:* Pesonen and Sänkiaho, 1979, p.116.

Among the four large Finnish parties, SKDL's vote has been geographically the most evenly dispersed. Thus, as table 3.2 illustrates, its support in 1975 was only marginally weaker in the outlying and less developed northern and eastern provinces than in the capital Helsinki and the constituency of Uusimaa in its hinterland. Indeed, one-fifth of the radical left's following has derived from the north and east (where only one-sixth of the electorate is situated), compared with 21.3 per cent for Helsinki and Uusimaa and only 17.6 per cent of the populous, industrialized region of the south-west. The extent of Finnish Communism in the geographic and economic periphery has attracted much attention and has obvious parallels with the strength of the radical left in the rural Massif Central in France or the agrarian provinces of Tuscany and Umbria in central Italy. Various attempts to explain the phenomenon, however, can be summarized only very briefly here (see, for example, Nousiainen 1968, pp.243—52).

In his pioneering work in the 1960s Erik Allardt contended that support for peripheral or 'backwoods Communism' was drawn in large part from the type of marginal men that Kornhauser (1959) alludes to in his *Politics of Mass Society*: rootless, isolated and alienated smallholders and lumberjacks making up a 'Forgotten Nation'. The fundamental radicalizing factor in Allardt's view was economic modernization, which led to rural depopulation and a demographic drift southwards. Indeed, he was able to link support for radical leftism to areas affected by high levels of migration (Allardt, 1970). In his review of the existing literature on the sources of West Europen Communism in 1971, Walter Korpi suggested that instead of seeing anomie as the vital link variable, Finnish 'backwoods Communism' could just as feasibly be regarded (if not more feasibly) as a rational, instrumental response to such problems of regional deprivation as high unemployment (Korpi, 1971). Finally, Pertti Laulajainen's (1979) study takes a historical tack, stressing the importance to an understanding of peripheral Communism of the organizational foundation laid in the north and east in the 1920s by the Socialist Workers' Party.

It is worth emphasizing that all the above interpretations link electoral support for post-war radical leftism in Finland with endogamous factors related in the main to the restructuring of the national economy, and not to any voter emulation of, or even direct influence from, the Soviet Union. In short, support for modern Finnish Communism has had little or nothing to do with the country's proximity to Russia, although *historically* this did play its part in the radicalization and subsequent bifurcation of the Finnish labour movement. As a postscript to this present discussion, it might be noted that a majority of bourgeois voters in the peripheral regions have also preferred the more radical options, the Agrarian Centre and, more recently, the Rural Party to either the Conservatives or the Liberals. Indeed, dating back to the 1890s there have been two distinct political cultures in Finland: a radical north and east and more moderate south and west (Rantala, 1967). Post-war modernization has accentuated rather than integrated these two Finlands.

As in Finland, radical leftism in Iceland emerged in a developing rather than a developed economy, but, unlike Finnish radicalism, it drew its initial strength almost exclusively from the urban sector. In other words, though Iceland was more agrarian and maritime than any other Scandinavian economy at the time of the completion of mass democracy, its Communism was, paradoxically, industrial rather than of the 'backwoods' variety. Similarly, after the war the radical left continued to recruit from interests central to the national economy and not among the marginal men of the Finnish case.

In the context of the Scandinavian left as a whole, Iceland is interesting because she represents the exception to the rule of the dominance of large Social Democratic parties. On first consideration, this fact might be attributed to the primacy of the national question frustrating the rational interest-centred patterns of electoral behaviour found elsewhere in the region. Certainly, during the twenty-five-year period of domestic sovereignty between 1919 and 1944, the bourgeois parties presented nationalism and the class struggle as leading Iceland in contradictory directions, and the Independence Party even charged the Social Democrats with being an arm of the Danish Social Democratic Party (Kristjánsson, 1979, p.10). In fact, however, the evidence points to a high incidence of class voting in Iceland in the 1930s, with approximately three-quarters of the manual working population supporting one or other of the two left-wing parties. It seems more likely, therefore, that the relatively poor showing of the *combined* left in Iceland was connected to the only weak impact of industralization during the formative era of mass politics, coupled with the absence of a real basis for class conflict in the countryside. The fact that factories were small also tended to deter the development of adversary owner–worker relationships.

The combined left in Iceland has remained relatively weak in Scandinavian terms in the post-war period, although in 1942 the United Soicalist Party overtook the Social Democrats to become its leading force. The supremacy of radical over moderate left since then has owed much to the projection and exploitation of a model of Iceland as an essentially subject nation – a pawn in the dominant Great Power imperialism. In this connection the radical left has stressed the importance of Icelandic neutrality, has mobilized anti-NATO sentiment by focusing on the American military presence at the Keflavik base and opposed British jingoism during the Cod Wars of the 1970s. Ironically, then, the radical left has profited from preaching Icelandic nationalism and national self-interest rather than internationalism, let alone international socialism as might have been expected. Indeed, despite the fact that a pro-Soviet group controlled the party between 1949 and 1962 – the United Socialist Party changed its name to the People's Alliance in 1956 – the party has been predominantly reformist, participating in coalition governments to further particular domestic interests. It does not, in consequence, receive financial support from Moscow, and shortly after the People's Alliance's strong denunciation of the Russian invasion of Czechoslovakia, the Stalinists left and, in 1969, formed a party of their own.

Polling a minimum of 15 per cent of the vote throughout the postwar period, the radical left in Iceland has been one of the largest of its kind in Western Europe. Its success has been based on two factors above all. First, as mentioned above, it has been sensitive to the need to protect native industries like fishing, to deal with fundamental economic issues such as unemployment and to protect the subject Icelandic culture against the cosmopolitan culture of the Americans. Secondly, it has been able to target a base in the labour movement, for, by contrast with its Finnish counterpart, the radical left, in co-operation with the Progressive Party, controls the Icelandic Labour Federation. At the same time, it should be remembered that the People's Alliance has remained a small party in absolute terms, currently with only about 2500 members. In addition to its working-class membership, the party has succeeded in attracting generally moderate teachers and intellectuals, together with fishermen and fish-processing workers (Tannahill, 1978, pp.12, 194). In short, it recruits from interests central to the Icelandic economy. Yet if Icelandic Communism has been industrial rather than 'backwoods', the historic propensity of a significant section of the working class to favour the conservative Independence Party has restricted support in its primary constituency – just as it has in the case of the Social Democrats.

*The rise of Christian Democracy as a national factor in post-war Norway*

The basic five-party Scandinavian model was modified in 1945 by the emergence at national level of the Christian People's Party (*Kristelig Folkeparti*) in Norway. In that year it received 7.9 per cent of the poll and eight *Storting* seats, and by 1977 this had increased to 12 per cent and twenty-two seats. The Christian People's Party has participated in all three post-war non-socialist coalitions, providing the Prime Minister of the last one between 1972–3, formed after Norway's referendum decision not to accede to the EEC. Developments in Norway were followed by the formation of interest-specific religious parties in Finland (1958), Sweden (1964) and Denmark (1970). This section considers all four in the context of *institutional diffusion*, though with primary emphasis on the Norwegian case. It also considers the importance of the moral dimension for an understanding of the structuring of the party systems and electoral alignments of the Scandinavian region.

A Christian party had been discussed in Norway as early as 1919, at a time when there was a small Christian Workers' Party in Finland. Its inception in 1933, however, owed much to growing dissatisfaction with the Liberals, *Venstre*, who were criticized for failing to identify with the highest Christian standards in public life. More specifically the Liberals, it was feared, lacked resolution in defending the established faith against the threat of socialism and atheism from the reunited Labour Party, and had also reneged on their hardline prohibitionist stance by presiding over the reopening of liquor outlets – some 300 in Bergen – despite the local option which followed the repeal of 1926 (Madeley, 1977, p.282). Indeed, it was a former Liberal, a Bible school headmaster, who was elected as the Christian People's Party's first parliamentary delegate in 1933, and three years later a second representative was returned for the same south-western province of Hordaland.

Properly to understand the nature of Christian democracy in Norway, it is necessary to say a word about traditional Church–State relations. Precisely as elsewhere in the region, the impact of the Reformation had been total, and the Church had been reduced to no more than an arm of the state. Indeed, by contrast with Sweden and Finland, no measure of ecclesiastical self-governance whatsoever was permitted in Norway in the nineteenth century, making all Church questions at once political issues. During that century various revivalist movements, beginning with the Haugians (cf. the Grundtvigians in Denmark and the Laestadians in the northern provinces of both Sweden and Finland), emerged to challenge the role of the clerical estate, claiming that it was neglecting its pastoral responsibilities in favour of such worldly affairs as maintaining its privileges or even cultivating the land! The failure of the state to act in sanctioning these various revivalist groups allowed them to consolidate a position as Churches within the Church, as well as to found missionary societies with the express objective of converting the (largely rural) nation to a personal and living faith. This scenario of considerable pietistic pluralism within the confines of the Evangelical Lutheran Church was fairly typical of the whole Scandinavian region by the time of the initial thrust of political and economic modernization in the last quarter of the nineteenth century. Moreover, in Norway the struggle for parliamentarism in the 1880s rendered partisan the religious differences within the revivalist camp. The radical revivalist groups led by men like Jakob Sverdrup and Lars Ottedahl backed the anti-establishment Left, *Venstre*, while the Right, *Høyre*, was favoured by the more conservative clerical and pietist groups represented by Gisle Johnson (Madeley, 1979, pp.9–10). Indeed, the left–right split of Low Church revivalism survived into the twentieth century, when a series of issues, culminating in the repeal of prohibition in 1926, united elements in the moderate and radical wings of the revivalist constituency against the established party system and provided a potential support base for the Christian People's Party.

Before the Second World War the Christian People's Party was a very small regional group recruiting its support from the western coastal 'Bible Belt'. However, as its first election manifesto made abundantly clear, the party's struggle against secularization had important implications for the mobilization of the Christian vote across the entire national territory. The party's decision to put up national slates of candidates in 1945 was in line with the emergence of significant religious parties across Western Europe in the immediate aftermath of war. The organizational impetus came from the affiliation of the Oxford Group movement, a revivalist body concentrated in the 1930s among the upper middle classes in Oslo, which provided two of the Christian People's Party's best-known leaders, Erling Wikborg and Olav Bryn. The character of the party, however, remained fundamentally unchanged, and, as John T. S. Madeley has observed, it represented, in the context of the confessional parties of the period, a rather distinctive type: a non-denominational party directing itself at individual Christians (Madeley, 1977).

Support for the Norwegian party in the post-war period has typically come from those scoring highly on two measures: first, *religious activity*, calculated on the basis of church attendance and/or membership of a religious (revivalist) organization; and, secondly, *teetotalism*. In Valen and Rokkan's survey of Norwegian voters in 1965, over one-third of those registering high levels of religiosity supported the Christian People's Party, while the latter was the most popular non-socialist choice among a large sample of active teetotalers (Valen and Rokkan, 1974, pp.300–1). The party has continued to recruit extensively in its original stronghold in the south-west and also polls well among the urban middle classes (ibid., pp.331, 353, 363). During the 1970s the party's main gains were at the expense of the Centre Party, Labour and the Liberals (Valen, 1978, pp.83–107).

The establishment of interest-specific religious parties in Finland, Sweden and Denmark by 1970 is an outstanding example of *institutional diffusion* within the Scandinavian region, for all three based their programmes on that of the Christian People's Party and took as their 'Bible' the pamphlet on Christianity and politics, *Kristendom og politik*, by the Norwegian pastor Karl Marthinussen. In turn, the Norwegian party played a paternal role in encouraging the sibling Christian parties. An influential member of the Finnish Christian League (*Suomen Kristillinen Liitto*), for example, has related how in 1965, at the invitation of the Christian People's Party secretary, he operated as an election speaker among the Finnish settlements in northern Norway and became convinced, in the process, of the potential viability of a similar type of party in Finland. The initiative for formal co-operation between the Scandinavian Christian parties also came from the Norwegian party, and a first regional conference was convened in Stockholm in 1964. By 1974 these gatherings included representatives of the Swiss Evangelicals and the two Dutch Protestant parties. Only in Iceland has no Christian Democratic party formed, despite a number of proposals to that end.

In terms of their origins, leadership, rank-and-file support and programmatic priorities, the three new Christian parties have much in common. They were all formed at a time of accentuated cultural secularization in the face of party systems that appeared not only to eschew but actively to challenge Christian standards in the formulation of policy. Thus in Sweden, at the time of the creation of the Christian Democratic Union (*Kristen demokratisk Samling*) in 1964, 2 million people signed a petition opposing a proposed reduction in the levels of religious education in schools. In Norway, incidentally, nine Lutheran bishops lobbied the *Storting* on precisely the same matter the following year. In Finland the Christian League achieved its first parliamentary delegate in 1970, after four years of a Popular Front government (including Communists) which became synonymous with permissive legislation. It was a similar story in Denmark, where the Christian People's Party, formed in 1970, specifically opposed the relaxation of the laws relating to pornography and abortion.

Like that of the Norwegian party, the leadership of the new Christian parties has drawn heavily on the various Low Church revivalist organizations within the Evangelical Lutheran Church as well as on non-comformist groups such as the Baptists and the Pentecostalists outside it. An investigation of leaders (active members) of the Finnish Christian League in 1979 revealed that 55 per cent identified with a revivalist organization — an overwhelming preponderance of whom belonged to the National Missionary Society (*Kansanlähetys*) founded in 1967 — while no fewer than 12 per cent adhered to nonconformist organizations (Arter, 1980a). In the latter context it is significant that in Sweden the involvement of a well-known Pentecostal pastor contributed much to the Christian Democrats' 1.6 per cent poll in their inaugural year. At the founding meeting of the Danish party the revivalist Inner Mission was strongly represented, as were both the Low Church Grundtvigian and the High Church wings of the Evangelical Lutheran Church (Andersen, 1975).

The rank-and-file supporters of these parties have included mainly active religious persons, again with a strong tendency to align with one of the revivalist organizations. Eighty per cent of the Swedish Christian Democrats' support in 1968 derived from Low Church adherents (Särlvik, 1974, p.418) and in Finland no fewer than 90 per cent of those National Missionary Society members who admitted to a party allegiance in 1970 preferred the Christian League (Kauppinen, 1973, p.65). Finally, all three parties, in line with the Norwegian Christian People's Party, view themselves as centre parties: closer to the left in social policy matters but on the non-socialist side in protecting the basic inviolability of private property. Their fundamental objective, however, is the wholesale Christianization of political society, and this, in turn, amounts to little short of a moral revolution.

From a European perspective there are two striking and somewhat paradoxical features about the emergence of interest-specific Christian parties in the Scandinavian region: first, that they have appeared at all in mono-religious nations lacking the religious *verzuiling* of Holland or Switzerland; second, that, given the extremely high membership of the Lutheran Church, comparable only with that of the Roman Catholic Church in Ireland, their support has remained relatively small.

Clearly, the extent of their electoral backing has been delimited by entrenched patterns of religious affiliation and partisan alignment built up over the initial period of mass democracy. In all four states there has been an historic alliance of High Church clericalism and the political right, while the traditional link between Low Church revivalism and liberalism (in Denmark, Norway, Sweden) and agrarianism (in Finland) has significantly reduced the availability of the active Christian constituency for recruitment by religious parties. By the 1960s the massive passivity of the majority of Christians minimized the salience of the moral perspective as an electoral factor. Indeed, it is precisely this decline in the traditional norms of religious observance that goes much of the way to explaining the post-war emergence of Christian Democracy in Scandinavia. Put another way, spiritual regeneration and the cause of moral rearmament have rallied active Christians despite the traditional differences between them. This is not to say that old religious—political allegiances have lost their significance: outside Norway the Christian parties have not exceeded 6 per cent of the vote at general elections, although the Finnish party's candidate, Raino Westerholm, achieved a creditable 8.8 per cent at the presidential election of 1978. But the interest-specific religious parties in post-Christian Scandinavia have gone some way to undermining the partisan disunity that was the historical corollary of pietistic pluralism in the region.

## *The decline of agrarianism as a political force*

At the same time as interest-specific religious parties emerged in post-war Scandinavia, the interest-specific farmers' parties formed earlier in the region experienced declining support as the number of persons transferring from the primary to the non-primary sector of the economy increased. By the mid-1960s all three Agrarian parties had transformed themselves into Centre parties with a view to penetrating the urban—industrial vote market. The Swedish Agrarians were the first to adopt the new designation in 1957, followed by their Norwegian counterpart two years later and finally the Finnish party in 1965. This section briefly examines the reasons for the diminishing electoral base of agrarianism, the significance of its decline as an independent political force and the success of the new Centre parties in their bid to become catch-all parties.

TABLE 3.3: THE DECLINE IN THE POPULATION ENGAGED IN FARMING, FISHING AND FORESTRY IN THREE SCANDINAVIAN STATES, 1950—70

| *Year* | *Sweden* | *Norway* | *Finland* |
|---|---|---|---|
| 1950 | 25.0 | 27.0 | 45.9 |
| 1960 | 13.8 | 19.5 | 35.5 |
| 1970 | 8.1 | 11.6 | 20.1 |

Source: *Statistical Yearbooks* of Norway, Sweden and Finland.

The common denominator in the decision to modernize the Agrarian parties was a sharp drop in the numbers engaged in agriculture, forestry and fishing after the Second World War. As table 3.3 illustrates, the decline was most marked in absolute terms in Sweden, where the name change occurred first, and greatest in relative terms in Finland, where the party was the last to reorientate. It is important, however, to note that there was no direct correlation between a fall in the agricultural population and declining support for agrarianism. In Norway the size of the population engaged in farming, fishing and forestry fell by 7.5 per cent between 1950 and 1960, and yet the Agrarians *increased* their support throughout the decade. In Finland the population engaged in the primary sector dropped by over 10 per cent in the same period, whereas the Agrarian Party was only 0.2 per cent worse off at the general election of 1962 than in 1951 and was, in fact, the largest single party when it changed its name. The salient point is that the Scandinavian Agrarians were never catch-all parties within the agricultural sector; rather, they relied on a core constituency of generally medium-sized farm proprietors which was declining more slowly than that of smallholders, labourers and the rest of the agrarian population. Indeed, industrialization, in tending to attract the non-independent agricultural elements away from the land, was electorally less injurious to the Agrarian parties than was the structural rationalization of farming (i.e. the amalgamation of holdings into larger, more viable units), for this attacked the very foundations of their support base.

The precipitating circumstances surrounding the transformation of Scandinavian Agrarian Parties into centre parties varied from one country to the next. In Sweden it was the electoral nadir reached in 1956 when, following a Red–Green coalition with the Social Democrats, the Agrarians managed to poll a mere 9.4 per cent of the vote at the general elections that year. In Norway it was, ironically, an improvement (albeit a modest one) on the Agrarians' electoral failures in the 1950s which contributed to the decision to modernize. In particular, the Norwegian party hoped to fashion and lead a distinctive non-socialist centre bloc with the Christians and Liberals, so isolating the Conservatives on the right (Elder and Gooderham, 1978, pp.219–20). In the Finnish case the change of name was associated with the election in 1964 of a new chairman, Johannes Virolainen, and gained added immediacy from the Swedish party's success in winning its first seat on Stockholm City Council the same year. Indeed, the case for modernizing the respective parties undoubtedly profited from the formal co-operation and informal personnel interchange which developed between the Scandinavian Agrarian parties after the Second World War.

Before considering the outcome of the name changes, a note on the demise of Finnish agrarianism is needed — partly because it could justifiably be said to have dominated national politics for over forty years, and partly because it was never a single-interest party to anything like the same extent as its counterparts in Norway and Sweden.

The first and overwhelmingly the largest of the Scandinavian Agrarians, the Finnish party, participated in government far more than any other party. Like the Radical and Radical Socialist Party in the French Third Republic, in fact, it functioned as a 'hinge group' in coalition-building (Arter, 1979a, pp.108—27). Indeed, the peculiar conditions of the Finnish party system enabled it to occupy a position at the centre of the political spectrum and, by holding the balance of power between left and right, to be at once indispensable to the achievement of majority governments and decisive in determining their party composition. The Agrarians also supplied three presidents, including the long-serving head of state, Urho Kekkonen (1956—81).

Prior to 1929 the Finnish Agrarians were essentially a party of cultural opposition, combining several of the causes of the 'old' non-socialist Left (*Venstre*), in Norway with the functional representation of the interests of the small farmers in the geographical and economic periphery of northern and eastern Finland. The party took the side of the predominant rural language, Finnish, against the Swedish spoken by much of the urban middle class; it made inroads into the liberal vote, first by providing a mouthpiece for various revivalist groups in opposition to the High Church clerical elite and then by taking the prohibitionist line against the liquor 'libbers'; finally, the party mobilized support in the larger farming districts of the south-west by identifying republicanism with a wide range of rural grievances during the constitutional crisis of 1918. In sum, the Finnish Agrarians emerged as the party *per excellence* of the 'bumpkin' against the 'bigwig' — its rhetoric hostile to the towns and to the sybaritic and hedonistic classes supposedly dominating them. Even when it joined the political establishment in 1919, it retained much of its early cultural radicalism.

By the 1930s the Agrarian Party had become far more narrowly a farm producers' party, but after the 1944 Armistice it effected a policy coup by claiming to be the first party to appreciate the geopolitical realities of Finland's situation and to advocate what became the official post-war presidential line of firm but fraternal Fenno-Soviet relations.

It was an important watershed in the party's history, for the electoral *cachet* accruing from the Agrarians' wholehearted identification with — and, arguably, monopolization of — Kekkonen's deft handling of relations with the Soviet leadership served to offset the electoral logic of a declining agricultural population. At the same time several Agrarian leaders developed a close relationship with Moscow and were especially trusted there — a factor contributing to the centrality of the party's role in the post-Second World War period.

With the significant exception of the Swedish party, the Centre parties have not thus far proved successful in adapting to the structural imperatives of developed industrial economies, and their vote has remained anchored in the farming population and smaller towns based on agricultural hinterlands. In Norway the Centre (*Senterparti*) has maintained its stronghold in the Trøndelag — where its poll is about twice its national average — and the west, while nowadays competing for the vote in the North. As elsewhere in the region, the farm electorate has remained loyal: an estimated three-fifths of the farm owners and their families supported the Norwegian party in 1965, compared with only 4 per cent of industrial workers and the same proportion of the white-collar population who did so (Berglund and Lindström, 1978, p.108). In Finland the Centre Party (*Keskustapuolue*) still recruits the lion's share of its poll from its original core areas in the outlying north and east and has held the support of over two-thirds of the farmowners who in the mid-1970s contributed over two-fifths of the overall poll (Pesonen and Sänkiaho, 1979, p.121). In 1975 the correlation between the size of the Centre Party poll and the numbers engaged in agriculture and forestry by province was +0.85 (Vanhanen, 1978). Both parties have been conspicuously unsuccessful in penetrating the larger urban–industrial areas. The optimal urban vote of the Norwegian party was 3.6 per cent in 1969 — only just over one-quarter of its rural vote — and at the general elections of 1973 and 1977 this dropped sharply. Neither Norwegian nor Finnish party has returned a parliamentary delegate in the national capital at a general election, and although the latter has managed to claim about 6 per cent of its vote in the capital city and surrounding dormitory province, Uusimaa, it has regularly been surpassed in Helsinki itself by Vennamo's Rural Party!

At this point it might be noted that the last Scandinavian agrarian party — albeit one with a small 'a' — to refurbish its name was the nineteenth-century non-socialist Left in Denmark (*Venstre*, heretofore translated as 'Agrarian Liberals'), which adopted the suffix 'Denmark's

Liberal Party' to become *Venstre—Danmarks liberale Parti* in 1970. This left the Progressive Party in Iceland as the only one of the predominantly farmers' parties of the inter-war period not to amend its historic designation, and until late in the 1970s it retained the support of between one-fifth and one-quarter of the electorate. Three factors formed the background to the Danish party's change of name; first, the election in 1965 of a new chairman, Poul Hartling, which ended divisive discussion within the party's ranks about a possible merger with the Conservatives; next, its participation in a three-party bourgeois coalition with the Radicals and Conservatives between 1968 and 1971; and, last, a very gradual decline in its support during the 1960s. Indeed, the adjustment to the party's name was partly designed to strengthen the party's appeal in the towns, particularly among the growing number of salaried employees. Significantly, in 1965 an internal party faction primarily based in Copenhagen and concerned, among other things, about the Agrarian Liberals' inability to attract a sizable urban vote, had broken away to form the Liberal Centre (*Liberalt Centrum*) (Thomas, 1973, pp.31—3).

Certainly, in the mid-1960s the Danish Agrarian Liberals provided the most outstanding example of a class party in Scandinavia. No fewer than 78 per cent of Danish farmers supported the party — representing the highest level of political cohesion among farmers in the region — while fewer than one Agrarian Liberal voter in twelve was a blue-collar worker and only one in nine a white-collar worker. At the 1968 general elections, moreover, they polled a mere 3.4 per cent in Copenhagen, compared with 18.6 per cent nationally and 26.5 per cent in rural Jutland. The loyalty of the party's farm vote disguised the same type of contraction in the primary sector occurring elsewhere in the region: the size of the agriculture, forestry and fishing population declined from 17.8 to 10.6 per cent in the course of the 1960s, though the Agrarian Liberal vote fell by only 2.2 per cent in the same period. In the 1970s support for the Danish party, notwithstanding its modified name, was subject to considerable fluctuation: it undoubtedly lost some of its agrarian following to Glistrup's Progress Party in the earlier part of the decade, while its success in the towns was largely confined to traditional agriculture-related centres like Ringkøbing and Skjern in western Jutland.

The only interest-specific farmers' party successfully to transform itself into a catch-all party has been the Swedish Centre Party (*Centerpartiet*), which by the late 1960s drew almost equally on the support of farmers and of industrial workers, with considerable backing too from lower-grade clerical workers and small entrepreneurs. Traditionally strong in the agricultural districts of the south, especially the counties of Halland, Kronoberg and Gotland, the Swedish party has retained the favour of just under three in four active farmers and their wives. However, the party has managed to shed its agrarian image, initially by expanding northwards to capture a substantial vote in the medium-sized towns of around 30,000, and latterly by making considerable inroads into the southern conurbations. By 1968 the party's decision to modernize its name and programme seemed vindicated: at the general elections that year the Centre Party doubled its 1956 vote and, gaining an extra 2.7 per cent of the poll, overtook the Liberals as the largest non-socialist and leading opposition party. An estimated 11 per cent of the new support was gained at the expense of the Liberals, but, perhaps more interestingly, another 9 per cent came from the Social Democrats, who themselves increased their share of the poll by 2.8 per cent (Särlvik, 1970, p.248). In 1973 the Swedish Centre Party reached its optimal vote of over one-quarter of the total active electorate and won nine parliamentary seats in Stockholm city and province.

Why has the Swedish party proved an effective adaptive structure when its sister parties have patently been less successful? Briefly stated, our contention is that while macro-trends affecting the occupational structure of all three economies created differences in the size of the prospective vote market for Centre parties, it was the favourable political environment during the critical fifteen-year period following party modernization which enabled the Swedish Centre to recruit a significant non-primary electorate. Put another way, the fact that the Swedish party enjoyed a uniquely favourable tactical position in opposition facilitated the projection of radical policies at a time when the governing Social Democrats, with almost forty years in office behind them, were beginning to look increasingly conservative. In Finland, by contrast, the Centre Party has been out of office for a mere six months since changing its name in 1965, and in promoting the agriculturalists' case against its predominantly consumer-based left-wing coalition partners, it has found it hard to shed its agrarian image. The same fate has befallen the Norwegian party, albeit on a lesser scale, notably in its alliance with the farmers against EEC membership.

Extrapolating from the data in table 3.4 on the occupational structure of the Swedish Centre Party's vote, and excluding the traditional farm support, at least four distinct party clienteles can be identified

TABLE 3.4: THE OCCUPATIONAL STRUCTURE OF THE SWEDISH CENTRE PARTY VOTE IN 1968

| Occupational grouping | Percentage of total Centre Party vote |
|---|---|
| Professionals and senior managers | 6 |
| Small businessmen/entrepreneurs | 11 |
| Lower clerical grades | 17 |
| Foremen/shop assistants | 3 |
| Industrial workers | 26 |
| Farm/forestry workers | 7 |
| Farmers | 29 |
| Students and others | 1 |
|  | 100 |

n = 469

Source: Särlvik 1970 p. 279.

and motives for their partisan alignment suggested. First, the Swedish Centre appears to have attracted blue-collar workers in the smaller firms — particularly those situated at a distance from the regional concentrations of industry — where levels of unionization tend to be somewhat lower and owner–worker relationships more solidary. Secondly, it has appealed to new recruits to the urban salariat, particularly those in the lower clerical grades, many of them recent immigrants to the town with histories of personal or parental allegiance to the Agrarians. Thirdly, it has recruited a younger generation of electors — students, graduates, etc. — disaffected with the ethos of social democracy, large-scale bureaucracy and centralized state management of the economy. Indeed, as Elder has argued, the Centre Party capitalized on the frustration and anti-materialism of the *avant-garde* New Left, with its radical, ecological credo (Elder and Gooderham, 1978). Finally, the Swedish Centre has targeted small businessmen and entrepreneurs, their position threatened by the major thrust of economic development. In the latter context, Särlvik, underlining the importance of regional imbalance, has noted that in the 1960s the Swedish Centre profited from its ability to articulate the grievances of the population on the periphery of the highly urbanized and industralized centres — rural, small-town Sweden — where there were evident signs of recession (Särlvik, 1970, p.255).

In addition to the considerable advantage accruing from the Centre Party's status as an untried alternative to the ruling Social Democrats, its mobilization of support was predicated on a set of innovative policies stressing decentralization in all its facets: in small-scale ownership, industrial democracy, conservationism and parity between the regions. On the other hand, the Centre Party's strenuous opposition to the development of nuclear energy in the 1970s, a policy associated with the election of Thorbjörn Fälldin as chairman in 1971, was less obviously an electoral asset. After all, as mentioned above, the environmentalist lobby aligned itself with the party as early as the 1960s, and in 1976, when the nuclear power issue was central to the general election campaign, the Centre Party lost ground. Indeed, by 1979 it had been overhauled as the largest non-socialist party by the Conservatives (*Moderata Samlingspartiet*), just as the Finnish Centre Party had been in 1970, after fifty years of supremacy. With the vote for the Norwegian Party also waning, the future of the Scandinavian Centre remains problematical. While obituary notices are certainly premature, the Centre parties, even allowing for the Swedish case, have yet to become stable catch-all parties.

*Fissures in social democracy and the rise of a new radical left*

The Social Democratic parties maintained their position as predominant parties in Denmark, Norway and Sweden after the Second World War and, despite the re-emergence of Communism as a significant electoral factor, remained the largest single party in Finland too. By far the largest of the four parties was the Swedish Social Democratic Party, which polled a goodly 45 per cent of the vote after 1945 and in 1968, the year after Rokkan's celebrated observation about the viscosity of West European party systems, achieved an absolute majority of 50.1 per cent of the active electorate. Next in order of size was the Norwegian party, an omnipresent member of government for the twenty-year period after the war, polling nearly as many votes as its Swedish counterpart during much of the period. In Denmark the Social Democrats established a hold on power from 1953 to 1968, with approximately 40 per cent of the poll. Even in Finland the Social Democrats contrived to capture around a quarter of the popular vote, though this fell to below one-fifth in 1962, and only four years later did it become a regular member of coalitions (Arter, 1980b). This section examines briefly how the Social Democrats have managed to hold on to their electoral primacy; the extent of their success in attracting support outside their traditional blue-collar following; and why in the 1960s there was fragmentation in the Social Democratic ranks leading to splinter groups especially on the radical left.

The continuing supremacy of the Social Democrats at the polls was due in no small measure to the fact that the structural changes in all the post-war Scandinavian economies had left the core constituency of social democracy largely unscathed. True, there was some shrinkage in the size of the farm worker population which detracted from the Social Democrats' support. But there was little appreciable change in the percentage of the economically active population engaged in secondary industry in Denmark and Sweden in the 1950s, and the size of the labour force employed in mining, manufacturing and electricity increased in Norway, Finland and Iceland. Moreover, while the blue-collar population remained at between one-third and one-fifth of the active workforce in the region, the political cohesion of the working class remained high. It has been estimated that in the 1960s 80 per cent or more of the working-class vote went to parties of the left in Denmark, Finland and Sweden and 71 per cent in Norway, and that really only in Iceland was the phenomenon of working-class conservatism a significant electoral factor. Table 3.5 illustrates this point. In particular, the middle-aged and older cohorts of blue-collar workers, together with pensioners, have been the bastions of post-war Scandinavian social democracy. In

TABLE 3.5: THE POLITICAL COHESION OF THE WORKING-CLASS ELECTORATE IN FOUR SCANDINAVIAN STATES IN THE MID-1960s

| Party | Percentage working-class support | | | |
| --- | --- | --- | --- | --- |
| | Denmark | Finland | Norway | Sweden |
| Communists | 2 | 34 | 1 | 6 |
| New radical left | 10 | 4 | 7 | — |
| Social Democrats | 73 | 42 | 63 | 78 |
| Non-socialists | 15 | 20 | 22 | 16 |
| Non-voters | — | — | 7 | — |
| n = 100% | 8216 | 669 | 684 | 841 |

Source: Adapted from Berglund and Lindström, 1978, p.108.

TABLE 3.6: THE SIZE OF THE ECONOMICALLY ACTIVE
POPULATION ENGAGED IN MINING, MANUFACTURING AND
ELECTRICITY IN SCANDINAVIA, 1960–70

| Year | Denmark | Finland | Iceland | Norway | Sweden |
|---|---|---|---|---|---|
| 1960 | 29.7 | 22.8 | 25.6 | 26.9 | 36.0 |
| 1970 | 28.6 | 27.4 | 26.2 | 28.5 | 30.5 |

Source: *Yearbook of Nordic Statistics*, 1978, p. 42.

Sweden in 1968, for example, probably as much as one-quarter of the Social Democratic vote came from persons between 61 and 84 years of age — the largest percent of any age group voting for one party (Särlvik, 1974, p.428).

The 1960s, however, were a watershed decade for the Social Democratic parties, as table 3.6 demonstrates, for there was a *relative* decline in the size of the economically active population engaged in secondary industry in Denmark and Sweden and a considerable levelling out elsewhere in the region. The blue-collar workforce, in short, entered a period of contraction as the numbers in service industries expanded. By 1970 between about one-fifth and one-quarter of the economically active population in the region was employed in the tertiary sector, as table 3.7 shows. The effect of these changes was to blur, though not to undermine, the class basis of electoral politics and to dictate the need for the Social Democratic parties to reach beyond their traditional blue-collar support in order to attract the growing salariat. Indeed, prompted

TABLE 3.7: THE PERCENTAGE OF THE ECONOMICALLY
ACTIVE POPULATION IN SERVICE INDUSTRIES IN
SCANDINAVIA, 1960–70

| Year | Denmark | Finland | Iceland | Norway | Sweden |
|---|---|---|---|---|---|
| 1960 | 20.9 | 14.8 | 15.2 | 17.4 | 19.8 |
| 1970 | 26.8 | 19.9 | 19.0 | 22.4 | 24.9 |

Source: *Yearbook of Nordic Statistics*, 1978, p. 42.

by the precedent of the Bad Godesberg programme of the SPD in the German Federal Republic, the Scandinavian Social Democrats took steps to modernize themselves in an attempt to become catch-all parties.

In the main, their response to the white-collar revolution has involved modifying the rhetoric and moderating the historic policies of social democracy. In Denmark, for example, the Social Democrats' refurbished programme of 1961 did not refer to the working class as such but instead simply spoke of 'wage-earners' (Miller, 1968, p.111). In Sweden in the late 1960s, as Bengt Lundberg's (1979) analysis of the party's policy declarations and manifestos demonstrates, the Social Democratic Party intensified the lip-service it paid to the widely appealing though rather anodyne notion of equality. In Norway Knut Heidar has noted that from the late 1950s the strategy favoured by the Labour Party's right wing of projecting moderate, centrist policies with a multi-group appeal gained ground in the party (Heidar, 1977, p.301). Furthermore, long-serving leaders like Tage Erlander in Sweden, with his style of Harpsund Democracy — bringing the main sectoral interests into an informal but regularized relationship with the government — created the popular image of a safe establishment party. In sum, the Social Democrats in central Scandinavia attempted to find new support by making more explicit the gradualism that had characterized the parties since the 1930s.

In truth, it cannot be said that the Social Democrats have met with any greater success in attracting the crucial class of salaried employees than have the modernizing farmers' parties. In Sweden in 1968 the Centre Party gained 1 per cent more of its electoral clientele from lower-grade clerical workers and 4 per cent more from senior salaried staff, while there is evidence that in the same year the Danish Social Democrats were actually more reliant on the industrial working-class and farm-labourer vote than they had been fourteen years earlier (Thomas, 1977, p.241). To be fair, both parties improved their position among white-collar workers during the 1960s, but in their attempts then and since to recruit more broadly to become catch-all parties, there have been a number of fundamental problems to be resolved.

First, any moderation or dilution of policies to attract the salariat has risked alienating elements among their traditional blue-collar constituency, for whom it is imperative that social democracy sustain a radical image. Tacit recognition of this fact can be found in the Social Democrats' recent emphasis on industrial democracy and the Swedish Social Democratic Party's flirtation with an employee investment scheme which might eventually transfer control of company finances to the trade unions. In the 1960s the Swedish party, concerned not to appear to lose its central reformist dynamic, set about reappraising the social welfare system that it had built, subsequently focusing more attention on underprivileged minorities such as the unemployed, the elderly and the infirm. Indeed, a Social Democratic Party study group under the chairmanship of Alva Myrdal confirmed that there was still substantial progress to be made in order to achieve their historic goal of social and economic equality (Castles, 1974, p.180). As with the farmer—Centre Party relationship, survey data suggest that the Social Democrats have done enough to keep the allegiance of the vast majority of the industrial working class.

A second problem for the predominant Social Democratic parties of central Scandinavia in winning a broader recruitment base has been to create a political climate conducive to the socialization of the younger and, more particularly, educated voters and to avoid the inertia and lack of programmatic renewal associated with parties experiencing long periods in office. Indeed, declining support for the Social Democrats in Denmark in the 1960s, and in Denmark, Norway and Sweden in the early 1970s (outlined in table 3.8), suggested a loss of potential recruits among the younger generation of workers and intellectuals. It was not that social democracy ceased to be an innovatory force; rather, it failed either to generate or to identify with causes appealing to the newer electors of the late 1960s. Put another way, it did little to excite the imagination of a generation that simply assumed the security and prosperity that the Social Democrats had had a large hand in creating. In fact, the youth in Sweden at least began increasingly to challenge the twin gods of growth and materialism and to seek an alternative set of values in ecology movements. The very achievement of social democ-

TABLE 3.8: THE FALL IN THE SOCIAL DEMOCRATIC VOTE IN DENMARK, NORWAY AND SWEDEN IN THE FIRST HALF OF THE 1970s

| Country | Social Democratic vote (%) | |
|---|---|---|
| Denmark | 37.3 (1971) | 29.9 (1975) |
| Norway | 46.5 (1969) | 35.3 (1973) |
| Sweden | 45.3 (1970) | 42.7 (1976) |

racy, in short, became electorally counter-productive as more spurned the social bureaucracy, corporatism, even 'new totalitarianism', imputed to it (Huntford, 1971).

Finally, in modernizing themselves the Social Democratic parties needed to make incursions into the salariat, and to do this it was necessary to recognize that in practice this was not one class but at least two. As early as the inter-war period, the Social Democrats in Sweden and Denmark had gained a following among the middle class. Bo Särlvik has speculated that the white-collar proportion of the Swedish party's vote approached one-fifth in the 1920s — a share significantly greater than that of its British counterpart at the time — and in the 1930s the Danish party also made important inroads into the middle-class electorate (Särlvik, 1974, p.395). The 'old' middle class, comprising predominantly professional groups and civil servants, was doubtless attracted to the gradualist strategy of the Social Democrats and their ambition to realize a society based on equality of opportunity. By the 1960s, however, the Social Democrats were confronted with the task of marrying the interests of this established middle class, its mood increasingly radical as the socio-economic status of some of the older professions declined, with the needs of the 'new' middle class of service employees, many from working-class or farming backgrounds, who, as upwardly mobile persons, tended inherently to be more conservative. It is possible that the Social Democratic parties did not recognize fully the extent of internal differentiation within the middle class or the need to espouse policies attractive to the whole of this heterogeneous stratum. Reforms of the national systems of taxation, with a shift away from direct to indirect taxes, constituted one such policy, and it was one which the Danish party furthered in the mid-1960s. However, it took the rise of populist anti-tax parties in the early 1970s fully to convince the Social Democrats elsewhere in the region that something needed to be done. In any event, middle-class support for social democracy has remained fairly stable over the years. There has been a small decline in traditional middle-class socialism and a modest growth in salariat socialism.

In terms of the geography of its support, social democracy has varied relatively little over the post-war period. The Danish party, historically more urban and white-collar in character than its sister parties in the region, has remained weak throughout most of rural Jutland but continues to dominate the shipping district of Lolland-Falster. The Finnish party has consolidated its strength in the southern, 'developed' third of the country while remaining significantly weaker in the peripheral north and east. By contrast, support for the Norwegian Labour Party has straddled the economically central provinces in the east and the outlying regions in the far north, though it has been less well ensconced in the south-west. The south-west, along with the island of Gotland, has been the only real electoral blind spot of the Swedish Social Democrats, who have also made inroads into the electorate of the north. All in all, the Scandinavian Social Democratic parties have lost ground in the capital cities and larger urban centres as these have become less industrial and the size of the blue-collar population has diminished, while at the same time 'nationalizing' their support bases by eroding the differential between town and country.

Before considering defections from the Social Democratic camp to new parties on the radical left, a note on the contribution of social democracy in Scandinavia is in order. Perhaps its most distinctive achievement has been to combine the requirements of central government planning with the continuing private ownership of much of industry. Thus the Social Democrats have been responsible for building modern welfare states and for investing more in welfare spending than almost anywhere else in West Europe, while at the same time avoiding wholesale nationalization. Womb-to-tomb protection schemes have coexisted in Sweden, for example, with one of the most developed forms of monopoly capital in the world. In the 1960s the 100 largest companies employed 43 per cent of all workers in Swedish manufacturing industry (Scase, 1977, p.316). True, the development of welfarism has proceeded at a differential rate: a comprehensive system of protection was in existence in Sweden and Norway by the 1960s, whereas in Denmark and particularly in Finland its realization came about more slowly. In the Finnish case this was in no small measure because the Social Democrats were in opposition for close on a decade commencing in 1958, having lost favour in high places in Moscow. Deep divisions in the Finnish labour movement have also prevented the close co-operation between the Social Democratic Party and the central labour federations so characteristic of Sweden. But the very fact that the welfare state is no longer a bone of contention between the parties (outside the radical right) is in itself a measure of the Social Democratic achievement in Scandinavia.

As in the case of the British Labour Party, the Scandinavian Social Democrats have been 'broad churches', with left wing and right wing divided over such fundamental questions as the role of the market in the national economy and (in Denmark and Norway) the position of the nation in the international arena. In the latter context two issues in the 1960s, membership of NATO and the EEC, created internal tensions, splits and an overall vote loss. Strictly speaking, the Socialist People's Party, founded by Aksel Larsen in Denmark in 1959, was a Communist rather than a Social Democratic splinter group, although it recruited the majority of its initial 6.1 per cent poll from disaffected Social Democrats. Its Norwegian counterpart of the same name, however, which polled 2.4 per cent of the vote at its first general elections in 1961, originated in the ranks of the Labour Party.

In the 1950s Larsen, who had been a Communist delegate in the *Folketing* since 1932, began to articulate the case for a middle course between servile Kremlinism and a social democracy which appeared to have lost sight of socialism (Thomas, 1977, p.249). He was consequently expelled from the Communist Party, and by 1966 his Socialist People's Party had polled a creditable 10.9 per cent – the Communists, by contrast, managed to claim less than 1 per cent – much of it recruited from working-class electors concentrated in, but not confined to, the Copenhagen area. Indeed, the left obtained a parliamentary majority in 1966 for the first time in Danish political history: informal co-operation between the governing Social Democrats and the Socialist People's Party in opposition led to agreements on the introduction of VAT and other fiscal measures. That said, there were major disagreements between the two over the EEC, which the Socialist People's Party strenuously opposed. In 1968 the Socialist People's Party itself split on the question of devaluation, with a dissident faction leaving to found the Left Socialists. The picture in Denmark in the late 1960s was thus one of fragmentation on the radical left; but in 1973 the Social Democrats also had to contend with the secession to the right of the Centre Democrats, initially over the issue of excessive taxation of house-owners.

The Norwegian Socialist People's Party's opposition to the EEC revitalized a party which in the 1960s had enjoyed considerably less success than its Danish sister party, although remaining well ahead of the Communists. Moreover, when the Labour Party decided on a consultative referendum on the Common Market issue in 1972 a sizable number of members in the Workers' Information Committee left the party and joined the Socialist Electoral Alliance – an umbrella organization formed specifically to fight the 1973 elections – of which the Socialist People's Party was one of the leading members. The Alliance managed to seize a remarkable 11.2 per cent of the poll in 1973. In general, the Norwegian Socialist People's Party prompted a better electoral response in the urban than in the rural areas and, in addition to its working-class constituency, has been supported (though dominated much less than in the Danish case) by a core of highly educated intellectuals. Finally, it should be noted that in Finland a Social Democratic Opposition party left the mother party in the second half of the 1950s primarily over what it saw as the capture of the Social Democratic leadership by anti-Soviet elements (Arter 1980b, pp.373—5). The Social Democratic Opposition co-operated with the Finnish People's Democratic League from the outset and gradually merged with the radical left. The splinter party was a timely reminder that, as elsewhere in the region, social democracy had constantly to be looking over its left shoulder.

The immediate post-war surge of Communism in Finland and Iceland, the rise of Christian Democracy in Norway and subsequently across Scandinavia, the decline of agrarianism as an independent political force in Sweden, Norway and Finland and the rise of a new radical left, mostly at the expense of social democracy, are the four major developments that occurred in the region between the 1930s and late 1960s which challenge Rokkan's point about the freezing of the West European party systems a decade or so after the First World War (Lipset and Rokkan, 1967, p.50). There were others too. The year 1968 in Sweden, for example, marked the end of a remarkable post-war recovery of the Liberal Party, which, under the forceful leadership of Bertil Ohlin, had displaced the Conservatives as the leading non-socialist party in 1948, a position held for twenty years with the exception of a two-year break between 1958 and 1960. The other Liberal parties in the region declined, though not evenly: the Danish Radical Liberals revived somewhat at precisely the point when the Swedish party took second place to the Centre Party among the non-socialists. The trend, however, was definitely downwards. The only sizable ethnic party in the region also lost ground, for the Swedish People's Party in Finland faced a fall in the numbers speaking the minority language as well as defections to social democracy on the part of Swedish-speaking blue-collar workers. If these within-party trends seem unduly harsh on Rokkan's generally valuable observation, the latter was, in any event, written before the 1970s — a decade that marked a rapid thaw in the Scandinavian party systems.

## THE SCANDINAVIAN PARTY SYSTEMS IN THE 1970s: DECLINING CONSENSUS?

In the 1970s the five-party Scandinavian model was challenged by a decade of electoral volatility and party proliferation which posed fundamental questions about the extent of political consensus in the region. Thus at the Danish general election in 1973 no fewer than eleven parties gained at least 1.5 per cent of the vote, compared with only six ten years earlier. In Finland in 1975 ten parties exceeded the same minimum of the active vote, whereas a decade earlier only six succeeded in doing so. It was the same story in Norway, for between 1965 and 1973 the number of parties obtaining 1.5 per cent of the poll rose from six to nine, while even in Iceland the general election of 1971 saw the parties attaining the same percentage increase from four to five. Only Sweden seemed immune from the contagion, and the number of parties gaining 1.5 per cent of the vote stayed at six. This final section examines the heightened multi-partism of the 1970s (the extent of which can be seen in table 3.9) and considers the causes and overall significance of the protest elections during the decade.

The numerous new parties of the 1970s can be ordered into three basic types. First, *there were splinter groups caused by factionalism within the ranks of established parties*. Such parties comprised the Danish Centre Democrats, the Constitutional People's Party and People's Unity parties in Finland and the Union of Liberals and Leftists in Iceland. The Centre Democrats in Denmark were formed in 1973 by dissident Social Democrat Erhard Jakobsen, in opposition to the growing influence within the Social Democratic Party of the newly formed left-wing Socialist Debate faction. It found a place on the political spectrum to the right of the mother party. The Constitutional People's Party in Finland was founded in 1973 by Georg Ehnrooth, a break-away delegate of the Swedish People's Party, in protest against the alliance of all the established parties which the same year passed exceptional legislation enabling Parliament to elect the President, Urho Kekkonen, for a further four-year term of office without recourse to the popular elections prescribed by the Constitution. The Finnish People's Unity Party broke away from the Rural Party in 1973 in revolt against the dictatorial manner of its leader, Veikko Vennamo (Matheson and Sänkiaho, 1975, pp.217–23). Finally, the Union of Liberals and Leftists in Iceland was set up in 1969 by two non-Marxist delegates of the People's Alliance and in 1971 realized no less than 8.9 per cent of the vote. The next most successful of these splinter parties was the Centre Democrats,

TABLE 3.9: ELECTION RESULTS IN SCANDINAVIA SINCE 1969

| Denmark | 1971 Votes | 1971 Seats | 1973 Votes | 1973 Seats | 1975 Votes | 1975 Seats | 1977 Votes | 1977 Seats | 1979 Votes | 1979 Seats | 1981 Votes | 1981 Seats |
|---|---|---|---|---|---|---|---|---|---|---|---|---|
| Social Democrats | 37.3 | 70 | 25.7 | 46 | 29.9 | 53 | 37.1 | 65 | 38.2 | 68 | 32.9 | 59 |
| Socialist People's Party | 9.1 | 17 | 6.0 | 11 | 5.0 | 9 | 3.9 | 7 | 6.0 | 11 | 11.3 | 21 |
| Left Socialists | – | – | – | – | 2.1 | 4 | 2.7 | 5 | 3.6 | 6 | 2.6 | 5 |
| Communists | – | – | 3.6 | 6 | 4.2 | 7 | 3.7 | 7 | – | – | – | – |
| Centre Democrats | – | – | 7.8 | 14 | 2.2 | 4 | 6.4 | 11 | 3.2 | 6 | 8.3 | 15 |
| Conservative People's Party | 16.7 | 31 | 9.2 | 16 | 5.5 | 10 | 8.5 | 15 | 12.5 | 22 | 14.4 | 25 |
| Agrarian Liberals (*Venstre*) | 15.6 | 30 | 12.3 | 22 | 23.3 | 42 | 12.0 | 21 | 12.5 | 22 | 11.3 | 21 |
| Radical Liberals | 14.4 | 27 | 11.2 | 20 | 7.1 | 13 | 3.6 | 6 | 5.4 | 10 | 5.1 | 9 |
| Justice Party | – | – | 2.9 | 5 | – | – | 3.3 | 6 | 2.6 | 5 | 1.4 | – |
| Christian People's Party | – | – | 4.0 | 7 | 5.3 | 9 | 3.4 | 6 | 2.6 | 5 | 2.3 | 5 |
| Progress Party | – | – | 15.9 | 28 | 13.6 | 24 | 14.6 | 26 | 11.0 | 20 | 8.9 | 16 |
| Faroese representatives | | 2 | | 2 | | 2 | | 2 | | 2 | | 2 |
| Greenland representatives | | 2 | | 2 | | 2 | | 2 | | 2 | | 2 |
| Total | | 179 | | 179 | | 179 | | 179 | | 179 | | 179 |

## Finland

| | 1970 Votes | 1970 Seats | 1972 Votes | 1972 Seats | 1975 Votes | 1975 Seats | 1979 Votes | 1979 Seats |
|---|---|---|---|---|---|---|---|---|
| Social Democrats | 23.4 | 52 | 25.8 | 55 | 25.0 | 54 | 24.0 | 52 |
| People's Democratic League | 16.6 | 36 | 17.0 | 37 | 19.0 | 40 | 17.9 | 35 |
| Centre Party | 17.1 | 36 | 16.4 | 35 | 17.7 | 39 | 17.4 | 36 |
| Coalition Party (Conservatives) | 18.0 | 37 | 17.6 | 34 | 18.4 | 35 | 21.7 | 47 |
| Liberals | 6.0 | 8 | 5.2 | 7 | 4.4 | 9 | 3.7 | 4 |
| Swedish People's Party* | 5.7 | 12 | 5.3 | 10 | 4.7 | 10 | 4.3 | 10 |
| Christian People's Party | 1.2 | 1 | 2.5 | 4 | 3.3 | 9 | 4.8 | 9 |
| Rural Party | 10.5 | 18 | 9.2 | 18 | 3.6 | 2 | 4.6 | 7 |
| Unity Party | | | | | 1.7 | 1 | | |
| Constitutional People's Party | | | | | 1.6 | 1 | | |
| Total | | 200 | | 200 | | 200 | | 200 |

* Including Åland Alliance.

## Iceland

| | 1971 Votes | 1971 Seats | 1974 Votes | 1974 Seats | 1978 Votes | 1978 Seats | 1979 Votes | 1979 Seats |
|---|---|---|---|---|---|---|---|---|
| Independence Party | 36.2 | 22 | 42.7 | 25 | 32.7 | 20 | 37.9 | 22 |
| Progressive Party | 25.3 | 17 | 24.9 | 17 | 16.9 | 12 | 24.9 | 17 |
| Social Democrats | 10.5 | 6 | 9.1 | 5 | 22.0 | 14 | 17.4 | 10 |
| People's Alliance | 17.2 | 10 | 18.3 | 11 | 22.9 | 14 | 19.7 | 11 |
| Left Liberals | 9.0 | 5 | 4.6 | 2 | | | | |
| Total | | 60 | | 60 | | 60 | | 60 |

## Norway

| | 1969 Votes | 1969 Seats | 1973 Votes | 1973 Seats | 1977 Votes | 1977 Seats | 1981 Votes | 1981 Seats |
|---|---|---|---|---|---|---|---|---|
| Labour Party | 46.5 | 74 | 35.3 | 62 | 42.4 | 76 | 37.3 | 65 |
| Socialist Electoral Alliance | | — | 11.2 | 16 | 4.1 | 2 | 0.7 | — |
| Conservatives | 19.6 | 29 | 17.5 | 29 | 24.7 | 41 | 31.6 | 54 |
| Centre Party | 10.5 | 20 | 11.0 | 21 | 8.6 | 12 | 6.7 | 11 |
| Christian People's Party | 9.4 | 14 | 12.2 | 20 | 12.1 | 22 | 9.3 | 15 |
| Liberals | 9.4 | 13 | 3.5 | 2 | 3.2 | 2 | 3.9 | 2 |
| New People's Party | | — | 3.4 | 1 | | — | 0.6 | — |
| Progress Party (Lange's) | | — | 5.0 | 4 | | — | 4.5 | 4 |
| Socialist Left | | | | | | | 4.9 | 4 |
| Communist Party | | | | | | | 0.3 | — |
| Total | | 150 | | 150 | | 150 | | 150 |

## Sweden

| | 1970 Votes | 1970 Seats | 1973 Votes | 1973 Seats | 1976 Votes | 1976 Seats | 1979 Votes | 1979 Seats |
|---|---|---|---|---|---|---|---|---|
| Social Democrats | 45.3 | 163 | 43.6 | 156 | 42.7 | 152 | 43.2 | 155 |
| Communist Left | 4.8 | 17 | 5.3 | 19 | 4.7 | 17 | 4.6 | 20 |
| Centre Party | 19.9 | 71 | 25.1 | 90 | 24.1 | 86 | 18.1 | 64 |
| Liberals (People's Party) | 16.2 | 58 | 9.4 | 34 | 11.1 | 39 | 10.6 | 38 |
| Moderate Alliance (Conservatives) | 11.5 | 41 | 13.9 | 51 | 15.6 | 55 | 20.3 | 72 |
| Total | | 350 | | 350 | | 349 | | 349 |

*Source*: Based on tables in *Nordisk Kontakt (passim)*.

which polled 7.8 per cent at its first attempt in 1973, largely, as in the Icelandic Party's case, at the expense of the Social Democrats. The two Finnish parties each polled just under 2 per cent at their first general election in 1975, the Constitutional Peoples' Party recruiting some former Swedish People's Party and Conservative voters, and the People's Unity Party, naturally enough, disgruntled Rural Party supporters. By the end of the decade the survival of all four remained at best problematical.

Secondly, the proliferation of the 1970s included *the emergence or re-emergence of parties with established roots in the region*. This category is made up of the Justice Party in Denmark, together with the Christian parties already discussed, which modelled themselves on the Norwegian Christian People's Party. After a period of gestation in the 1960s, they entered the parliamentary arena in the 1970s: the Danish party achieved its best vote of 5.3 per cent in 1975; the Finnish party increased its percentage poll throughout the 1970s to gain 4.8 per cent in 1979; but the Swedish party, although polling consistently, has thus far failed to beat the 4 per cent electoral threshold. The appearance of interest-specific religious parties further exacerbated the traditionally high fragmentation in the non-socialist camp. The Justice Party is less easy to locate on a left—right continuum. Its heyday stretched from 1947 to 1960: it obtained 8.2 per cent of the poll in 1950 and participated in a coalition government with the Social Democrats and Radical Liberals between 1957 and 1960. After a depressing period in the late 1960s, when it managed to claim a mere 0.7 per cent of the poll, the Justice Party's opposition to Danish membership of the EEC facilitated its reappearance in the *Folketing* in 1972, and after a set-back in 1975 it went on to poll 3.3 per cent in 1977, its best vote in twenty years. In that year its support was divided between Central Jutland and Copenhagen and comprised in both regions a disproportionately large percentage of lower-grade white-collar workers. The party's belief in the free play of market forces, albeit to promote equality and social justice, place it firmly in the non-socialist camp, though on issues such as defence, land reform, housing and so on it has been much closer to the left (Fitzmaurice, 1979).

Thirdly, the 1970s witnessed the appearance of *significant populist parties constituting a radical right on a scale unprecedented in the Scandinavian region*. The 'unholy trinity' was made up of the Danish Progress Party, the Finnish Rural Party and the Anders Lange (later Progress) Party in Norway. The impact of radical rightism was felt first in Finland. The origins of the Rural Party date back to 1958 when Veikko Vennamo, its founder and (until 1979) leader, broke with the Agrarians. Consistently and personally critical of Kekkonen, Vennamo opposed the incumbent head of state with some success at the presidential election of 1968, and it was hardly coincidental that his party went on to poll 10.5 per cent of the vote at the next general election in 1970 – a tenfold improvement on its performance four years earlier. Even that was bettered in Denmark three years later, when the Progress Party founded by Copenhagen tax lawyer Mogens Glistrup polled 15.9 per cent of the active vote to become at once the second largest party. Indeed, the achievement is all the more remarkable when it is remembered that the party was registered only a year before the December 1973 election and was, in contrast to the Rural Party, totally lacking in an organizational infrastructure. Finally, in Norway the Anders Lange Party, emulating much of the anti-tax rhetoric of Glistrup, polled 5 per cent of the vote in 1973. It subsequently admitted its programmatic debt when, following Lange's death in 1975, it adopted the designation of the Danish party, but its support has fallen away badly in recent years. Indeed, the Rural Party too, weakened by defections to the People's Unity Party, seemed quickly to be running out of time. Nevertheless, at the last general election in 1979 there was a modest revival in its fortunes: it polled 4.6 per cent of the vote, and shortly afterwards the leadership of the party passed to Vennamo's son. Glistrup's party has also lost ground over the decade, being overhauled as the second largest party by the agrarian Liberals in 1975 and the Conservative People's Party four years later, but in 1979 it still boasted a significant twenty of the 179 *Folketing* seats.

A further measure of the electoral volatility of the period can be seen from the fact that there were several dramatic short-lived winners and an equal number of catastrophic short-term losers among the established parties in the region, although by the end of the decade there had been a return to something approaching the *status quo ante*. In Denmark, for example, the agrarian Liberals gained an astonishing 11 per cent of the poll in 1975, immediately after their two years as a single-party minority government, only to lose it all a couple of years later. In similar fashion, only in reverse, the Danish Social Democrats lost 12 per cent of the active electorate in 1973, following a single-handed two-year period in office, but had regained it in total by 1977. It was precisely the same story in the case of the Norwegian Labour Party between 1965 and 1977, the party conceding over 11 per cent of its vote in

1973 and then recovering most of it four years later. In Sweden too the Centre Party picked up an extra 10 per cent of the poll between 1968 and 1973 but saw it considerably eroded over the next two general elections. Finally, as if to emulate events elsewhere in the region, the Icelandic ballot of 1978 witnessed the Progressive–Independence Party coalition lose no less than 18 per cent of its support — the greatest swing against a government since 1908!

As far as any general trends may be observed over this electorally volatile phase, it appears that across much of the region by the end of the 1970s centre-based parties and the new radical right were losing ground, while the moderate right and social democracy were making up the arrears of earlier in the decade. The fortunes of the radical left were more variable. More specifically, the Conservatives improved their position to overtake the Centre parties in Finland and Sweden, to equal the agrarian Liberals in Denmark and, in Norway in 1977, to gain a seat in every constituency for the first time in their history; the Liberal parties throughout Scandinavia, together with the Radical Liberals in Denmark and Swedish People's Party in Finland, declined (often appreciably); social democracy either held its own or gained ground, coming within a whisker of replacing the non-socialist coalition in Sweden in 1979; and of the two strongest radical left parties, the Finnish People's Democratic League surrendered support, while the People's Alliance in Iceland strengthened its hand. Curiously, the Left–Communists in Sweden achieved their best result for thirty years in 1979 — with twenty of the 349 *Riksdag* seats — at the same time as the Danish Communists were eliminated from the *Folketing* altogether. Though there had been some reduction in their numbers by the end of the decade, there were still ten parties represented in the Danish legislature and eight in the Finnish at the start of the 1980s — a considerably heightened incidence of multi-partism compared with the bulk of the post-war period. What causes can be adduced for this instability?

A number of nation-specific factors aside, three macro-political and economic factors contributed greatly to the instability affecting Scandinavian party systems in the 1970s. First, there were high levels of personal taxation needed to fund the rising inertia costs of developed welfare states (Sweden and Norway) and increased welfare provision in those nations (Denmark and Finland) rapidly making up the leeway. Secondly, there were structural and sectoral changes in the Scandinavian economies associated with advanced industrialization (in central Scandinavia) and accelerated industrialization (in Finland). Last, international relations, notably Norway and Denmark's proposed membership of the EEC, Finland's special relationship with the Soviet Union and Iceland's role in NATO, were central to the factionalism, volatility and populism of the period. These three points are worth examining briefly in turn.

High taxation became a sore point with Scandinavians in the 1970s. In Sweden, for example, it prompted a disgruntled undercurrent which was occasionally articulated at the public level. The celebrated film director Ingmar Bergman's flight from the taxman drew attention to the matter (in Denmark Glistrup was defending himself against no less than 240 charges of alleged tax evasion), while the taxation question took on an explicitly political guise in the spring of 1976, when Astrid Lindgrén, the well-known author of children's books, wrote a strong attack on Sträng, the Minister of Finance, in the form of a fable in an evening newspaper. Three weeks before the general election the same year, Lindgrén wrote an open letter to the governing Social Democratic Party in which, having again criticized the stultifying effect of high income tax, she signed herself 'formerly a Social Democrat now simply a Democrat'. It cannot be doubted that the issue bolstered the cause of the non-socialist opposition.

In essence, the problem in Sweden, and indeed in Norway, was that the price of a highly developed welfare state had grown to the point where both countries were living beyond their means, so placing an increasing financial burden on the individual. Sweden, for example, with its womb-to-tomb protection, is one of the six Western nations cited by Rose in which the costs of public policy had been growing at a yearly average of 7.1 per cent between 1951 and 1977, whereas the national economy had grown at an average annual rate of only 4.2 per cent in the same period (Rose, 1979, p.357). In Denmark and Finland, where the welfare state was much less developed at the beginning of the 1970s, a marked increase in welfare spending during the decade pushed up levels of personal taxation. Thus in 1967 Denmark was a low-tax country by Scandinavian standards, but five years later she had the highest overall level of taxation in the region (Berglund and Lindström, 1978, p.199). In Finland, too, there were significant tax increases between 1972 and 1973. Indeed, it cannot be pure coincidence that radical rightism had its greatest success in the two Scandinavian states where the *relative* increase in personal taxation was greatest. Certainly, when the three-party non-socialist Baunsgaard coalition in Denmark between 1968 and 1971 did nothing to meet a widespread demand for tax cuts, Glistrup's pledge to abolish income tax altogether may have been irresistible to many of his bourgeois constituents.

Taxation apart, the electoral volatility of the 1970s was connected with the sectoral changes associated with advanced or advancing industrialization, which, in concentrating production in a number of highly developed areas and causing problems of regional imbalance, militated for protest in the peripheries. The Swedish Centre and Finnish Rural parties were obvious beneficiaries of this type of unrest. The Swedish case has already been discussed; suffice it here to re-emphasis the tactical way in which the Centre Party exploited the theme of decentralization. In Finland, where a significant primary sector survived longer than in metropolitan Scandinavia, the Centre Party (historically, of course, the farmer's party) signed its own execution warrant in its core support areas in the outlying north and east by presiding over the amalgamation of small farms as part of a broader programme of rationalizing agriculture. This contributed further to radicalizing an already radical regional culture, allowing former Agrarian, Veikko Vennamo, to appeal to what he called 'Forgotten Finland'. Interestingly, however, only 53 per cent of the Rural Party's vote in the breakthrough election of 1970 derived from these peripheral northern and eastern areas, underlining the fact that the party's appeal was much broader than its name implied. Vennamo's wide-ranging, non-specific but colourfully expressed antielitism clearly attracted elements in the highly taxed salaried employee category, as well as those disaffected with the ruling centre-left government's managerial style. Indeed, throughout the region endogamous changes integrally related to the achievement of post-industrialization created conditions of social and geographical mobility which were reflected in the marked increase in electoral mobility.

In the present context it is worth noting that the international recession following in the wake of the Yom Kippur war in 1973 precipitated no greater degree of radical rightism in the region than had the Great Depression of the 1930s – slightly surprising, perhaps, when it is remembered that the contrast between the prosperity of the 1960s and the austerity of the 1970s was far more sharply delineated than in the economic climate of the two inter-war decades. To be sure, the effects of the increase in oil prices were felt throughout the region, particularly in terms of domestic inflation and a disastrous decline in overseas trade. Thus with her shipbuilding industry decimated and steel-making run down, Sweden experienced a drop in annual national income for the first time since 1939–45. In 1977 Sweden's GNP actually fell by over

2 per cent. In Norway and Finland it was timber-based exports that were badly hit, while in Denmark, with her lack of natural resources, a massive external deficit built up. Everywhere in the region, in fact, it was the same catalogue of rising inflation, growing unemployment (or concealed underemployment), contracting overseas markets and, ultimately, devaluations with a view to improving export performance. Yet the full impact of all this was not felt until the middle and second half of the 1970s, when populism was already in decline. Indeed, in bespeaking the need for expedients based on harsh reality rather than Glistrupian panacea-peddling, the international recession may well have been a factor that actually *contributed* to the decline of populism in Scandinavia in the second half of the 1970s.

A final ingredient of instability in the parliamentary and electoral arenas in the region during the 1970s was the international relations dimension. In Finland, in particular, this constituted an important, albeit much understated, component of the protest groundswell of the decade. Thus it was hardly a coincidence that Vennamo, who implied, when breaking with the Agrarians, that the nation was leaning too far towards the East and who was personally critical of Kekkonen throughout the 1960s, should achieve his party's breakthrough only two years after opposing Kekkonen at the presidential elections of 1968. Vennamo, it should be noted, favoured former President Paasikivi's tough but friendly line with Moscow but refused to honour his successor by referring to official policy by its generally accepted title of the Passikivi– Kekkonen line. In like manner, the Constitutional People's Party (nowadays Constitutional Rightist Party) voiced the sentiments of precisely those late middle-aged persons with recollections of the Winter War who most feared the prospect of insidious Finlandization and who were incensed at the failure of senior politicians to explain the urgency of the situation which dictated Parliament's decision in 1973 to extend the long-serving head of state's period in office. Clearly, Finnish radical rightism owed much to mistrust of 'the Management'.

Elsewhere in the region the focal point of foreign relations in the early 1970s was Brussels – either as the home of the Common Market or as NATO headquarters. In Denmark and Norway proposed membership of the EEC brought the party systems into competition with popular movements for or against accession which broke down party loyalties on both left and right. This was particularly true in Norway, where the People's Movement Against the EEC, founded in 1965, conjoined farmers, *småbruker* and a number of idealists and intellectuals against the high-status professional and business interests that were in favour of joining the Market. Indeed, the opponents of the EEC, reviving something of the nationalism of the 'old' nineteenth century Left — *Venstre* was ironically divided on the issue — gained 53 per cent of the poll at the consultative referendum in 1972, despite the fact that the *parliamentary* opposition to membership, based on the Centre Party and the radical left, had commanded only 35 per cent of the active electorate at the foregoing general election. Social democracy was split on the issue, and although its leadership was in favour of Norway's application for membership, the rank and file was distinctly less enthusiastic, and there were clearly defections both at the referendum and at the ensuing general election, for the Labour Party's vote was down by over 11 per cent in 1973 compared with the 1965 poll. By contrast, the radical left, in the form of the Socialist Electoral Alliance, which joined together Communist and Socialist People's parties specifically to contest the 1973 elections, gained appoximately 7 per cent more than the combined vote for the two parties four years earlier. Indeed, although Anders Lange's party made its first appearance at this dramatic post-referendum election in 1973, Norway differed from both the Danish and the Finnish cases in seeing a growth of radical leftism *as well as* radical rightism in the early 1970s. Unlike Denmark, too, the Norwegian party system quickly regained control of events, and the death of Anders Lange in 1975 marked the effective end of his party and a return of most of its votes to the Conservatives.

In Denmark the EEC question shook the party system rather less, and nearly two-thirds of the votes at the 1972 referendum were cast in favour of entry. Even so, division in the Social Democratic and Radical Liberal camps contributed to a sharp drop in their respective poll at the general election of 1973, while, interestingly, the Socialist People's Party, the only party united in opposition to the EEC, also lost ground. The splinter Centre Democrats obviously recruited their 7.8 per cent vote mainly at the expense of the Social Democrats, with the entry into the electoral arena of Glistrup's party, polling 15.9 per cent in 1973, accounting for the significant losses suffered by all three established non-socialist parties (Thomas, 1975).

In both Norway and Denmark the EEC issue represented, in Stein Rokkan's terms, a return to territoriality: a resurrection of the conflict between the rural *nation* and urban *state* (and, beyond that, the super-state in Brussels) which had characterized the initial period of late nineteenth-century Scandinavian bipartism (Lipset and Rokkan, 1967, pp.41f.). In Norway the countryside was generally against the EEC and the towns for it; in Denmark it was the competitive export farmers in the countryside who were in favour and the towns largely against. In Iceland, too, the radical left consistently profited in the 1970s from an identification with territorality and, in particular, the interests of the Icelandic nation against NATO imperialism. 'Iceland out of NATO and NATO out of Iceland' ran the familiar slogan of the People's Alliance, a party which gained almost 6 per cent of the active electorate between 1971 and 1978. True, these advances have owed as much to deep-seated economic problems and the inability of the centre-right government after 1974 to deal with a national inflation rate reaching almost 50 per cent in 1978. The Social Democrats, the junior party of the left in the post-war period, have also made considerable gains in the same economic milieu. But whereas the rise of radical leftism in Norway in 1973 proved to be short-lived, Iceland was unique among the five Scandinavian nations in witnessing a steady growth in support for the radical left throughout the 1970s.

To conclude this chapter it is important briefly to consider whether the electoral volatility of the 1970s was an expression of declining support for the Scandinavian political systems or, somewhat paradoxically, a measure of deep-seated consensus in the political society of the region. Gordon Smith clarifies the latter view when he insists that while 'one result of a declining intensity of political cleavage may be the catch-all party, it is just as conceivable that sections of the electorate – secure in the knowledge of the basic consensus in society – will be inclined to lend their support to marginal parties' (Smith, 1979, p.140). In this light, support for Glistrup *et al.* could be construed as a symptom of a basic consensus over values – albeit in the context of a temporary inability of the party system to deliver desired policy outcomes – rather than a real indicator of declining popular legitimacy (i.e. fundamental disagreement over objectives). Richard Rose, on the other hand, asserts that 'the increasing volatility of voters in the past decade is another sign of growing *civic indifference* . . . . voters have shown a readiness to abandon what were once thought to be stable and strong party identifications without shifting support to anti-regime parties' (Rose, 1979, p.367). Rose uses the notion of civic indifference rather loosely, encompassing things as substantively different as tax evasion and electoral abstentionism. However, the existence of wholesale apathy, if proven, would scarcely be consistent with describing the Scandinavian states as consensual democracies.

On the face of it, two facts favour Rose's interpretation. First, electoral volatility did not generally go hand in hand with increased voter mobilization. In Denmark electoral participation fell by over 2 per cent in 1973 when the Progress Party crashed on to the scene; turnout dropped by nearly 3 per cent in Finland in 1970, the year the Rural Party achieved its breakthrough, and was down by a similar margin in Norway in 1973 when the Anders Lange Party made its notable gains. In Iceland, too, the largest swing against a government in seventy years in 1978 was accompanied by a 2 per cent drop in turnout. Only in Sweden did the protest elections of the 1970s witness an increase in voter participation. Secondly, the Communist parties have not really profited from the swings of recent years, while their anti-regime character has, in any event, been open to doubt. In Finland and Iceland the two largest radical left parties in the region have both participated in government in the 1970s: in the former the hardline Stalinists, led by former delegate Taisto Sinisalo, make up an opposition minority of eleven out of the Finnish People's Democratic League's parliamentary group of thirty-five, and in the latter the People's Alliance has been 'Eurocommunist' from its inception. Moreover, there is clearly room to debate Sartori's inclusion of the Danish Progress Party in his class of anti-system parties (Sartori, 1976).

In fact, it is arguably less important in contemporary Scandinavia to establish whether a particular party possesses an anti-system ideology than to note the existence of sizable parties with a low to zero eligibility for governing. While it may be countered that the preclusion from coalitions of the likes of the Danish Progress and Finnish Rural parties is simply a consequence of their protest character, the 'outcast' status of the moderate right in Finland, which has gained 8 per cent of the active electorate over the course of the fifteen years since it last participated in government in 1966, carries more serious implications (Arter, 1978b, pp.422—36). Obviously, when significant sections of the electorate are denied a voice in government, for whatever reason, this is bound to have a negative feedback effect on levels of popular consent. As John Frears has noted in relation to the French Fifth Republic, the best test of legitimacy in a liberal democracy is to observe the alternation of power from government to opposition (Frears, 1978, p.11). In Finland the possibility of alternation, if not actually foreclosed, has not been realized in a decade and a half.

Even so, the balance of evidence points to the fact that much of the electoral mobility of the 1970s stemmed from a protest against the inability of the established party system to maintain, through a period of declining economic growth, the affluent living standards to which the Scandinavians had grown accustomed. Indeed, in line with Gordon Smith's observation cited above, increased support for marginal parties was the consequence of the temporary inability of the established elites to produce economic prosperity, over which there was widespread popular consensus. True, the protest incorporated those adopting a questioning attitude to growth as well as those opposed to the secularism of a materialist era. But the increased level of personal taxation needed to support the rising relative costs of government lay at the heart of the matter in so far as it affected lifestyles and work incentives. Moreover, it was less an upturn in the respective economies than an acceptance of the harsh realities of the situation and the need for *concertation* between government and the main sectoral interests of society to deal with it that gradually eroded the basis of Scandinavian populism. As an adjunct to *realpolitik*, governments introduced measures of tax reform designed to reassure the electorate that prosperity remained a primary goal.

By the second half of the decade the decline in levels of class voting that had gone hand in hand with the electoral mobility of the earlier 1970s had been halted; some of the splinter groups had disappeared from the parliamentary stage; and there were at least some signs of the five-party Scandinavian model reasserting itself. True, while Anders Lange is dead and Veikko Vennamo has retired, Mogens Glistrup cannot yet be counted out. But with his Progress Party on the retreat, the vote for the Swedish Centre Party falling and the new radical left diminished, it was evident that the worst of the protest mood in Scandinavian politics had passed by 1980. Even at its height, between 1972 and 1973, electoral behaviour was largely faithful to the socialist–non-socialist ordering of the parties on the political spectrum. Thus although the Danish Progress Party gained support from previous Social Democrats and the Finnish Rural Party from elements on the radical left, the bulk of their support came from disaffected non-socialists. In short, the radical right recruited mainly from bourgeois electors and the radical left from socialist voters. Indeed, the functional voter alignments characterizing the formative pre-war period of the Scandinavian party systems survived the turmoil of the 1970s. The vast majority of blue-collar workers continued to support the parties of the left; the bulk of the farmers remained with the centre; and a majority, albeit a modest one, of the white-collar middle classes favoured the non-socialist parties.

When the social structure was dichotomized into working class and middle class (including farmowners) and a simple bipolarized socialist—non-socialist scheme was employed in Finland in the mid-1970s, a high class index of voting of +39 was obtained — and that in reputedly the most fragmented political culture in the region!

CHAPTER FOUR

# Political Structures in Scandinavia

In the previous chapter we examined the socio-political landscape of the Nordic countries, mapping the regularities of behaviour which have influenced Scandinavian political relationships. In the following pages our intention is to examine the institutions which have been built in that landscape to regulate political activity. The aim throughout will be to illustrate the distinctive solutions developed by the Scandinavian states to some of the perennial problems of regulating political activity, while at the same time there has been a process of diffusion and adaptation of institutions between the countries of the region, with their close affinities to each other and their willingness to learn from each other's experience.

After a comparative discussion of constitutional frameworks, we shall examine the powerful executive machinery of the state. Some of the more significant parliamentary, legal and administrative checks on that power will then be considered, and this chapter will conclude with a comparative discussion of the electoral systems which regulate one of the important ways in which political representation is accorded to social forces and with a brief survey of political recruitment. This will provide the context for an examination in the following chapter of the political process in action, including the ways in which a consensus has been developed and maintained in both the legislative and the corporative arenas for particular sets of policies.

## CONSTITUTIONS

Constitutions are commonly drawn up when a sharp break occurs in a country's history. This certainly holds true of four out of the five initial constitutions of the modern era in Scandinavia. In the case of the metropolitan states, the break was with a previous phase in the country's domestic history. Thus Denmark in 1849 marked the end of centuries of royal absolutism with a constitution based on the principle of the separation of powers. Sweden in 1809 had already adopted the same principle after successive periods of parliamentary hegemony (1718–72) and monarchical absolutism (1772–1809), culminating in an unsuccessful war with Russia, the loss of Finland and the enforced abdication of Gustav IV. In the case of the non-metropolitan states, Norway and Finland, the break was with another power and represented an assertion of independence. In the fifth instance, Iceland, the situation was less clear-cut, and the first modern constitution of 1874 is best regarded as a first instalment of home rule from Copenhagen.

Political development in Scandinavia has followed a general pattern of evolution from early separation-of-powers systems towards a thoroughgoing acceptance of the principles of parliamentary government, whether explicitly written into the Constitution or not. Finland, however, forms an exception to this generalization: here elements of both systems have coexisted, illogically but workably, ever since independence in what may be called a hybrid presidential/parliamentary regime. The differences in origin of the various constitutions of the region have meant that on the whole they exhibit more variety than uniformity and owe more to national evolution than to intra-regional diffusion.

Denmark and Sweden have both replaced their early modern Constitutions with fresh ones incorporating the principles of parliamentary government – Denmark in 1953, Sweden in 1975. The Danes observe 5 June, Constitution Day, as a national holiday: this was the date of the 1849 model and has since become the traditional date for the entry into force of new Constitutions. Intervening models took effect in 1866 and 1915. This comparative frequency is less a sign of political instability than of a periodically felt need to update a set of written rules which are unusually hard to amend. The new Swedish Constitution of 1975 was similarly a tidying-up exercise. In this case the relatively flexible Constitution of 1809 had become so patched up and amended that it had lost coherence. The lawyers therefore rationalized what the politicians had begun.

The Norwegians, Finns and Icelanders tend to attach a more special significance to their Constitutions as symbols of nationhood. The Norwegian Constitution of 1814 was adopted by a representative assembly at Eidsvoll which proclaimed the country's independence in the brief interregnum between the end of Danish and the beginning of

Swedish rule. Drawing intellectual inspiration in part from two of the more liberal constitutions of the French Revolutionary era, it remained in force domestically, in all essentials, during the union with Sweden and served to protect Norwegian liberties and to limit the power of the Swedish kings. Although inevitably much amended, it remains technically in force today, and the date of its adoption – 17 May – is celebrated as National Day. The names given under it to the legislature and the subdivisions of the legislature – *Storting, Odelsting, Lagting* – deliberately evoke echoes of the early medieval period of Norwegian independence, in accordance with the spirit of nineteenth-century romantic nationalism. So too did the title of Haakon VII, assumed by the Danish Prince Carl, who was voted to become the country's king by a majority of four to one in a referendum after the break with Sweden in 1905. But, more to the point in the present context, the rules inherited from the era of the separation of powers affect present-day Norwegian politics more powerfully than those of any other Scandinavian state. Thus the *Storting* continues to be indissoluble during the four-year span between elections, and Ministers must resign their seats in Parliament on taking office (they may, of course, continue to speak there).

The Finnish Constitution of 1919 and the Icelandic of 1944 are both the Constitutions adopted on achieving national independence. The drafting process for the former began, in fact, while the country was still under the rule of the Russian provisional government in 1917, and the parliamentary principle was written in partly with a view to heading off any imposed regime. American and French (Third Republic) sources were drawn upon for inspiration, and at the same time much of the pattern laid down for the administrative and judicial sectors reflected practice inherited from the period of Swedish rule and subsequently preserved, largely intact, under the tsars. The Constitution was adopted by the Finnish Parliament in the wake of civil war and bitter division between republicans and monarchists: the provision of a potentially formidably strong presidency was a sop to the latter once they had been defeated on the question of principle. Over time the Constitution has come to command much the same degree of respect and support as had its predecessor from pre-independence days, the 1772 (Gustavian) Constitution Act, which preserved a considerable measure of Finnish political liberty during the period of tsarist rule. One peculiarity at least has significantly been carried over from pre-independence days, namely, the possibility of passing statutes that give dispensation from constitutional rules in particular cases. These dispensing statutes have to be passed by the same procedure as constitutional amendments — that is, *either* by passage in two successive Parliaments, the second time with a two-thirds majority, *or* by the urgency procedure, requiring a vote of five-sixths of Parliament for activation, followed shortly afterwards by a two-thirds vote in favour of the measure. By 1970 no fewer than 600 dispensing statutes had been passed (Kastari, 1970), thus allowing a strict interpretation of the Constitution to be combined with flexibility in crises and emergencies, provided there is a pretty general consensus in favour. It is of particular relevance that the tough majority requirements act as an inducement to the parties in the system to compromise and to horse-trade: in other words, the Constitution itself is a force for consensual policy-making.

The Icelandic Constitution of 1944 was approved unanimously by the Althing and by 95 per cent of those voting in the subsequent popular referendum. It builds largely upon the earlier Constitutions of 1874 and 1920 and draws much of its content from Danish and Norwegian sources, particularly the former. The chief innovation in 1944 was the design for the presidency, based essentially on the role of the Danish constitutional monarchy but chosen by direct popular election.

The formal powers of the Icelandic President include the authority to appoint the Cabinet, to determine the number of Ministers and their duties, to preside over the State Council, to summon, adjourn and dissolve the *Althing*, to make appointments of senior officials and to conclude treaties with other states. But the office has not been developed by its incumbents to the same extent as in Finland. A continuation of precedents created by regents under the Danish monarchy has emphasized its non-political nature, although the list of powers indicates a potential for political significance. In the 1968 election, for example, the candidate with the support of the governing parties was defeated in what was seen as a judgement by the electorate on their record (Griffiths, 1969, p.109). The successful candidate was Professor Kristjan Eldjarn, an archaeologist and director of the National Museum, who held office for twelve years. The view of the presidency as a position of intellectual, social and cultural representation rather than political power was confirmed by the election in 1980 of Ms Vigdís Finnbogadóttir as the country's fourth President. Previously the manager of Reykjavík Theatre Company, she had never been a member of a political party, but she will require political skills, especially in influencing the formation of new governments.

Finland and Iceland are republics, and the other three Scandinavian countries are monarchies. In Denmark and Norway the wartime role of the monarchs profoundly strengthened their significance as symbols of national unity. In Sweden the new constitution of 1975 removed all possibility that the monarch could influence the course of events in a confused party political situation by exercising discretionary power to choose a Prime Minister: this function is now entrusted to the Speaker. Only the Communist Left and a small minority of the Social Democrats could be described as convinced republicans, however, even though the latter party showed their coolness towards the introduction of female succession to the throne (following the Danish precedent of 1953) by abstaining in the parliamentary vote that brought this into effect in 1980.

All three Nordic monarchs, Margrethe II of Denmark, Olaf V of Norway and Carl XVI Gustaf of Sweden fulfil all the usual duties of dignified heads of state, though without any conspicuous show of wealth or social distance. The Danish and Norwegian monarchs can still influence the process of government formation, although in the Danish case this function was partially delegated by the Queen, shortly after her accession, to the Chairman of the *Folketing* in January 1975, with the support of a large majority of the political forces represented in the *Folketing*. Nevertheless, this drew some adverse comment from constitutional purists and is a precedent unlikely to be followed.

While the Danish, Icelandic and Norwegian Constitutions are codified, Finland follows Swedish practice in that her Constitution, strictly speaking, comprehends not one basic law but several: in other words, the special procedures for constitutional amendment have to be followed in respect of a number of basic texts. The 1919 Finnish and 1975 Swedish Instrument of Government Acts set out most of the key arrangements. Otherwise Finland has (for example) the 1928 Parliament Act, Sweden the 1810 Act of Succession and the 1949 Freedom of the Press Act. Swedish amendment procedure, it may be added, is comparatively simple: straight majority votes in two successive *Riksdags*, with a general election intervening. Iceland also follows this model, while Norway — like Finland, in the case of non-urgent amendments — requires a two-thirds majority vote after a general election at which voters have, theoretically at least, had the opportunity to consider the issue.

Until 1980 Denmark was alone in introducing a significant measure of direct democracy into her constitutional provisions. Thus constitutional amendments require not only passage by two successive Parliaments but also approval by a majority comprising at least 40 per cent of the total electorate in a popular referendum. Moreover, government Bills can be forced to a referendum on the initiative of a third of the members of the *Folketing*: a Bill is then rejected if the majority against it comprises at least 30 per cent of the electorate (Denmark, Constitution of 1953, paragraphs 20, 29, 42: Himmelstrup and Møller, 1958). Elsewhere in Scandinavia referenda may in practice occur (in Sweden, constitutionally) if Parliament so decides, and they are then consultative in character. There have been some notable (though infrequent) examples – for example, the introduction of prohibition in Norway (1919–27) and its rejection in Sweden (1922); the rejection, by a large majority, of right-hand driving in Sweden (1955; subsequently rejected by a conference of party leaders); the Norwegian and Danish votes on the Common Market (1972); and the Swedish decision in favour of the nuclear power programme (1980). In 1980 Sweden introduced a new element into her constitutional amendment process: it has an obvious affinity with the Danish procedure for ordinary legislation. On the proposal of one-tenth of the membership of the *Riksdag*, and with the support of one-third, a draft amendment that has already received one favourable vote in Parliament must be put to a referendum held at the same time as the next general election. The amendment is decisively rejected if there is an adverse majority equivalent in size to over half of those casting valid votes in the election. Otherwise the *Riksdag* votes for a second and final time on the draft. In other words, a valid negative referendum vote is decisive; a positive referendum vote is consultative.

## EXECUTIVES

In Scandinavia as in other parliamentary democracies, political leadership is exercised by an executive comprising a Prime Minister and a group of political Ministers with responsibility for defined functional policy areas. In Finland, however, the President has come to wield great power and influence both in the conduct of the country's foreign affairs (especially with the USSR) and in the supervision of the country's governmental and party-political affairs. Thus, while the other Scandinavian countries conform quite closely to the classic model of a parliamentary executive, Finland has a semi-presidential government somewhere between parliamentary and presidential models, in a category which would also include the bicephalous presidentialism of the Fifth French Republic (Duverger, 1980). In both models the role of political leadership involves the functions of initiating policies, elaborating and developing these policy initiatives in consultation and collaboration with the interests affected by them, steering the resulting legislation through the legislature and then exercising some supervision over its implementation by the administrative machinery.

Cabinet government began in Scandinavia (as, for instance, in Prussia) as a college of senior officials to advice a monarch in whom all executive power was formally vested; the officials acted within a highly formalized set of procedures and in a spirit of legalism reinforced by the legal training which was the normal prerequisite of a career in the court bureaucracy. The growth of constitutionalism during the nineteenth century, associated with the expanding ripples of liberalism, brought with it moves towards the differentiation of executive from legislative and judicial functions, while the monarchs continued to appoint those whom they considered best fitted to serve in their advisory councils: in practice they chose men qualified as much by professional experience as by political ability. Cabinets became politicized relatively late by British standards, and only as a result of prolonged struggle during the latter part of the nineteenth century between the monarchy, the aristocracy, the officials (many of whom were also aristocrats) and the large landowners on the right against the forces of liberal constitutionalism and democracy, represented with growing parliamentary strength by the Left. The legislatures finally gained control of the party composition of Cabinets first in Norway in 1884 and last in Sweden in 1921. This process converted the king into a ceremonial leader and the Cabinet into an executive committee of parliament.

The parliamentary principle was achieved almost without constitutional amendment but was consolidated in each country as part of more comprehensive constitutional revisions some time later. In Sweden even the power to appoint a Prime Minister has passed to the Speaker of the *Riksdag* under the 1975 Constitution. The Danish and Norwegian monarchs still formally preside over a Council of State, but this simply registers decisions taken by Ministers meeting under the chairmanship of the Prime Minister. The Finnish President, however, retains (and sometimes uses) decisive powers to overrule his Ministers, while the Finnish Basic Law makes a distinction between the functions of the President in Council and those of Ministers in Cabinet. The constitutional powers of the Finnish President include the conduct of foreign affairs, dissolution of the *Eduskunta,* appointment of leading civil servants and the right to reject or revise proposed government legislation and veto Bills approved by Parliament. The latter powers over legislation are more far-reaching than those of the French President: the extent to which they are put into effect makes the presidency in Finland an office without parallel in the Scandinavian countries.

Finnish presidential authority is strengthened by four factors. The elective nature of the office provides the incumbent with an independent constituency. The tangled complexities of Finland's multi-party system emphasize the need for a figure of national unity. (Both these factors also apply in France and Iceland.) As also in Iceland, the Finnish President may seek re-election for an unlimited number of terms, while the French President may only serve two. But perhaps most important of all, the need to keep on the right side of the Soviet Union has placed the President in a position of special power, particularly during the long incumbency (1956–81) of Urho Kekkonen. Finnish presidential power in foreign affairs rivals that of French presidents in scope, while the Icelandic President has no such power.

Since the adoption of the parliamentary principle, all Nordic governments must retain the confidence of a majority in the legislature. But this support can be purely tacit: the Cabinet need not seek a formal vote of confidence on taking office, but governs until overturned either by a defeat on a major issue or a formal vote of no confidence. The power of Parliament to dismiss the government is balanced, however, by the latter's power to obtain a dissolution and new elections, although this power is limited in Norway and Sweden (as is explained below in our discussion of Parliaments). While the Norwegian *Storting* cannot be dissolved between the regular four-yearly elections, the opposition parties have nevertheless held back from turning out a minority Cabinet when there was no viable alternative. This has happened only once since 1945, when non-socialists and the Socialist People's Party combined in 1963 to turn out the Labour government for a month, citing its failure to act effectively to prevent mining accidents at the state-owned King's Bay coal-mines in Svalbard (Spitzbergen). But two successive Labour administrations have been able to rule since 1973 simply because their opposition on left and right could not combine against them in any lasting manner: to oust a government in such circumstances would appear irresponsible and in conflict with the norms of Nordic political culture. Instead there was a series of 'crises' over aspects of Labour policy, allowing the opposition to feel they still had a part to play and usually resolved by some compromise involving only minor concessions by the government.

The constitutional separation of legislative from executive roles means that Ministers are not required to hold seats in the legislature and in Norway are prohibited from doing so: any member of the *Storting* who joins the Cabinet must surrender his parliamentary seat to an alternate while holding office. The number of Cabinet members not elected to Parliament varies with political circumstances. In Denmark over the past fifteen years there have been about four in each Cabinet, but seven of the twelve members of Hartling's 1973–5 Cabinet were not MFs, thus eking out the Liberal Party's very narrow parliamentary base. The Swedes used to be required by the Constitution to appoint two (usually non-party) legal specialists as Ministers without Portfolio to help keep the forms of legislation in proper order, but this necessity disappeared in the 1975 Constitution. Ministers with little or no party affiliation may be selected for their technical expertise. A case in point was the appointment of Jens Evensen, Norwegian Trade Minister in 1973–4 because of his knowledge of the EEC and then Law-of-the-Sea Minister, a short-term post created to deal with an issue of great national importance by virtue of his experience in international law. Others are appointed because they are acceptable to a client group important to a Ministry. Conversely, in Sweden in 1979 the Energy Ministry went to a non-partisan appointee, Carl Axel Petri, because the non-socialist coalition Cabinet could not agree on which of the three parties should hold a post made particularly controversial by the divisive nuclear power issue. The Finnish President quite frequently resorts to the expedient of caretaker Cabinets composed largely of civil servants, although perhaps also containing some party politicians, as in May 1970 or following the 1975 elections. Pending agreement on the composition of a party government, it was necessary to have a government to greet participants in the Helsinki European Security Conference. The 1970 government was installed by the President in preference to a conservative minority government which had the tacit acceptance of the centre-left, for reasons of foreign policy and relations with the labour market. These caretaker Cabinets are short-lived and come about either because the parties are unwilling to co-operate during the approach to an election or, particularly latterly, as an element in a wider presidential political strategy. In addition, most of the partisan Cabinets in Finland have had one or more non-party members.

As head of government, the powers of the Prime Ministers who occupy this office in all five Nordic countries are limited first and foremost by the extent of the parliamentary support on which they are able to rely. The region is rich in the variety of support relationships which have been developed, ranging from broad or all-party coalitions (usually in times of national peril), through coalitions which at various times have spanned most ideological hues, to sometimes precariously based minority governments or even the non-party governments mentioned above. A Prime Minister's choice of Cabinet colleagues is limited by the constraints imposed by the other parties with which he is working in Parliament and also by the major organized interests whose acquiescence is essential to acceptance of his government's policies. In Finland the Prime Minister is overshadowed in this by the President. The ways in which these problems are managed and the influence these have on the policy process will form the theme of chapter 5. Here we will concentrate on the organization, structure and values of the executive branch of government in the Nordic countries.

TABLE 4.1: PUBLIC EXPENDITURE AS PERCENTAGE OF GNP, SELECTED COUNTRIES, 1950–76

| Country | Year | Public expenditure % (GNP) |
| --- | --- | --- |
| Denmark | 1971 | 31.0 |
|  | 1975 | 42.3 |
| Finland | 1950 | 35.2 |
|  | 1975 | 38.7 |
| Norway | 1950 | 31.8 |
|  | 1974 | 50.1 |
| Sweden | 1950 | 23.6 |
|  | 1975 | 44.8 |
| UK | 1950 | 35.3 |
|  | 1976 | 51.7 |

*Source*: Sharpe, 1978.

The scope of the state's activities has expanded vastly over the past century in all European countries, and not least in Scandinavia. One indicator of this is the proportion of GNP devoted to public expenditure by the state, which has risen from under 10 per cent in 1869–70 to well over 40 per cent a century later. Much of this rise has occurred in recent years, as is shown in table 4.1. While the proportion of resources at the state's disposal has increased substantially, their value in absolute terms has increased many times more, in line with the growth of population and the even faster growth of GNP per head. A major organizational concern of Nordic public administration since 1945 has been the evolution of acceptable ways in which to cope with the tremendous increase of work produced by the construction of far-reaching welfare schemes, the adoption of long-term planning techniques and a commitment to large-scale state intervention in virtually all aspects of economic and social life. As elsewhere, the problem has acquired two central and frequently conflicting aspects: how to keep the administration up to an acceptable standard of efficiency, and how to keep it accountable and responsive to both Parliament and the public. Solutions adopted have included changes in personnel and structure in central and local government, the increasing integration of organized interests into the process of administration, the extension of the jurisdiction of ombudsmen, moves to promote more open government and continuing emphasis on very careful consultative procedures when preparing legislation.

With growth in the scope and extent of state functions has come a corresponding growth of legislative and administrative activity. One consequence has been a considerable increase in the number of civil servants. Another has been that decisions have been taken at lower administrative levels, partly through the delegation of authority within departments and partly through decentralization to directorates or local authorities. A third has been an expansion in the size of Cabinets.

In Denmark, Iceland and Norway the structure of central administration is based on government departments, each headed by a Minister with a seat in the Cabinet, and with several directorates subordinate to, but with various degrees of independence in, their relationship with the Departments. A permanent secretary heads the official establishment of each Department and may to a limited extent act on behalf of the Minister, while a directorate will be headed by a (permanent) director who acts on behalf of his own organization. This ministerial system is broadly similar to British arrangements but rather different in origin to the Swedish pattern. There the central administration is not formally organized as a group of services, each fully integrated under the control of a Minister. Instead the supreme body is 'the Government', each of whose members is still, if anachronistically, known as *statsråd* (literally 'state counsellor'). One effect of this distinctive organizational principle is that central government authorities cannot take formal instructions

TABLE 4.2: CABINET COMPOSITION IN THE NORDIC COUNTRIES, 1980, IN ORDER OF PRECEDENCE

| Denmark | Finland | Iceland | Norway | Sweden |
|---|---|---|---|---|
| Prime Minister (1914)* | Prime Minister | Prime Minister | Prime Minister | Prime Minister |
| Foreign Affairs (1848) | Foreign Affairs | Foreign Affairs | Foreign Affairs | Foreign Affairs |
| Finance (1848) | Justice | Finance | Agriculture | Economy |
| Economy (1971) | Interior | Education | Local Government and Labour | Budget |
| Industry (1908) | Deputy Interior | Fisheries and Communications | Oil and Energy | Justice |
| Culture (1961) | Defence | Trade | Environment | Defence |
| Church (1916) and Greenland (1955) | Finance | Justice and Church | Social Affairs | Social Affairs |
| Social Affairs (1924) | Deputy Finance | Agriculture | Finance | Deputy Social Affairs |
| Justice (1848) and Interior (1848) | Education | Social Affairs, Health and Social Security | Justice and Police | Communications |
| Education (1916) | Deputy Education | Industry | Trade and Shipping | Deputy Communications |
| Environment (1971) | Agriculture and Forestry | | Defence | Agriculture |
| Agriculture (1896) and Fisheries (1947) | Traffic | | Church and Education | Trade |
| Public Works (1894) | Trade and Industry | | Industry | Labour Market |
| Defence (1950) | Foreign Trade | | Communications | Deputy Labour Market |
| Labour (1942) | Social Affairs and Health | | Consumer Affairs and Public Administration | Industry |
| Housing (1947) | Deputy Social Affairs and Health | | Fisheries | Local Government |
| Tax and Duties (1975) | Employment | | Planning | Housing |
| Energy (1979) | | | | Deputy Housing |
| | | | | Personnel |
| | | | | Energy |
| (18) | (17) | (10) | (17) | (20) |

*Dates show year of establishment of Ministry.
*Source: Nordisk Kontakt*, no. 4, 1980.

directly from the Minister concerned but only via a decision taken by the King-in-Council, that is, by the government as a whole (Vinde, 1971, p.13). Thus the head of a Swedish administrative organization is not under orders from a superior body as to the interpretation and application of a statute and is not part of a hierarchical structure surmounted by a Minister, so that, for example, complaints are not amenable to ministerial intervention but must be dealt with through the administrative courts or by an ombudsman.

As in other ways, Finland is something of a hybrid between the Swedish and the Danish/Norwegian patterns, having a number of central offices coexisting with the ministerially headed Departments. While the two underlying organizational principles remain distinct, in practice there has recently been some convergence in appearance, as both Denmark and Norway have extended the outgrowth of directorates over the past thirty years (Bloch, 1963, p.130). Vinde lists seventy-three Swedish administrative authorities in 1971 with at least a hundred employees, in relation to the relevant Ministries (Vinde, 1971, pp.78–86). Moreover, the gap between myth and reality in Swedish arrangements has been steadily widening as direct and informal contacts between Ministries and Boards have greatly increased (Molin *et al.*, 1969, p.353).

The Danish administrative pattern dates from 1848, when it was established initially with seven Ministries, on the Napoleonic model then widespeard in Europe. There were twelve Ministries by 1910, sixteen in 1948 and twenty-one in 1978, a growth rate paralleled in the other countries. Impetus for this growth came from the expansion of state activities, but it has been constrained by the need to keep Cabinets viable as decision-making bodies. In Denmark the Cabinet was reduced a little in size in the late 1970s by some Ministers holding portfolios jointly, Agriculture with Fisheries, or Justice with the Interior, or Church Affairs with Greenland, for example, thus more than compensating for the subdivision of economics Ministries into Finance, Economy, Taxation, and Industry earlier in the decade. Ministerial initiative and control has been strengthened by the appointment of political assistant Ministers or State Secretaries on the Swedish or West German pattern. In Sweden the 1976 Cabinet included five *konsultativa statsråd*, to assist Ministers, while in the 1980 coalition there were four members of the Cabinet with the title of assistant Minister, of different parties from their chiefs'. Finland follows the Swedish pattern, which dates back to 1917, while Norway follows Denmark in appointing joint Ministers.

The division of responsibilities between Ministries varies considerably, reflecting separate national concerns and developments. Thus, Norway and Iceland boast a Fisheries Ministry, reflecting the importance of this industry in the economy; Denmark and Norway responded to the environmentalist concerns of the 1960s and 1970s with a special *Miljöminister*; and Denmark, Norway and Sweden each set up Energy Ministries in the late 1970s to meet pressing new tasks in this area. Generally, of course, structural correspondence between the Cabinets of the Scandinavian countries is greatest in the traditional areas of state activity — foreign affairs, the interior, justice, finance and later trade, communications and education — and least in the economic and social fields which became areas of concern more recently. The interests of important organized sectors of society such as labour, agriculture or industry are each visibly catered for by a Ministry with a corresponding title, and indeed the organization may even be in a position to dictate which incumbent would be acceptable: for example, in a Norwegian Labour Cabinet at least one Ministry is virtually in the gift of LO, the trade union confederation. Sometimes a portfolio will be created to accommodate the special constellation of interests of a senior politician, as when the Radical Liberal, K. Helveg Petersen, was appointed Minister for Cultural Affairs and Minister for Technical Co-operation with Developing Countries and Disarmament Questions in the 1968—71 Danish coalition.

Limits on the size of Cabinets, together with real fears for the health of Ministers with heavy work loads, have prompted further politicization of the top reaches of the Ministries with the creation of ministerial staffs of political appointees. In Sweden State Secretaries and in Norway the Under-Secretaries of State (*statssekreterare, statssekretær*) are usually politically appointed, youngish civil servants who hold office on the understanding that they will change with a change of Minister, with the task of assisting the Minister by co-ordinating the Ministry's work and with sufficient authority to do so — an arrangement which in Norway dates back to 1947 and was recognized by the Constitution in 1976. Although Norwegian Ministers have no formal 'cabinet' or private office, their personal secretaries, information officers, *statssekretær*, and other advisors are coming to fill such a role. There has been a similar informal development in Denmark, but recurrent proposals for State Secretaries have never received the support of Ministers or civil servants (Lund-Sørensen, 1970). In 1965 an extensive review of the Swedish ministerial structure standardized the organization for a Ministry, with the Minister assisted by three chief officers: the Under-Secretary of State (*statssekreterare*), the Permanent Secretary (*expeditionschef*) and the Chief Legal Officer (*rättschef*).

Two distinct Nordic traditions of government structure retain their influence today. In Sweden and Finland a sharp and consistent division is formally made between the work of policy formulation on the one hand and day-to-day administration on the other: Ministries establish directives and policies which are executed by agencies. The former are fairly small bodies which function as staffs for their political chiefs. The latter number well over a hundred and are technically responsible directly to the government rather than to an individual Minister. The great advantage claimed for this is that Ministers are not burdened with numerous executive decisions. But given the increasing integration of politics and administration in modern circumstances, the distinction is of decreasing importance. An appeals system will give the government an opportunity to exercise its own judgement in a really controversial case. But a sense of responsibility is said to be engendered in the agencies which makes for greater efficiency, allowing Ministries to remain fairly small units devoted mainly to planning future developments (Vinde, 1971, p.53). While the legalistic distinction is maintained between *policy* and *administration*, in practice there is direct steering of the decentralized administration by the political Ministries. This takes place informally, through personal contacts, meetings over lunch and telephone conversations: there is likely to be contact at least once a week, usually initiated by the State Board rather than the Ministry, so as to obtain guidance on politically controversial issues. Another means of political steering used increasingly is the nomination of political sympathizers to Board positions (Molin, 1968, p.354). In the Danish and Norwegian systems the distinction is much less clear-cut, despite the Norwegian policy since 1955 of increasing the number of directorates to deal with specific technical or routine tasks.

In a detailed review of the development of Danish central administration, Niels Petersen (1973) distinguishes three types of directorate (although some go under such other titles as General Directorate, Inspectorate or close synonyms of the latter such as *tilsyn* or *kontrol*). Some are equivalent to the Departments of a Ministry; most are external to a Ministry but subject to ministerial decision if a case is transferred or referred for appeal to the ministerial office under which they belong; and some are subsidiary to a Department within a Ministry. The guiding principle has been that the juridical expertise required to prepare a law, advise on how it is to be executed and decide disputed interpretations of general rules should be located within a Ministry, while 'field work' in the form of technical and expert executive activity should be left to bodies which are institutionally separate from a Ministry. Sometimes exceptions have been made for reasons of economy or speed of administration, to to play down the prominence given by such an organizational pattern to technical rather than juridical expertise, so illustrating the emphasis on a legalistic interpretation of responsibility. Lines of *political* responsibility have become increasingly blurred, and earlier devices for safeguarding political control over the government have been weakened as tight party discipline has been consolidated and, more recently, as decision-making has shifted to informal bodies. In Sweden Cabinet minutes are examined by the *Riksdag* committee on the Constitution, but its role is roughly analogous to the British Statutory Instruments committee (*Regeringsformen* (Instrument of Government), ch. 12, para. 1). The Norwegian *Storting*'s power to examine the minutes of the Council of State is of little importance now that the real decisions are taken in Cabinet. Its power to impeach Ministers was of great constitutional significance in 1884, when it was used successfully to uphold the will of the *Storting* against the monarch, so initiating the democratic era. The possibility of impeaching government Ministers for their behaviour at the time of the German invasion was considered in 1948 but the *Storting* protocol committee majority thought that there was no case for impeachment, while the non-socialist minority believed there was a case but that it should not be pursued (Popperwell, 1972, p.165). It is now hard to envisage circumstances in which the procedure might be invoked. While parliamentary finance committees remain busy and prestigious bodies, their power of the purse has been eroded by growing state involvement in comprehensive economic strategies, particularly wage settlements, agreed with groups outside Parliament.

While parliamentary control has declined, despite the development of specialized parliamentary committees and other organizational adaptations, the influence of the state has grown, exercised through a Civil Service of greatly expanded size and expertise. Denmark illustrates the growth in numbers of university-trained (i.e. senior) civil servants: there were 184 in 1850, 644 in 1946, 2240 in 1962 and probably 3000 in 1972 (Damgaard, 1975, p.277) — more than a match for the 179 members of the *Folketing*, with their limited staff and resources. Similar numerical relationships exist in Norway — 2212 higher civil servants in 1970 (Higley *et al.*, 1975) — and the other Nordic countries. The Civil

Service tradition is one of a highly bureaucratic, rule-bound and hierarchic structure designed to promote objective decision-making on the basis of appropriate laws or regulations in obedience to the current government, whatever its political complexion. This neutrality has sometimes been questioned: in the closing years of the nineteenth century in Denmark, when there was bitter constitutional conflict, politicians of the Left had a very hostile attitude to the civil servants who were implementing the policies of the government of the Right and doubted whether they could be loyal to any future government of the Left. With complete obedience demanded from civil servants during this time, they could either show overt support for Conservative policies or stay out of politics entirely, as neutral non-political administrators. This episode reinforced the latter attitude, and helps to account for modern opposition to politicized State Secretaries. More recently, Swedish and Norwegian Social Democratic and Labour governments were frequently accused during their long spells in power of packing the Civil Service with party appointees, but the evidence fails to support such claims (Lægried and Olsen, 1979). In Finland, conversely, this issue is far more contentious, with claims having wide currency that most civil servants act in the interests of their party rather than impartially.

The Continental tradition which regards public administration, like judicial decision-making, as the application of legal rules meant that jurists long dominated the senior Civil Service posts. In Norway throughout the second half of the nineteenth century they had a near monopoly and in 1915 held 86 per cent of these positions. The proportion of lawyers among newly recruited civil servants declined from 60 per cent before 1945 to 48 per cent between 1957 and 1965, while economists increased from 6 to 10 per cent over the same period. This shift was even more marked at the higher levels of *byråsjef* (equivalent to Under-Secretary) or above, where lawyers declined from 72 to 38 per cent and economists increased from 5 to 29 per cent in the period since 1945 (Higley *et al.*, 1975). There has been a similar but less marked change in Denmark, where a 1970 study showed that 80 per cent of civil servants in the generalist grade were jurists and 17 per cent were economists (quoted by Damgaard, 1975). New tasks and the political desire to moderate what was considered a one-sided and over-narrow recruitment have encouraged the appointment of graduates in other disciplines such as engineering, architecture, medicine, the social sciences or the liberal arts, but they tend to be employed in directorates with specialized functions rather than in the Ministries themselves. Promotions are on a merit system and in Denmark are generally only within the Ministry where the civil servant was initially appointed, so that, typically, a whole career is spent in a single Ministry, with entry at about 25, promotion over the next twenty-one years and the final twenty years spent in a top position. Only recently have the innovations of movement between Ministries or limited-term appointments been tried (ibid.).

In Norway a more general public-sector career is commoner, with people joining the Civil Service from the judiciary, politics, other public institutions, education or international organizations and others leaving the Civil Service for other areas of the public sector: the boundary between the Civil Service, narrowly defined, and the larger public sector is relatively permeable, while the boundary between the Civil Service and the strictly private sector is crossed much less frequently (Higley *et al.*, 1975). The concept of a government employee is generally drawn widely in Scandinavia, taking in army officers, clergymen and university staff, for instance, as well as administrators.

In Sweden recruitment of civil servants is firmly in the hands of separate administrative authorities. In 1947 52 per cent had law degrees, 19 per cent natural science degrees and 10 per cent degrees in business and economics (Landström, 1954, p.130). The predominance of lawyers was particularly noticeable in the Departments of State and the older and more traditional parts of the administration. If anything, it appears to have increased subsequently. At the same time the content of law degrees has been widened in Sweden to include the social sciences, and, of course, more social scientists and economists have entered the Civil Service. As a tradition of administration, this pattern can be traced to the close kinship of administrative and judicial functions, both being concerned with the application of the law, which is characteristic of the *rechtsstaat* (Kelsen, 1967, pp.312–13), now rather more in evidence in Sweden and Finland than in Denmark and Norway.

The tradition of a politically neutral Civil Service does not generally bar civil servants from party activity in their own time. In the last century, especially when the Right was in power, a substantial proportion of Ministers had been civil servants; the parliamentary principle has greatly reduced this, although it has not eliminated it. Of the fifteen civil servants in Danish Cabinets this century, six were diplomats serving as Foreign Ministers and the rest were not from top Civil Service posts. Under the Constitution civil servants are explicitly allowed to enter Parliament, but the number doing so in Denmark is no more than about 3 per cent of all MPs (Damgaard, 1975). In the circumstances peculiar to the small island community of Iceland, politicians have enjoyed a position of relative strength in relation to civil servants, who have complained of their unobjective intervention in details with which they should not be involved (Vilhjalmson, 1973). Both the growth of the party system and the increased burden of official work have reduced the chances of combining the two activities successfully and have greatly reduced the number of civil servant MPs during the past half-century. Even so, civil servants in all the Nordic countries are entitled, as is any other citizen, to stand for election. If successful, they are granted leave of absence, preserving their entitlement to promotion and pension while their representative function continues. The convention is well established, in Sweden and elsewhere, that political differences are not carried over into the administrative sphere, where loyal service is expected irrespective of political affiliation (Elder, 1970, p.102).

Several changes of administrative structure have been made over the past twenty years in order to accommodate more effectively the growth in scope of state activities. There have been extensive reforms of local government, in Denmark in 1972, Norway in 1973 and Sweden starting in 1964, in each case with the intention of creating larger and more economically efficient units of local government, but giving rise to much discussion of the citizen's remoteness from the day-to-day political process. Notwithstanding concurrent moves to devolve some administrative activities from the central authorities, allegations of 'distant democracy' (Martinussen, 1977) and demands for ways to bring citizens and administration closer to one another were much debated. The small central departments in Sweden overhauled their organization in 1965 in order to facilitate long-term planning and thereby, in effect, to tighten the steering of the extensive decentralized sector of the administrative apparatus (Elder, 1970, pp.81 and 86). In Denmark an official report (*Administrationsudvalget af 1960*, 1962) recommended changes in a similar direction, separating legislative and administrative policy, defined as the formulation of new ideas, from the functions of management according to established principles. But the inertia and the power structure of the established system, including links between the Ministries and between them and the organized interests, have meant (as with the Fulton recommendations in Britain) that except for some relatively minor reforms, the basic central administrative structure has not changed.

While the scope and functions of the Scandinavian states have increased very substantially especially in the past two decades, for the reasons discussed earlier, too much should not be made of the shift of power in favour of the executive. Ministers are still concerned to avoid parliamentary criticism, where question time, interpellation debates and the development of the committee system help to review government activity. The development and functioning of the unicameral Parliaments is examined in the following sections.

## UNICAMERALISM IN SCANDINAVIA

All five Scandinavian states have legislatures that are in structure either strictly unicameral or unicameral with modifications. In each case the national assembly is chosen directly and at the one election. This degree of parallelism has been arrived at by a process of separate development rather than by intra-regional institutional diffusion. The modified unicameralism of the Icelandic *Althing*, however, owed some of its inspiration to the Norwegian prototype; and the supporters of unicameralism in Sweden in the late 1950s and the 1960s — in particular, the Liberals — derived some impetus from the reform that had been put through in Denmark in 1953.

Norway, Iceland and Finland settled the present basic structure of their legislatures relatively early. Norway did so in the pre-modern political era, as part of the new constitutional order of 1814. Iceland and Finland did so in the first decade of this century, when their modern party systems were beginning to emerge — in Iceland's case as part of the growth of home rule under Danish sovereignty and in Finland's, in 1906, as a by-product of the Russian Revolution. Denmark and Sweden have both had bicameral legislatures — in each case the two Chambers enjoyed equality of power — but abolished them in 1953 and 1970 respectively in the course of a more general process of constitutional recasting. In both countries the final result came about through hard political horse-trading rather than because of the force of arguments based on abstract democratic principle. In Denmark a Liberal–Conservative coalition government anxious for Radical and Social Democratic support conceded the long-standing demand of the latter parties for a single-chamber system in return for the introduction of an element of direct democracy as a check on majority rule in the new representative assembly (the *Folketing*). In Sweden the Social Democrats, who had owed much of their post-war ascendancy to their entrenched strength in the indirectly elected chamber, agreed to the abolition of that chamber in the wake of severe reverses in the local government elections of 1966. An adverse knock-on effect was to be expected in due course with respect to their parliamentary representation in consequence of these elections, and in return for speedy reform the Social Democrats won acceptance for both local and national elections to be held henceforth on the same day instead of being staggered as hitherto.

One major reason for the creation of a second chamber, namely, the federal principle, has never appeared necessary or desirable to any of the Scandinavian states. This may in part be read as a reflection of the comparative homogeneity of their societies. Other grounds for having a second chamber have either appeared irrelevant or else been successively discarded. Thus, for example, the aristocratic principle of representation could not have been invoked in 1814 in the case of the Norwegian *Storting* because the indigenous aristocracy had by then virtually ceased to exist (Derry, 1973, p.23). Similarly, an ordered system of local self-government, which might have formed the basis for an indirectly elected chamber, did not come into being in that country until two decades later. To Iceland, with her small population and egalitarian society, the cost and complexities of two sets of elections were always unnecessary.

The Icelandic *Althing* follows the Norwegian *Storting* in splitting itself, immediately after election, into two divisions. In the Icelandic case these divisions — *Efri Deild* and *Nethri Deild* — comprise one-third and two-thirds respectively of the total assembly membership of sixty. In late 1981 it was proposed to adopt a unicameral *Althing* of 66 or 70 members. In Norway the corresponding divisions are approximately one-quarter (the *Lagting*) and three-quarters (the *Odelsting*) of the total membership, currently 155. In neither country are special qualifications laid down for membership of either division; in both, membership is, under modern conditions, determined on a basis proportional to party strengths in the legislature at large. This structure was originally designed to ensure that legislation coming before the national assembly should receive at least two separate and distinct sets of scrutiny, one in each of two roughly co-equal bodies. In Norway, however, the committees of the *Storting* as a whole have come to play a much more significant role in the legislative process than the formal and largely archaic organization of the legislature into two divisions. Adventitious absences may give rise in the *Lagting* to an occasional political demonstration by parties not in government, but the rules have scarcely more effect than that. On the other hand, in Iceland both divisions of the *Althing* have a well developed committee system of their own. (The formal rules for modified unicameralism in Iceland and Norway are set out more fully in Andrén, 1964, pp.102–4, 123–6.)

Finland in 1906 passed directly from a medieval system of representation of four Estates in the Swedish mould (one Estate reflecting the aristocratic principle) to a single chamber, the *Eduskunta*, based on universal suffrage. The sweeping nature of this reform is explicable in view of the preoccupation of most Finnish political groupings at the time with the need to achieve maximum social mobilization in resistance to the process of Russification. National sentiment was also of great significance in both Norway and Iceland. The name chosen for the Norwegian legislature consciously harked back to the simple assemblies of the distant era before Danish rule. The *Althing* could claim the distinction of being the oldest legislature in the world — it celebrated its millennium in 1930 — and had come, however weakened and changed, to symbolize the national consciousness during the latter part of the long period of Danish ascendancy.

Denmark (1849, 1866) and Sweden (1866) both, as indicated earlier, began the modern political era with bicameral systems. Originally, the two co-equal chambers differed widely in each case, not only in span of service, method of election (direct/indirect, from local government units) and age requirements, but also because one of each pair was based on the plutocratic principle in accordance with the then prevailing liberal philosophy. The principle was indeed taken to an extreme in Sweden where joint-stock companies were given votes on a scale graded in accordance with the size of their assets. These differences in composition led to periods of discord and deadlock between the chambers. In the present century the property qualifications for members and voters were successively discarded, and the process of convergence made the bicameral division harder to justify in principle.

It would be mistaken to suppose that Norway and Iceland, with their modified unicameral legislatures, have thus provided a more effective restraint on the popular will as manifested through majorities in Parliament than have their neighbours with undivided single-chamber systems. The Danes have, for example, introduced a considerable check in the shape of the constitutional requirement that *one-third* of the *Folketing* can force a Bill already passed to be submitted to a referendum within eighteen weekdays of publication. Again, a similar proportion of the Finnish *Eduskunta* can ensure that a Bill is held over for final consideration until the next Parliament — i.e. until after the next general election — and qualified majorities are also required there for certain types of measure. The Finnish Grand Committee, to which all legislative drafts have to be referred, was also designed as a weighty consultative device more or less in the shape of a Council of Elders: it comprises forty-five out of the 200 members of the national assembly. It has, however, declined in significance and prestige (Helander, 1976). Despite this, the Scandinavian states furnish some striking examples of how a unicameral system can be combined with provision for an effective second consideration of proposed legislative measures.

## PARLIAMENTS: PLENARY SESSIONS

Parliaments in the Nordic countries enjoy relatively high levels of popular support, but their policy-making powers are modest by the standards of, for example, the legislature of the United States. Michael Mezey (1979, p.36) groups the legislatures of Denmark, Finland, Norway and Sweden with those of Britain, West Germany or the Fifth French Republic as being reactive in their relations with the executive, contrasting this with the active US legislature and the minimal legislatures of the USSR or Poland. Our task in this section is to give nuance to some of these broad structural comparisons.

As an index of popular support for a legislature, electoral turnout leaves much to be desired, influenced as it is by detailed arrangements for electoral registration as well as by many less tangible factors. It is nevertheless worth noting that turnout levels in Scandinavia in the 1970s averaged 88 per cent in Denmark, 82 per cent in Finland, 90 per cent in Iceland, 84 per cent in Norway and 88 per cent in Sweden, and that there has been a tendency for a rise towards these levels over the period since 1945, indicating perhaps a growth in the legitimacy of the parliamentary and party system.

The maximum interval between elections is four years except in Sweden, where since 1969 the constitutionally prescribed period has been three years, but lately there has been discussion about bringing Swedish practice into line with the other Nordic countries. In Norway there is no provision to vary this interval, but in the other countries an election may be called by the head of state on the advice of the Prime Minister or, in Finland, on his own initiative. This power is used sparingly, however, and elections are generally held in the constitutionally prescribed month: March in Finland, June in Iceland and September in Norway and Sweden. Sweden has only deviated from this pattern once since 1945, Finland four times, in 1954, 1962, 1972 and 1975. In Denmark, by contrast, the *Folketing* never runs its full four years: Prime

Ministers are tempted to take advantage of apparently favourable public opinion, and during the 1970s elections were called every two years. The Norwegian Constitution is unusual for a parliamentary rather than a presidential system in requiring fixed-term Parliaments. Although permitted in Sweden, a 'premature' election is discouraged by the requirement that it must be in addition to, and not in place of, a regular election. While the intention may have been to strengthen the Parliament by giving it a secure term of office, in Norway in recent years the converse has been found to be the case, and a *Storting* majority has been reluctant to oust a government, knowing the difficulties of constructing an alternative from the unchanged party strengths available.

The scope of parliamentary activity is indicated in table 4.3. Parliamentary sessions generally begin in early October, although the 1975 Swedish Constitution allows for an August start to accommodate a growing volume of business. The opening date is fixed by the Constitution, which adds to the legitimacy of the assemblies by removing the need for an initiative (by a government, for example) to summon them: they meet as of constitutional right. The normal parliamentary session lasts through to April/May in Iceland and no later than early June in the other countries, with breaks at Christmas and Easter and for about a week in February or March for the annual meeting of the Nordic Council. In Finland there are plenary sessions only on one or two days during the week: in the other Nordic Parliaments more of the week is used for this purpose, but Mondays may be reserved for committee work and Fridays for constituency contacts. The time spent in meetings compares more closely with the West German *Bundestag*, which sits for an annual average of forty-nine days or 273 hours, or with the US House of Representatives, where these figures were 139 and 726 respectively, than with the very long sessions of the British House of Commons, which average 160 days or 1480 hours (Lees and Shaw, 1979, p.369). Surprisingly, the time spent in the meetings of the Danish *Folketing* has scarcely changed in the past century, although four or five times as much legislation is produced, and the scope of that legislation is less specific and much wider in its social, economic and administrative effects. In about 300 meeting hours per year an average of thirty Bills were passed in 1870–1901, while for 1963–74 this figure was 153 (Damgaard, 1977, pp.56–7). Legislative activity has clearly expanded greatly during this century, and, despite time-saving devices, the legislator's job has become a full-time occupation.

TABLE 4.3: SELECTED STATISTICS FOR LEVELS OF ACTIVITY IN THE SCANDINAVIAN PARLIAMENTS

|  | Denmark | Finland | Iceland | Norway | Sweden |
|---|---|---|---|---|---|
| Population (millions) | 5.1 | 4.76 | 0.22 | 4.07 | 8.29 |
| Parliament | Folketing | Eduskunta | Althing | Storting | Riksdag |
| Number of Members of Parliament (1981) | 179 | 200 | 60 | 155 | 349 |
| Population per MP (thousands) | 28.5 | 23.8 | 3.6 | 26.3 | 23.8 |
| Sitting days/year(s) | 117 (1978–9) |  | 61 Upper House: 97 Lower House: 94 (1968–72) |  |  |
| Sitting hours/year(s) | 300 (1963–74) average |  |  |  | 647 (1979) |
| Annual number/year(s): |  |  |  |  |  |
| Government Bills | 148[1]  146[2] |  | 78[1] } 82[2] | 230[1] | 187[1] |
| Private Members' Bills | 86[1]  1[2] |  | 76[1] | 4[1] | 198[1] |
| Interpellations | 32 |  | 74[1] | 19[1] | 172[1] |
| Questions to Ministers | 1519[1] |  | 86[1]  28[2] | 464[1] | 519[1] |
| Resolutions | 107[1]  5[2] |  |  | 3[4] |  |
| Reports | 6[3] (1978–9) |  | (1968–72) (average) | 89[5] (1979–80) | (1977–8) |

[1] Introduced.  [2] Passed/approved.
[3] *Redegørelser*: oral or written ministerial statements which may subsequently be debated by the *Folketing*.
[4] Resolutions (*anmodninger*) to the government, adopted by the *Storting* with a vote.
[5] *Storting* reports (*Stortingsmeldinger*) are major statements of government policy, discussed in committee and debated *in plenum*, but not leading to a vote on realities. They account for a major part of *Storting* work, since many Bills are founded on them and are passed with reference to their conclusions.

The number of members in each Parliament in relation to the size of the population is shown in table 4.3. Except in Iceland, the average number of people represented by each Member of Parliament is relatively uniform and is small enough to allow for close contact between representative and represented. In Denmark, where distances are small, contact is often close and is encouraged, for example, by the Social Democratic Party's internal rules requiring annual renomination of candidates in each constituency and allowing party branches to take policy initiatives. But in the other Nordic countries, with their less frequent elections and no tradition of door-to-door canvassing, representatives tend to rely for their political intelligence less on direct contacts with the public than on the local press. In Finland Helander (1975) found in a survey of the 1972–5 Parliament that only 8 per cent had not turned to an interest group to confirm an opinion or to get detailed information, while Johansson (1966) and Martinussen (1977) both found that organizational membership was an integral component of political resources in Sweden and Norway. Agreement on local issues across party lines may be encouraged, in the *Storting* and the *Riksdag*, by the grouping of members geographically (by province or county) in the chamber, by contrast with the seating by party groups which prevails in the *Folketing* and the *Eduskunta*. Members normally speak from a rostrum beside the President of the Assembly and can await their turn at chairs nearby, but in the electronically well equipped *Riksdag* and, from 1981 in the *Folketing*, they may also speak from their own seats. It is the extensive preparation of legislation in committee, however, rather than the use of the rostrum, which removes some of the controversy from debates, since exchanges on questions or interpellations can at times be lively.

The reactive relationship of Scandinavian legislatures with their respective governments is illustrated by the fact that the great majority of Bills introduced and passed by the legislatures originate with the government, although individuals or groups of Members may also originate matters for consideration. In Sweden there is a distinction of terminology and procedure: government *propositions* make up the larger proportion of business and give structure to most of the *Riksdag*'s time; Members' *motions* are more numerous than propositions, are used to amend propositions and frequently set out the stands adopted by opposition parties or the detailed views of private Members. Such motions may be introduced only during limited time periods: for example, for fifteen days after the introduction of the Budget Proposition a member can move a motion on any subject; thereafter the normal time limit for submitting motions amending government propositions is also fifteen days.

There is something of a paradox in Finnish legislative–executive relationships: the formal status of the *Eduskunta* is inferior, in that it is subject to the presidential power of dissolution; but the status of the opposition (and therefore of the assembly as a whole) is enhanced by the system of qualified majorities which requires the government to obtain the support of more than a simple majority of Members, with all the opportunities for extracting concessions from the government which that implies.

Finnish procedures distinguish three different types of Bill: legislative Bills passing, amending, explaining or annulling a law; fiscal Bills concerning the state budget for the ensuing year; and petitionary Bills proposing that the *Eduskunta* urge the government to act on a matter over which it has jurisdiction. Private Members as well as the government may introduce legislative or petitionary Bills but, as in Sweden, there is only a short period (ten to fourteen days) in which to do so, unless there are exceptional circumstances. Government proposals in Finland run at the rate of some 220 per year, of which 75 to 85 per cent are adopted, about 5 per cent rejected and the remainder postponed. The numerous legislative Bills introduced by private members stand only about a 7 per cent chance of success; over half are decisively rejected; and the remaining 40 per cent do not come to any final resolution. Fiscal Bills average about three per year (some 200 in the sixty years since independence); it is these which enact governmental powers to give effect to agreements with the major economic interests, lasting perhaps one, two or even four years, securing employment, stabilizing prices and seeking to balance economic development and international trade. There are two distinct procedures for passing legislation, requiring one reading or three respectively (Nousiainen, 1977).

In Denmark such procedural distinctions are not made and Ministers introduce government legislation, including even the annual Finance Law, on their own motion and in just the same way as would an individual or group of private members. During the twenty years 1953–73, 90 per cent of Bills introduced and 99 per cent of Bills passed originated with the government, but the more turbulent inter-party relationships of 1973–9 reduced these figures to 63 per cent and 96 per cent respectively. There was also a significant growth of business, with about 150 Bills introduced per year in 1963–9 compared with 305 for 1973–9. The success rates for *all* Bills in the two periods were 77 per cent and

53 per cent respectively. But, taking the figures for government Bills only, the rates for the two periods are 83 per cent and 92 per cent, an interesting illustration of the way in which the minority Danish governments of the 1970s were able to manage the parliamentary support for their legislation (calculations from Marquard, 1979, p.3). The small *Althing* deals with about 150 Bills a year, about half from the Cabinet and half from individual members. In 1968–72 the success rate for Cabinet Bills was 78 per cent (Nordal and Kristinsson, 1975, p.133). Much of the purpose of private Members Bills is to gain publicity for an opposition party's point of view, but, to the extent that they are serious attempts to influence the direction of development of society, their relative lack of success follows from a lack of the resources necessary to draft Bills competently. Damgaard (1977, p.308) found that, in consequence, over half of the resolutions proposed by opposition parties in Denmark were demands for specific legislative initiatives, and most of the rest were requests for other governmental action.

It follows that while the balance between government and non-government parties may at times favour the latter to a much greater extent than is customary in Britain, for example, and the government still has to devote much effort to constructing and maintaining parliamentary support for its policies, it retains great organizational advantages over the members of non-government parties. It is in this sense, then, that Members of the Nordic legislatures 'shape their behaviour to meet the expectations of mass publics' (Mezey's (1979) description of a reactive legislature). But they are less constrained to do so in the multiparty circumstances of Scandinavia than in the British Parliament, especially if the government has no assured majority, as was the case in Denmark throughout the 1970s and in the other Nordic countries for parts, at least, of the decade. While this increases the possibility that governments have occasionally to accept policies not of their own making, more often either broad support will be negotiated in committee or else the proposal will be dropped at the committee stage. An extreme case of consensual, or at least non-partisan, decision-making occurred in the 'tied' Swedish parliament of 1973–6, when each bloc had 150 seats. Decisions (149 of them) were made by drawing lots, with the outcome in seventy-seven instances favouring the non-socialist parties and in seventy-two instances favouring the governing Social Democrats and their Communist Left allies. But the more important questions were settled by the government, which negotiated the support, issues by issue, of one of the three non-socialist parties.

The activities of legislators are not confined simply to the processing and passing of Bills, however: the Swedish tradition of circulating reform projects for comment from interested administrative agencies and interest groups has been formalized and extended to the other Nordic countries often, but not invariably, through the establishment of commissions to investigate the subject and make proposals for change. Members of the legislature often represent their parties on such commissions, and the resulting reports generally pay close attention to the experience of the other Nordic countries in reaching their conclusions. Government Bills are much the most comprehensive in their supporting documentation in Sweden, followed by Norway and then Finland and Denmark. Neither Denmark nor Iceland generally gives the divergent opinions of the administrative authorities consulted in the preparation of legislation: in varying degrees the others do. Commissions of inquiry are important in the gestation of legislation in all the Scandinavian countries, and this is also an important way in which Nordic legislation is harmonized, often with the underlying feeling that because each country is small none can afford mistakes and so should make the most of the experience of closely comparable neighbours. As well as this preparatory stage, in Denmark legislators often sit on the committees appointed to assist or control a Minister in executing legislation. The involvement of legislators in both the initiation and implementation of policy was frequent during the first half of the twentieth century but has increased significantly more recently (Damgaard, 1977, pp.46–7).

An important function of Parliaments in liberal democracies is to hold governments to account. The main procedures by which they can do so are, in order of increasing significance, questions to Ministers, interpellations and votes of confidence. Parliamentary questions have not achieved great significance as devices of accountability and are useful mainly for obtaining factual information, often bearing particularly on the affairs of a limited locality, although this can, of course, sometimes be controversial. The number of questions asked has grown considerably over the past thirty years – in Denmark by a factor of ten – and the procedure, modelled closely on British practice and subject to many of the same limitations, has grown most vigorously in Norway and Denmark, where it was adopted in 1926 and 1947 respectively. In Finland it was legislated in 1928 but barely came to life until the 1960s, when oral questions and a separate ministerial question time were introduced. In Sweden, however, there is a greater preference for interpellations, of which there may be 150 to 200 per year, although here their significance is hardly more dramatic than that of parliamentary questions. The scope of an interpellation is generally broader than a question, and the procedure is often used to permit a Minister to report on the policy area for which he is responsible as the basis for a debate. In Danish practice interpellations need not lead to a vote, since this requires an agenda resolution (*motiveret dagsorden* or 'motivated order of the day'), and the tactical purpose is either for the government to explain its intentions and obtain reactions to them or for non-government parties to make clear their own positions. Written notice and a specific parliamentary resolution to hold an interpellation debate are required, and a Minister may refuse an interpellation if he considers it not to be in the national interest, but naturally this is rare. Except in Sweden, the number of interpellations per year is generally in single figures, but in Denmark the frequency has grown beyond this since 1974–5, reaching twenty-eight in 1977–8 and thirty-two in 1978–9. Because government spokesmen must respond within a specified period of time, interpellations are among the most important tactical devices by which oppositions can hold governments to account.

Order is kept and inter-party conflict mediated by the presiding officer and his vice-chairmen or deputies, who collectively form the presidium. Usually the deputies preside in the absence of the chairman, but in Norway and Iceland, where the assemblies divide into two sections, there is a presidency for each section as well as for the assembly as a whole: the Norwegian president and vice-president alternate each month in the chair. These are elected offices, and their holders generally represent a spread of parties: in Denmark the election is by proportional representation but with no more than one official from any party, while in Finland, if the Prime Minister is from the Social Democrats, the Speaker is usually from the Centre Party and vice versa. Members of the presidium remain politicians and members of their party groups but are expected to exercise their office strictly impartially in the settlement of procedural disputes.

There is a strong tradition of party discipline in each of the Nordic Parliaments which is enforced more by group loyalties than by a whip system, although the Norwegian and some of the Finnish parties each have an official *innpisker* or whip. Party groups meet at least twice a week (each sitting day in Denmark) during the session, and a member who disagrees with his party's line is expected to give notice at this meeting rather than spring it publicly on his colleagues. The counterpart to this is that party spokesmen, in negotiations or on committees or in a coalition Cabinet, report regularly to their party groups. This emphasis on close consultation and party unity contributes substantially to the distinctive style of Nordic politics. It is offset by the individualism and relative incoherence of a populist party such as the Danish Progress Party, which is one reason why this party has met with parliamentary and governmental ostracism.

## PARLIAMENTARY COMMITTEES

We have already noted a great increase in scope of the activities of the Nordic Parliaments, measured crudely by a tenfold growth in the number of Bills per year since the closing years of the nineteenth century, with a corresponding qualitative increase in the impact of politicians and the public sector upon all aspects of society. Many organizational devices have been adopted to accommodate this development, such as the avoidance of unnecessary divisions, the use of written rather than oral presentations, limits on debating time and some increase in staff and other support resources (Damgaard, 1977, pp.58–65).

Much the most important organizational response to this development, however, has been the growth in the use and significance of parliamentary committees. Comprehensive standing committee arrangements have been in existence longest in the Swedish *Riksdag*, the Norwegian *Storting* and the Icelandic *Althing*, and in these Parliaments the committees show the greatest degree of autonomy and organizational differentiation in relation to their parent bodies. The Danish *Folketing* made the transition to a systematic pattern of standing committees during the 1970s, while committee arrangements in the Finnish *Eduskunta* resemble those which existed in Denmark before this transition. Table 4.4 gives the titles of the committees, and in the following discussion the countries will be considered in the order in which they have been mentioned above.

The strong and long-established committee system in the Swedish *Riksdag* dates back to the era of representation by Estates. It was further developed during the bicameral era, when the committees were composed of members from the two houses in equal numbers, a pattern which was distinctive to Sweden and Australia and which avoided the delays and possible conflicts inherent in a system such as that of the USA, where Bills finish their course in one chamber and its committee before being considered in the other. The outline organization of the committees is set out in one of the entrenched sections of the *Riksdag*

Act, and this in itself attests to their permanence and importance. The unicameral system adopted in 1970 preserved the idea of specialization but changed its basis, reduced the size of some of the larger committees and extended their number. All the committees now have fifteen members, but where there were ten committees before, there are now sixteen. Apart from the Prime Minister and the Minister of Trade, each of the twelve Ministries (as listed in 1971) has a corresponding committee. In addition, there are *Riksdag* committees on the Constitution and on Cultural Affairs, and in the field of finance there is also a separate committee on Taxation. There is also a Committee on Laws which deals with legislation on land, the family and commerce.

*Riksdag* procedure is based on a compulsory committee stage, which precedes any plenary consideration and applies to all propositions, motions or reports from *Riksdag* organs. This ensures that proposals can first be considered in private and in an informal arena rather than in a plenary session, and it also ensures consideration of the proposals or objections of minority groups or individual Members, not least because a committee has an obligation to consider and report on matters referred to it and cannot simply ignore them. A further indication of the strength of *Riksdag* committees is their independent right of initiative on matters within their domain: they are thus able to operate as a source of new proposals and specialized knowledge independent of the executive. The committees are expected to co-operate with each other, and Special Committees and Joint Committees may also be set up. Committee deliberations result in a report, which goes to the chamber for decision.

In the Norwegian *Storting* there is also a long-established system of fourteen standing committees, again subject-specific and intended to correspond as closely as possible to the division of functions between government Departments. The Departments without direct coverage by a *Storting* committee are those of Trade, Wages and Prices, and Family and Consumer Affairs. Conversely, there are committees on Administration and on Protocol. The former deals with regulations and appropriations for government Departments, the Council of State and the royal house, including the pay and pensions of civil servants. The Protocol Committee has power to examine papers relating to military and diplomatic secrets and also acts as a final board of investigation in auditing and accounting matters. The committees vary in size from nine or ten members up to sixteen in the case of the Finance Committee. The Constitution and Foreign Affairs Committee has twelve members but for some purposes is doubled in size. The membership reflects

TABLE 4.4: STANDING COMMITTEES IN THE SCANDINAVIAN PARLIAMENTS

| Denmark[1] | Finland | Iceland | Norway[4] | Sweden[5] |
|---|---|---|---|---|
| Standing Orders (21) Market Affairs Foreign Affairs Nationality | Constitution Foreign Affairs | Foreign Affairs[3] | Constitution and Foreign Affairs | Constitution Foreign Affairs |
| Justice | Legislation | General[3] | Justice | Justice Laws |
| Defence Social | Defence[2] Social[2] | Social and Local Government | Military Social | Defence Social Affairs Social Insurance |
| Local Government Planning Environment |  |  | Local Government | Physical Planning & Local Government |
| Church Education Culture Scientific Research | Education[2] | Health and Welfare Education | Church and Education | Education Cultural Affairs |
| Agriculture and Fishery Industry | Agriculture and Forestry[2] | Agriculture and Fishing Industry | Agriculture, Water and Industry Shipping and Fishery | Agriculture Industry |
| Public Works | Transport[2] | Communications | Communications | Transport and Communications |

| Denmark | Finland | Iceland | Norway | Sweden |
|---|---|---|---|---|
| Housing | Legislative and Economic[2] | Economic Affairs[3] | Finance | Labour Market |
| Labour Market | Economic[2] | | Elections (37) | |
| Energy Policy (21) | | | Administration | |
| Political-economic | | | Protocol | |
| Taxation | Bank | Finance[3] | | Taxation |
| Finance | Finance | Finance and Trade | | Finance |
| Proof of elections | | Credentials[3] | | |
| | Grand Committee (45) | | | |
| | | | Renumeration of MPs[3] | |
| | | | Pensions for MPs | Salaries |
| | | | | *Riksdag* Administration |
| Folketing | | | Storting Library | Election Review |
| Library | | | House Committee | |
| | | | Restaurant | |

[1] Apart from the Standing Orders Committee and the Energy Policy Committee, which comprise twenty-one members, all committees have seventeen members.
[2] Extraordinary committees, regularly reappointed.
[3] Committees of the United *Althing*; others exist in both divisions.
[4] Apart from the Elections Committee, which comprise thirty-seven members, all committees have between nine and sixteen members.
[5] All committees have fifteen members.

*Sources*: Denmark – *Forretningsorden for Folketinget*, 1975; Finland – Nousiainen, 1971, p.192; Iceland – Nordal and Kristinsson, 1975, p.132; Norway – *Stortinget 1965/6 – 1968/9*; Sweden – Landén, 1978, p.6.

party strengths in the main assembly; an attempt is made to sustain a regional spread of representation, and a proportion is also maintained between the membership of the *Odelsting* and the *Lagting*. As with the Swedish Joint Committees before 1970, this obviates conflict between the two divisions: this is especially important because Bills receive only one reading in each division.

By contrast, the other divided Nordic assembly, the *Althing*, has nine standing committees in *each* of the two houses, eight dealing with specific areas of legislation and the ninth covering 'General Affairs'. These committees also have the power to introduce Bills, although this power is shared with the Cabinet and with individual Members. Each Bill undergoes three readings in each house and, if the two houses fail to agree on a text, there is provision for up to three more readings, the last to be held in the united *Althing*. A two-thirds conditional majority is necessary for approval, but a ninth reading has not been necessary for many years. Almost all draft legislation and most draft resolutions go to committee, which in due course issues a written report. The united *Althing* also has committees (on Finance, Foreign Affairs, Economic Affairs and a General Committee) to deal with drafts introduced there rather than in one of the houses. The first two of these are the most important, and they sometimes convene between as well as during *Althing* sessions, a power also available to the Danish Finance Committee.

In Denmark until the late 1960s the nine standing parliamentary committees had administrative (internal) or only limited legislative functions. Legislation was remitted to an ad hoc committee, usually with seventeen members, specifically set up to consider one (or at most two or three closely related) Bills. Once those Bills had run their course of three readings and one or occasionally two considerations in committee, the committee disbanded automatically. While it helped members to retain a broad view of developing legislation, this ad hoc arrangement lacked co-ordination and discouraged the emergence of centres of expertise or criticism. It also had the important practical disadvantage that, as the volume of business increased, it became increasingly difficult to find a time when all members of a committee could meet, especially towards the end of the legislative session. For these reasons the transition was made in 1970–2 to a system of seventeen-member standing committees which corresponds closely to the areas of ministerial responsibility. In addition, there are committees on energy policy, on nationality law (with the duty of examining each application for naturalization) and on the Common Market. The latter has to agree a Minister's negotiating position in advance and to approve any changes in it, if necessary by telephone from Brussels: it is thus able to exert a veto power on behalf of the *Folketing* as a whole. Although there is a Minister for Greenland, there is no corresponding parliamentary committee in this area, since Greenland has its own representative institutions. The number of committees requires *Folketing* Members to sit on between three and six each, depending on the size of the party group (Damgaard, 1977, p.172–3). Some of the consequent pressures are relieved by allowing each party on a committee to appoint one or two deputies to whom a committee member may temporarily relinquish his place, although the deputy does not have the right to vote or to put forward proposals for the committee's report. Most of the committee chairmanships are held by the governing party or coalition unless its parliamentary position is very weak. This contrasts with the Norwegian tradition, which calls for the chairmanships to be distributed among the parties in rough proportion to their numerical strength. The main function of the committees is legislative: it is in committee that objections to aspects of legislation are sometimes met and concessions negotiated and that concerted opposition becomes apparent. Although a committee may be required by the *Folketing* chairman to report out a measure (*Forretningsorden*, 1975, para. 8, stk. 8–13), it is at the committee stage that a Bill may die of neglect. The use of ad hoc committees has now been greatly reduced but not entirely eliminated. Ministers can be asked to come to the committees for consultations, and other interested parties can submit evidence to hearings of the committee.

Although committee arrangements in the Finnish *Eduskunta* evolved from Swedish origins and occupy a similarly central position with respect to the work of the assembly, they are perhaps the least organizationally developed and differentiated of the Nordic parliamentary committee systems. There are only five standing committees, the jurisdiction of each defined by the Diet Act, their titles being the Constitutional, Legislative, Foreign Affairs, Finance, and Bank committees. Each has at least seventeen members except for the Banking and Finance committees, the minimum sizes of which are respectively eleven and twenty-one. The large Finance Committee has taken on a special importance. It is divided into nine sections, in which both full members and deputies sit. In sectional meetings the deputies have precisely the same status as full members, but in plenary meetings of the Finance Committee they may take part only if the full member is away. The committee considers the budget and hears the opinions of experts on a sectional basis. In recent years the Finance Committee has become heavily overworked, and it has been suggested by a former parliamentary secretary (Salervo, 1976) that this might be remedied by the creation of a special Budget Committee or else by distributing the budget load among the other parliamentary committees in accordance with their topic specialisms. The standing committees are supplemented by extraordinary committees, many of which are regularly reappointed at the start of each Parliament and have thus become institutionalized, although not legally recognized. There is also a Grand Committee, the forty-five members of which are elected by a plenary session of the *Eduskunta*. Its purpose is to consider legislative matters, but it has become party-politicized and has not achieved the status of a 'council of elders' intended for it, lacking the distinction of the Foreign Affairs Committee, for example. Its meetings are open to other Members of Parliament and to civil servants but (as with other committees) not to the public. Its reports generally contain neither supporting arguments nor dissenting opinions but have the character of *ex cathedra* statements. The arrangement is peculiar to Finland and operates to give the unicameral legislature some of the advantages of bicameralism.

Finnish parliamentary committees do not have independent powers of initiative or decision, and their function is essentially to ensure that a proposal of any importance is given extensive preparatory consideration, if necessary involving outside expertise, before it proceeds to final plenary consideration: often it then passes through subsequent stages quickly and without significant change. Committee members are chosen by an electoral college composed of forty-five Members of Parliament which remains in being for the duration of each Parliament. The committee chairman is selected by the committee from among its members and he, rather than the constitutional but redundant rapporteur, presents the committee's views to a plenary session. The committees are serviced by a secretary who is a civil servant. They have power to appoint subcommittees but seldom do so, preferring instead to divide into working groups: an official subcommittee would report directly to the *Eduskunta*, while a working group contributes to the report of the main committee.

In addition to committees dealing with legislation, each Parliament has others with administrative, oversight and housekeeping functions, the most important of which are also shown in table 4.4. All except the *Eduskunta* have a credentials committee or its equivalent with powers to check the validity of election returns and to authorize substitutes, normally persons who received the next largest number of votes on an electoral list at the previous election, for members applying for leave of absence or relinquishing their parliamentary mandate between elections. These powers emphasize the independence enjoyed by the Parliaments in each country.

The relationship of Ministers to parliamentary committees is still affected by the constitutional separation-of-powers doctrine. In Denmark, Finland and Norway Ministers appear before committees only if invited, and until 1970 in Sweden they were constitutionally prohibited from doing so; since then the discretion to ask for their views rests with the committees.

While helping to speed up parliamentary business, committees also allow their members to specialize in their own interests, and if there is continuity of membership over several years, committees may develop into centres of criticism to rival the Civil Service resources on which the government may call. Indeed, it was to avoid the re-emergence (Huntington, 1968, pp.116–17) of strong committees that twentieth-century British governments resisted the establishment of permanent specialized (standing) committees until 1979–80. Stjernquist (1966, p.330) considered that in Sweden seniority was usually the most important factor influencing committee placing but conceded that many committees recruited members with relevant career experience: farmers for the Agricultural Committee, directors and businessmen for the Bank Committee, teachers for the School Committee, trade unionists for the Wages Committees and lawyers for the committee which received the Ombudsman's report. There is no reason to think that this pattern has changed with the introduction of the new committee arrangements. Hernes (1973, p.11) found that in the *Storting* one member of the Shipping and Fishery Committee was a shipowner and all the rest came from the main shipping and fishing districts: several had been fishermen and had worked with the fishery organizations. Similarly, all the members of the Agriculture Committee had close farming connections. Damgaard (1977, pp.299, 301) found that 'policy area does matter in terms of who gets on the committee dealing with it.' Compared with a calculated chance distribution, leading Danish politicians were heavily over-represented on the Standing Orders Committee, the Political Economic Committee and the Market (EEC) Committee, although not on the important Finance Committee. Committee members were found to be very frequently affiliated with the sector of society relevant to their committees and had related interests outside the legislative arena.

For methodological reasons it should not be inferred that sectoral affiliation is always the independent variable explaining committee membership. Nevertheless, a collective portrait of the committee membership indicates that there were close sectoral affiliations for about two-thirds or more of the members of the committees on education, local government, commerce, scientific research and the labour market; for about half of the members of the agriculture, foreign relations, culture and defence committees; and for about one-third of members of the committees on taxation, welfare, transport, the chuch and housing. We can conclude, with Damgaard, that 'in sum, the findings indicate that legislative policy in the various areas to a high extent is controlled by groups of legislators characterized by special relationships with the segments of society most directly affected' (Damgaard, 1977, p.301).

ADMINISTRATIVE CONTROL

The reactive nature of much parliamentary activity is reinforced by the power and permanence of the state's administrative structures, contrasting with the transitory careers of party politicians in Parliament and their often ephemeral political concerns. While Members of Parliament may be able to hold Ministers, as political heads of government Departments, to account for many of the larger issues, they are not well equipped by inclination or resources for the close investigation of administrative malfunctions which so often underlie a real or imagined grievance held by the citizen against an arm of the state. Sweden has been a model, followed in the past quarter-century first by the other Scandinavian countries and then on a worldwide scale, for improvements in Civil Service accountability to the public.

Extensive measures were taken in Sweden in the eighteenth century to set limits to the powers of the corrupt and arbitrary officials of the time, thus laying lasting foundations for the distinctive safeguards which now exist in very different modern administrative circumstances. In 1713 an Ombudsman was appointed, six years later renamed the Chancellor of Justice, with independent authority under the King-in-Council to supervise the legality of state administration. In 1766 a much more elaborate system of control of the bureaucracy was introduced: criminal liability for official breach of duty was reinforced, efficient supervision of officials by their superiors was required; procedures to prevent nepotism and to promote objectivity in making appointments were adopted; and the freedom of the press was established as a means of bringing to light abuses or power (Wennergren, 1971). With the 1809 Constitution a *Justitieombudsman* (JO), responsible to the *Riksdag* rather than to the King-in-Council, was added to counter the argument that the Chancellor of Justice was insufficiently independent of the government to give citizens adequate protection. While some of these arrangements have become common features of most administrative systems, in Sweden their deep roots remain significant for current practice and add point to our discussion of the development and diffusion to the other Nordic countries and beyond of the Ombudsman institution and of arrangements for administrative publicity.

Discussion of the Ombudsman in the English-speaking world has concentrated on whether the institution can be adapted sufficiently to make it constitutionally and politically acceptable. Among the most useful of these discussions are the work of D. C. Rowat (1965), which includes essays by some of the Scandinavian Ombudsmen themselves, and of Frank Stacey (1978); both include useful bibliographies. But some of this discussion and diffusion has obscured distinctive features of the original model which it is now worth outlining, while at the same time bringing developments up to date.

The main duties of the Chancellor of Justice in Sweden were summarized in 1947 as (1) to act as the principal legal advisor to the King-in-Council; (2) to represent the crown as Attorney-General in cases affecting the state's interest; (3) to exercise supervision on behalf of the crown over all public servants and to take action in cases of abuse (Rudholm, 1965, p.19). Most complaints come to him from administrative agencies rather than from members of the public, since his functions are to provide authoritative interpretations of administrative law and to conduct an internal administrative 'audit', so there is little overlap with the JO, with whom he liaises informally. The work of the JO has expanded considerably, so that in 1975 3202 complaints were dealt with (Stacey, 1978, p.7). This necessitated a reorganization of personnel: in 1968 three JOs had been appointed, with co-equal powers, and two deputies; in 1976 this was changed to four full *Justitieombudsmen*, with one of their number elected as Chief Ombudsman. Their powers of investigation are wide, covering all areas of central and local government, excluding only the activities of elected Members or Ministers. The latter exclusion is justified by the concentration of Swedish Ministers on policy formation, discussed above, by contrast with the wider administrative functions of British Ministers (which can be investigated by the

British Parliamentary Commissioner for Administration). Thus the Swedish JOs can examine complaints against the police, the prisons, all the activities of the Foreign Office and the security services, the nationalized industries (unless these are run as private companies although wholly or partly state-owned), the health service and local government services — all areas excluded wholly or partly from the remit of the British counterpart. In addition, one JO supervises public access to official documents under the freedom of the press legislation. Moreover, a JO has the power to initiate his own investigations, sometimes acting on newspaper stories to do so, and may inspect the working of the law courts, hospitals, prisons and other closed state institutions — a power which emphasizes his role as guardian and spokesman especially for citizens unable to act for themselves. This power was used on 400 occasions in 1975. Over half these investigations were found to be justified, as were about one-quarter of the complaints cases investigated (Stacey, 1978, p.7). The terms of reference cover the reasonableness of decisions and prosecutions can be brought against officials and even judges, although there has been a preference recently for the use of disciplinary proceedings.

Common eighteenth-century administrative history meant that both Ombudsman and Chancellor of Justice were readily adopted in Finland in 1919. The Ombudsman there has had an assistant since 1971 and has wider powers and terms of reference than his Swedish counterparts, in that he can also prosecute Ministers and local councillors. Another Swedish official served as the first precedent for Norway: Sweden had a *Militieombudsman* (MO) from 1915 until his activities were merged with those of the JOs in 1968, with duties similar to theirs but in relation to the military administration. The Norwegian Ombudsman for the Armed Forces, modelled loosely on this office, was instituted when it was felt that the system of representatives from each military unit, given impetus especially during the conditions of wartime resistance, should be accorded greater official recognition. He combines his role of investigator of individual complaints with one as guarantor and head of the system of representative committees which take up general questions in such spheres as welfare arrangements or leisure activities. Many of the complaints he receives concern conscription, exemption from military service, transfer or demobilization, and his functions at times resemble those of a trade union official.

In Denmark the Ombudsman idea was taken up as part of the comprehensive 1953 reform of the Constitution, as a way of providing increased guarantees of the lawful conduct of the government's civil and military administration. The transfer to Denmark, with a political system more closely resembling the British, coupled with the publicizing flair of the first Danish Ombudsman, Professor Hurwitz, encouraged a process of diffusion which came to extend far beyond Scandinavia. The Danish Ombudsman has a slightly narrower jurisdiction than the Swedish: he cannot take up complaints against judges or the courts, but he can investigate the working of tribunals. In keeping with the different status of Ministers, he can investigate their actions as heads of Departments but not as Cabinet members. In local government he is confined to matters such as planning powers, over which there is an appeal to central government, and can investigate the activities of officials or council committees but not the decisions of a full council. Unlike Swedish complainants, Danes must first exhaust remedies of appeal to higher authorities, but the Danish Ombudsman will give advice on how to do so and also has powers of independent investigation which may sometimes be activated as a result of an apparently misdirected complaint. The Norwegian Ombudsman for Administration, established in 1962, closely follows the Danish model except that military cases are left to his military colleague. Local authorities were initially excluded in Norway but have been covered in part since 1969 and a separate Ombudsman for Consumer Affairs has since been added.

In all four countries the Ombudsmen are elected or re-elected by each new Parliament, and all except the first Norwegian Military Ombudsman have been legally qualified. The public has free access in each case and Members of Parliament are not involved in the filtering or transmission of complaints: very occasionally complaints may be channelled this way, but generally the involvement of MPs is thought to imply unwelcome politicization. In each case they investigate unreasonable administrative actions, disarming possible criticisms of this by emphasizing their function as independent critics of the executive rather than substitute administrators. Their powers of independent investigation are crucial to this role, although these are least used in Norway. In relation to their respective populations, the case load is heaviest in Sweden but has increased significantly in Denmark during 1971–81, after L. Nordskov Nielsen succeeded Stephan Hurwitz, as did the proportion found to be justified. Each Ombudsman was able to provide Stacey (1978) with abundant evidence that their services were widely used by all classes of society, and there seems little to support the allegation made in Britain that the Commissioner is mainly of use to the articulate middle class. Indeed, openness to public access and powers of independent investigation and inspection of state institutions strengthen both their image and their function as 'people's representatives' in the administrative process. The diffusion of the office among the Nordic countries is a good illustration of their willingness to seek and to adapt institutions developed in one country of the region to the needs and conditions of another.

A second aspect of the eighteenth-century package of Swedish administrative reforms which persists as a general principle of Swedish administrative law and has spread both to neighbouring countries and further afield is the principle of public access to official documents, whether of local or of central authorities. Introduced in the 1766 Freedom of the Press Act with the intention of abolishing 'that pernicious curtain of secrecy behind which self-interest, bias and unlawfulness could play their abominable game at the citizen's expense' (in the phrase quoted by Wennergren, 1971), the rule was successively reaffirmed in 1810 and 1949. It ensures that 'every Swedish citizen shall have free access to official documents', but in practice foreigners are not excluded, and the term 'documents' has been interpreted to include punch cards, tapes and computer memory, despite the difficulties which access to these has sometimes entailed.

Once again, Finland was first to emulate Sweden in enacting legislation on the publicity of official documents in 1951. Norway followed with an Administrative Publicity Act in 1968. Denmark was more cautious, beginning in 1964 with a law giving access to relevant documents to any party to an administrative matter, whether a decision had been made or was under consideration (*Lov om partsoffentlighed i forvaltning*). Later a parliamentary committee visited Sweden to compare experience, and in 1970 the scope of the legislation was extended: it now allows anyone access to documents on matters which have been or are being dealt with by the public administration, provided the topic is specified. Norway and Denmark do not allow the press to 'go fishing' in the way that is possible in Sweden or Finland: a reasonably specific description of the document is required, and in all cases working documents are excluded. The presumption of open access is counter-balanced by legislation, generally known in Sweden as the Secrecy Law, enumerating documents exempted from publicity and the periods of time for which the exemptions apply. Foreign or military affairs documents may be withheld for up to fifty years, but other main areas of secrecy include the prevention and prosecution of crime, the legitimate economic interests of the state, communities and individuals and the maintenance of appropriate individual privacy for which the period of limitation is often much shorter. Despite the length of the list of exemptions, the principle of publicity rather than secrecy is the one which predominates, extending, for example, to the summary of annual income and capital declared by each individual for purposes of taxation which is made accessible in Norwegian public libraries. Specific executive action is generally necessary to prevent disclosure in exceptional cases, by contrast with the British practice of guaranteeing secrecy unless disclosure is specifically authorized.

Some of the factors which have contributed to the growth of an attitude recognizing the right of the public to know the reasons for administrative decisions in the Nordic countries include acceptance of political pluralism, social and cultural homogeneity, a high degree of political participation, a minimal need to make concessions to external powers (in Denmark, Norway and Sweden, but not Finland) and the extensive rights to administrative outputs generated by welfare legislation (Galnoor, 1977). The willingness to grant very ready access to the administrative process, both vicariously through the Ombudsman and more directly through the enactment of administrative publicity, thus demonstrates the consensuality of the Nordic political style. It shows confidence in widespread agreement on the rules of the political game by accepting that openness is unlikely to be abused, and it implies that if the facts are sufficiently well known, there will be little difficulty in accommodating to them and evolving an objective and acceptable solution.

## ELECTORAL SYSTEMS

Before concluding our discussion of political institutions in the Scandinavian states, some consideration of the electoral systems and of the process of recruitment to political roles is necessary. Its location at this juncture will also provide the link between the analysis of structures in this chapter and the analysis of the policy process with which the next chapter will be concerned.

It is appropriate that this brief survey of Scandinavian electoral arrangements should also follow, and not precede, the analysis of the party systems of the region, because party-political considerations have been — in Scandinavia, as elsewhere — the chief determinants of the type of electoral system adopted. All five Scandinavian countries have now run their general elections on a PR basis for over half a century. In each of them multi-party groupings had begun to emerge *before* the decisions was taken to introduce PR, as shown in chapter 2. In short, PR was the consequence rather than the cause of multi-party systems. To assert this is not to deny that PR in some instances has contributed to the increasing complexity of multi-party systems by allowing fresh currents of party opinion to find ready reflection in the legislature and, though more debatably, by encouraging party splits. But these have not necessarily been the consequences of PR.

Commonly, though not universally, in Scandinavia PR was seen to provide a bulwark for the ruling non-socialist groups against the rapidly rising force of social democracy, and it was accepted by the Social Democrats in exchange for franchise and other concessions. At the same time it stabilized the political balance to the extent that it helped to maintain the identity of the various non-socialist parties.

The rationale here had its parallels in other smaller West European democracies — for example, Belgium. The same holds true of the use of PR to promote national integration by ensuring the representation of national minorities (Rokkan, 1968, p.16). Denmark was the pioneer in this respect and was, indeed, the first state anywhere to put a PR system into operation. This was in 1855, when the single transferable vote newly devised by Andrae, a Danish mathematician, was used on a limited basis for the return of Members to the upper chamber. The Slesvig-Holstein question then bulked large, and the country contained a sizable German minority. Similarly, one motive for the adoption of PR by Finland in 1906 was the protection of the interests of the numerically small but politically powerful Swedish minority. In this case the preferred variety of PR was the Belgian d'Hondt system, which gives a bonus to the larger parties in the allocation of seats, although there was a certain amount of intra-Scandinavian diffusion: one of the sources drawn upon while the issue was under consideration was a Swedish government inquiry report of 1903 recommending the d'Hondt method — which the Swedes in fact decided to adopt three years after the Finns.

PR was introduced in Finland in conjunction with the creation of a single-chamber legislature based on universal suffrage — Finland was the first European country to give women the vote — and it represented a compensating safeguard once the decision had been taken not to have a bicameral assembly. This radical reform package commanded the support of all political groupings, including the Social Democrats, and was passed almost unanimously by the archaic Diet of four Estates before that body finally dissolved itself (Törnudd, 1968, pp.30–5). It was a concession wrung from St Petersburg in the wake of the 1905 Russian Revolution. The concession may have appeared a hollow one in the ensuing years of Russification (Kirby, 1979, pp.31–4), but at least it provided a durable foundation for the Finnish political system after independence.

Iceland obtained PR and universal suffrage in 1915 as an instalment of home rule from Denmark. The PR arrangements paralleled the Danish and could be described as initially rather rough and ready. Only the capital city in each case formed a genuine multi-member constituency: otherwise the PR element in the system was limited to a small national pool of seats designed to lessen the discrepancy between votes and seats arising in the territorial areas. The effect was to strengthen rural and local interests.

Sweden, Denmark and Norway had had single-member plurality systems before switching to PR in 1909, 1915 and 1921 respectively. The first two had approximated to the British pattern, the Norwegian (from 1906 onwards) to the French double-ballot method. In Sweden the Conservatives conceded manhood suffrage in order to obtain the safeguard of PR (they had had the power to block franchise reform because of their strength in the indirectly elected chamber). But PR was to apply to *both* chambers henceforth, as part of the trade-off with the Liberals and Social Democrats. A similar deal was made in Denmark six years later, this time involving the introduction of universal suffrage — which the Swedes finally introduced in 1921, the last of the five countries to do so. In Norway the suffrage question had been removed from the political agenda before the adoption of PR, universal suffrage taking effect in 1913. In this case the double-ballot plurality system encouraged electoral understandings between Liberals and Conservatives to the disadvantage of the rising Labour Party. Thus in the last elections held under these arrangements the Liberals polled fewer votes than Labour but still managed to emerge with fifty-one seats to the latter's eighteen. The introduction of PR in 1921 represented a short-term concession by the non-socialist parties to secure a longer-term advantage. It could also be regarded as an incidental act of political pacification in view of the strong current of anti-parliamentarism which had been running within the ranks of the Labour Party.

For their general elections all five countries began with the d'Hondt system of PR, but only Finland and Iceland retain it. The others switched coincidentally, to the St Laguë method of apportionment in 1952–3. The ruling Norwegian Labour Party had prohibited electoral cartels in 1947, thus introducing more severe distortions into the representativeness of the electoral system. St Laguë diminishes the practical attractiveness of cartels (Rokkan, 1968, pp.14–15; Laakso, 1979). This consideration weighed heavily with the Agrarian Party (as it then was) in Sweden when it entered into coalition with the Social Democrats in 1951: it could more easily keep a distance from its former allies on the non-socialist side with the new type of PR in operation. In Denmark the change came about as part of a more general constitutional reform and has an attraction for all the established political groupings, not least because it has diminished the likelihood of party splintering.

Finland has made the fewest changes in her original electoral arrangements, having stipulated large multi-member constituencies in the Parliament Act of 1906. The redistribution of seats is carried out by the government before each election in strict accordance with population changes. Despite charges of gerrymandering levelled against the Agrarian Party in the sparsely populated northern constituencies, there has been little problem with the disproportionate weighting of rural in relation to urban areas, as has been the case in both Norway and Iceland. Only the Åland Islands, with their small population and single-member constituency, are an exception to the general pattern. Despite a relatively large number of small parties – four won representation in 1979, for example, in addition to the four large parties in the system – proposals to set up a special threshold qualification have never won acceptance. One powerful consideration here has been the danger of excluding the political organ of the chief national minority grouping, the Swedish People's Party, from the legislature. The possibility of forming electoral alliances, too, has always existed in the Finnish system and has often been exploited among the non-socialist parties. Perhaps the biggest change in the system was made in 1978, with the compulsory introduction of party primaries for the selection of candidates. This complemented the earlier distinctive Finnish arrangement under which electors rank-ordered party candidates in the absence of the predetermined ordering of party lists by voting for any *one* candidate from the choice proferred (details in Pesonen, 1968, pp.9–10).

Denmark, Iceland and Sweden all have a national pool of seats which are distributed between the parties so as to counter-balance discrepancies arising from the results in the territorial constituencies. Denmark currently reserves two seats each in the *Folketing* for the representatives of Greenland and the Faroes but otherwise has a pool of forty seats to supplement the 135 for the territorial constituencies, all of which are now multi-member (total, therefore, 179 seats). Iceland has a national pool of eleven seats out of a total of sixty: her territorial constituencies have since 1959 returned from five to twelve members apiece. Sweden followed Denmark in 1970 by adopting a pool of forty seats, but in this case for a legislature of 350 members. However, when the 1973 elections produced the embarrassment of a House exactly divided between socialists and non-socialists, so that many matters fell to be decided by lot, the numbers were reduced to thirty-nine and 349 respectively.

All these three countries specify certain conditions for a share of the pool. In Iceland one territorial seat must first be won. Denmark has a somewhat similar clause (Johansen, 1979, pp.47–8); otherwise 2 per cent of the national vote is sufficient to qualify. Sweden requires either 12 per cent of the vote in a territorial constituency or 4 per cent of the national vote. Denmark, it may be added, resembles Finland in giving voters the chance of voting for personalities. Parties in Sweden — especially those on the non-socialist side — regularly present differently balanced lists of candidates in different parts of the same large constituency in order to maximize their votes.

Throughout Scandinavia parties are in charge of their own nominating procedures, and the nomination process is firmly set at constituency or district level, with markedly less intervention from the national level than is the case in Britain. In some countries (e.g. Sweden) national party authorities have neither the opportunity to propose nor the power to veto candidates; and where they have these facilities, as with the Social Democrats in Denmark, they are more inhibited than British parties in using them because of the expected reaction at local level. Thus national candidate lists are not a Scandinavian phenomenon, and the carpet-bagger is virtually unknown.

Norway, like Finland, bases representation in the legislature on territorial seats only. A constitutional clause requiring two-thirds of the places in the *Storting* to be reserved for rural constituencies disappeared in 1952, along with the change in the type of PR used. But extra weighting is given to the sparsely inhabited provinces in the north of the country — as in Scotland, though in a very different context — so that a vote there counts almost thrice as much as one in Oslo. The imperfectly proportional system encourages the non-socialist parties in particular to make ready use of electoral alliances. General elections frequently produce the kind of paradoxical result more commonly associated with plurality systems, with both socialists and non-socialists often winning a majority of seats on a minority of votes. Thus in the 1977 elections — to take one of several possible examples from the post-war years — Labour and the Socialist Left between them obtained seventy-eight seats on a 46.5 per cent share of the poll as compared with seventy-seven seats for their combined opponents on a 52.3 per cent share of the poll.

One or two brief observations may be made about the impact of PR on Scandinavian party systems (for a lengthier survey, see Elder, 1975, pp.192–7). Danish experience shows that the adoption of PR does not automatically lead to an increase in the number of parties. In this case the four political groupings that had emerged under the old electoral system — Conservatives, Liberals, Social Democrats and Radicals — continued to dominate the scene until the 1960s. Similarly, in Iceland four parties have continuously had an overwhelming share of the popular vote. Elsewhere there has been a broad pattern of evolution from three- or four- to five- or six-party constellations, as was shown above in the section on electoral contours. The most significant, and the most distinctively Scandinavian, element in this evolution has been the appearance of relatively strong Agrarian (later, Centre) parties as an independent political factor.

The introduction (or reintroduction) of single-member plurality electoral systems could be expected to have different effects in the different countries of the region. These effects would depend chiefly on (a) the degree of geographical concentration of the vote for particular parties in the country concerned, and (b) the relative strength of the largest party in the constellation. Thus a first-past-the-post system would not reduce multi-partism in Finland, for example, to the extent that might be expected, given the persistence of regional differences in voting behaviour and also the division of the left into two major groupings. Sweden would lie at the other end of the spectrum in this respect because of the strength of the Social Democrats in relation to that of the next largest single party in so many constituencies throughout the country. Thus in a theoretical exercise based on the 1956 election returns — a long time ago, admittedly, but the point retains its validity — a report submitted to the Commission on the Constitution (SOU, 1963: 19, pp. 5–7) calculated that the Social Democrats would have obtained 200 seats rather than 106 that year under a simple plurality system and that the three non-socialist parties, in the absence of any combination, would have acquired only thirty-nine between them rather than 119. (The directly elected chamber was much smaller then than now.)

These considerations remain strictly academic, for the question of switching from PR to a majority system is not a live one. This still holds good despite the party turbulences of the 1970s, when PR facilitated the reflection of fresh currents of party opinion in some legislatures (notably among the Progressives in Denmark) and probably had some effect in encouraging party splits (Danish Centre Democrats, Finnish People's Unity Party). The Social Democratic and Labour parties have not on the whole been anxious for a change of system in the countries in which they enjoy the strongest relative positions (Denmark, Norway, Sweden), not least for fear of forcing mergers between their opponents. By the same token, their opponents have been anxious to maintain their several identities.

PR electoral systems have thus become an established element in Scandinavian political life. They are in force everywhere (except in Iceland) for the elections to local government councils, with the result that local government decision-making is commonly conducted on a coalition basis. PR is also used to choose the electoral college of 300 members which normally convenes every six years to elect the Finnish President: the same constituencies serve for both parliamentary and presidential elections. Protracted balloting in the electoral college is ruled out because the third ballot is confined to the two highest candidates in the second round — if, of course, nobody has secured an outright majority at an earlier stage — and in the event of a tie the outcome is decided simply by lottery. The Icelandic President is unusual in being chosen by direct popular plebiscite, simple plurality style, for an office which is more honorific than politically powerful.

In Scandinavia as elsewhere, PR has obviated the need for by-elections: in the event of a parliamentary vacancy, the next person on the party list (or the next most popular person bearing the party label) moves up to fill the place. This can have interesting consequences in the case of joint lists. By this method, for example, the Finnish Centre (Agrarian) Party succeeded in obtaining its one and only MP to date in Helsinki until the 1979 elections terminated the mandate (Arter, 1979b, p. 424). The national minority Slesvig Party was also given the possibility of representation in the Danish *Folketing* through a joint list arrangement with the Centre Democrats in South Jutland (1973–9).

In conclusion, some brief observations may be made about the significance of the principle of proportionality in Scandinavian political culture. First, established, settled patterns of co-operation between parties may make it harder for a new party, having surmounted the threshold of representation, to cross the threshold of political power. But the frequency of coalition rule at the local government level encourages easy inter-party working relationships which have relevance at the national level because of the relatively high degree of movement from the local to the national sector. This latter phenomenon owes much in turn to the close control of parliamentary candidatures by the constituency organizations. The point must not, however, be exaggerated. Political combinations entered into at the local level are formed on the basis of local issues and are not mirrored at the macro-level. There were, moreover, clear signs of a change of attitude at the local level in Sweden at least in the mid-1970s. In part these could be read as a by-product of the creation of larger and more politicized local authority units during the previous decade. 'In the course of the discussions', said the report of the Commission on Local Government Democracy, 'it has, for example, been maintained that local coalition government has led to the boundary lines between the political parties being erased. By marking off the majority more clearly from the minority it has been held that a livelier debate is likely to ensue' (SOU, 1975: 41, pp. 32–3). The same report recorded that the majorities on local and provincial councils were more and more frequently taking all the chairmanships — some 60 per cent in 1974, as compared with 30 per cent in 1971 — and its general tenor was plainly favourable to the practice.

Secondly, there is no strict application of a *Proporz* principle (Steiner, 1972, pp.390f.) in Scandinavian politics on the consociational democracy model (Switzerland, post-war Austria, Netherlands, Belgium). What can be asserted is that in specific respects there is a conscious effort to ascertain the proportionate division of political benefits; that this goes further than in states with adversary systems; and that it holds good both for those Scandinavian countries where no party has any immediate prospect of attaining a majority (Denmark, Finland, Iceland) and for those where a majority has been enjoyed by Labour/Social Democrats for considerable periods (Norway, Sweden). Thus public funds are distributed between the political parties in the system in proportion to their parliamentary strengths. Again, the norm at national level has been for committee chairmanships in the legislatures, speakerships and deputy speakerships, etc., to be shared out according to the same principle. But certainly nothing approaching a proportional distribution of political appointments occurs in the public sector. The Swedish Social Democrats, during their long ascendancy, appear to have given their political opponents rather more places — provincial governorships, embassies, directorships of public boards and so on — than a British government is in the habit of doing. Nevertheless, this aspect of government is handled in Scandinavia in accordance more with competitive than consociational principles.

PR, finally, plays a subsidiary and mechanistic part in diminishing the likelihood of landslide elections and in contributing to the rarity of sharp reversals of policy as governments succeed one another. The participation figures for elections show that the generally unspectacular nature of election results does not cause a decline of political interest in the electorate. The rarity of sharp reversals of policy means that the costs of adversary politics are largely avoided.

## POLITICAL RECRUITMENT

By the 1920s the major parties had developed a nationwide organization and had built up some form of national secretariat. The youth organizations of the parties date back to about 1920, as do the various auxiliary organizations typical of a class-structured party. The interest organizations also became significant political factors at about that time. The interventionist policies of governments between 1914 and 1918 and again during the economic depression of the 1930s tended to strengthen the economic organizations and to integrate them into the political system, taking on distributive tasks which had previously been performed by public agencies or which were newly created (Pedersen, 1976, p. 53). The other Nordic countries lagged somewhat behind Denmark in the pace of this social and political mobilization, but all except Finland had reached high levels of political participation by the 1930s, although social mobilization took another ten or twenty years to reach such levels (Kuhnle, 1975). These socio-political transformations provided opportunities for political training and experience for representatives of the lower and middle classes, who were then able to replace representatives belonging to higher social strata, a process of institutionalization which had the paradoxical result that while there was some broadening of the strata represented in the legislature, there was a rapid disappearance of an open legislative elite: security of tenure grew steadily and continuity of legislative careers increased as it became increasingly difficult to run for office without the endorsement of a party organization. Pedersen (1977, p. 85) found that while this process started in Denmark as early as 1840, it still goes on.

Intellectual professionalization brings with it a growing number of legislators recruited from professional-intellectual strata and a tendency to deal with political problems in terms of *saglighed og faglighed* (objectivity and expertise). Political professionalization, on the other hand, brings with it a legislature dominated by the officials of parties and organizations, by journalists and by others linked to the political infrastructure. In their interesting comparison of the professionalization of the Danish and Norwegian legislatures over the period 1814 to 1960, Eliassen and Pedersen (1973) found that although the typical legislator is still an individual who belongs clearly in neither of these camps, there were more full-time political professionals in Denmark than in Norway, while local political affiliations were almost twice as strong in Norway as in Denmark. The introduction of elected local councils in Norway in 1837 was followed immediately by a rapid increase in the proportion of MPs with political experience derived from this arena, and the number had increased to a very high level *before* the first large waves of electoral mobilization in the 1880s. In Denmark, by contrast, Poor Law and local government reform did not take effect until the beginning of the 1890s, after the start of significant political mobilization. The displacement of members of the legislature of high social status by professional politicians has been a slow, steady process in Norway; in 1945–60 it had reached the point at which about half were professional politicians and fewer than one in twenty had high social status. This is very different from the case of Denmark, where there were many more MPs in both categories until 1945 but the process of displacement had largely stopped by 1900.

Analysis of the social composition of the *Folketing* in 1968 and 1977 shows little significant variation overall: academics, company directors, landowners and others with high levels of responsibility (the upper middle class) predominated, and very few working class occupations were represented. The 'new' (post-1973) parties have, in total, done little to change the social composition of the *Folketing* as a whole: although the Progress Party has provided a channel for some lower-middle and working-class representation, this is counter-balanced by a predominance of upper- and middle-middle-class representatives, both in the Progress Party and among the Centre Democrats and the Christian People's Party (see table 4.5).

Comparisons with Norway, using the same analytical base (table 4.6), show far fewer representatives in Group I and far more in Groups II and III than in Denmark, a tendency which has become more marked in recent times than it was in the late 1960s. The Norwegian Labour Party

TABLE 4.5: DENMARK: OCCUPATIONAL COMPOSITION OF THE *FOLKETING* BY PARTY, 1968 AND 1977

| Occupational strata | Parties,[1] 1968 ||||||||||| Parties,[1] 1977 |||||||||||
| --- | --- | --- | --- | --- | --- | --- | --- | --- | --- | --- | --- | --- | --- | --- | --- | --- | --- | --- | --- | --- | --- |
| | SD | RV | KF | DR | SF | KP | CD | KrF | V | VS | FP | All | % | SD | RV | KF | DR | SF | KP | CD | KrF | V | VS | FP | All | % |
| I *Upper middle class and above* Academics, directors, landowners, others with considerable responsibility | 19 | 11 | 20 | | 2 | | | | 10 | | | 62 | 36.3 | 20 | 4 | 10 | 1 | | | | 6 | 5 | 7 | 2 | 8 | 63 | 35 |
| II *Middle middle class* 'Semi-academics' – teachers, social workers, most higher officials and office workers | 22 | 10 | 8 | | 2 | | | | 10 | | | 52 | 30.4 | 28 | 1 | 2 | 2 | 3 | 3 | | 3 | 1 | 6 | | 9 | 59[2] | 33 |
| III *Lower middle class* Lower office workers, independent tradesmen and craftsmen, larger farmers, etc. | 9 | 4 | 7 | | 1 | | | | 14 | | | 35 | 20.5 | 13 | 1 | 2 | 1 | 2 | 4 | | 2 | | 9 | 1 | 5 | 40 | 22 |
| IV *Upper working class* Skilled workers, smallholders, etc. | 8 | 2 | | | 1 | | | | | | | 11 | 6.4 | 4 | | | | 1 | | | | | 2 | | 3 | 10 | 6 |
| V *Lower working class* Unskilled workers | 3 | | | | 4 | | | | | | | 7 | 4.1 | 1 | | | | 1 | | | | | | 1 | 1 | 3 | 1 |
| *Others (unclassified)* | 1 | | 2 | | 1 | | | | | | | 4 | 2.1 | 1 | | 1 | 3 | 1 | | | | | | | | 6 | 3 |
| Totals | 62 | 27 | 37 | | 11 | | | | 34 | | | 171 | 99.8 | 67 | 6 | 15 | 7 | 8 | 7 | | 11 | 6 | 22 | 5 | 26 | 181 | 100 |

[1] SD = Social Democrats; RV = Radical Liberals; KF = Conservatives; DR = Justice Party; SF = Socialist People's Party; KP = Communists; CD = Centre Democrats; KrF = Christian People's Party; V = Liberals; VS = Left Socialists; FP = Progress Party.
[2] Includes one member of *Atássut*, elected in Greenland.

*Sources:* Data from *Sørensen 1968* and *Hividt 1977*. Classifications from Svalastoga, 1959, adapted by amalgamating his upper and upper-middle strata to produce stratum I above. Percentage of the adult population in each stratum was as follows: I – 2.65%; II – 8.05%; III – 29.86%; IV – 34.49%; V – 24.94%.

TABLE 4.6: NORWAY: OCCUPATIONAL COMPOSITION OF THE *STORTING* BY PARTY, 1969 and 1977

| Occupational strata[2] | Parties,[1] 1969 |     |     |     |     |     |      | Parties,[1] 1977 |     |     |     |     |     |     |      |
|---|---|---|---|---|---|---|---|---|---|---|---|---|---|---|---|
|   | A | V | KrF | Sp | H | All | % | SV | A | V | KrF | Sp | H | All | % |
| I   | 9  | 3  | 5  | 6  | 11 | 34  | 22.6 |   | 10 |   | 8  |    | 17 | 35  | 22.6 |
| II  | 27 | 7  | 5  | 6  | 14 | 59  | 39.3 |   | 34 | 2 | 10 | 4  | 17 | 67  | 43.2 |
| III | 25 | 3  | 4  | 8  | 4  | 44  | 29.3 | 2 | 18 |   | 4  | 8  | 7  | 39  | 25.2 |
| IV  | 10 |    |    |    |    | 10  | 6.6  |   | 12 |   |    |    |    | 12  | 7.7  |
| V   | 1  |    |    |    |    | 1   | 0.6  |   |    |   |    |    |    |     |     |
| Others | 2 |  |   |    |    | 2   | 1.3  |   | 2  |   |    |    |    | 2   | 1.3  |
| Totals | 74 | 13 | 14 | 20 | 29 | 150 | 99.7 | 2 | 76 | 2 | 22 | 12 | 41 | 155 | 100 |

[1] SV = Left Socialist; A = Labour Party; V = Liberals; KrF = Christian People's Party; Sp = Centre Party; H = Conservatives.
[2] For definitions of occupational strata, see table 4.5.

*Sources*: Data from *Stortinget 1969–73* and *Stortinget 1977–81*.

TABLE 4.7: SWEDEN: CLASS COMPOSITION OF SECOND
CHAMBER REPRESENTATIVES, 1968–9, BY OWN OCCUPATION
AND PARENTS' OCCUPATION

| Social strata | Parents' class % | No. | Own class % | No. | Comparison with 1978 electorate % |
|---|---|---|---|---|---|
| *Upper class* Directors of large businesses, landowners, higher civil servants, 'liberal professions', state and local councillors | 16 | 43 | 36 | 98 | 6 |
| *Middle class* Small businessmen, lower civil servants, foremen and supervisors, trade union and party representatives | 23 | 64 | 41 | 114 | 32 |
| *Farmer class* Farmers, both owners and tenants | 28 | 79 | 16 | 43 | 8 |
| *Working class* Agricultural, forestry and industrial workers, shop assistants | 33 | 92 | 7 | 19 | 54 |
| *Totals* | 100 | 278 | 100 | 274 | 100 |

Source: Holmberg, 1974, pp. 272–7.

(*Arbeiderpartiet*) is evidently more successful in recruiting members with working-class occupations than is its Danish counterpart (*Socialdemokratiet*). In the other instance in which direct comparisons between the parties can readily be made, the Norwegian Christian People's Party is both larger than its Danish sister party and is represented by a larger proportion of MPs in Groups II and III.

This type of analysis presents a number of methodological problems, however. Official publications of election results for Denmark or Norway classify their data by economic sector rather than by social class. Attempts to operationalize comparable systems of categorization of occupations meet with difficulties of translation and with different usages of similar terms. Individual self-descriptions may vary according to whether they are for use on a ballot paper or in a telephone directory. There is also the fact that we are dealing with an unusually mobile section of the population.

The latter point is well illustrated by Holmberg (1974, p. 273) who gives figures for the Swedish Second Chamber representatives in 1968–9 by both their own and their parents' social class (see table 4.7). (The Second Chamber, superseded by the unicameral *Riksdag* in 1970, was directly elected.) This shows that over three-quarters of the representatives had upper- or middle-class occupations themselves, a balance in sharp contrast to that of the electorate as a whole and a pattern characteristic, to various degrees, of the other Scandinavian countries – and, indeed, of all West European legislatures. If we turn our attention to a classification by parents' class, however, we find that over 60 per cent of representatives grew up in working-class or farming homes, a pattern much closer to that of the population as a whole: the economy a generation back was, of course, much more agricultural than in 1968. Clearly, many representatives have experienced significant personal social mobility before or during their legislative careers, and Holmberg conconcludes that election produces a pattern of recruitment that is socio-economically broader than the Swedish business or civil service elites which he also considers. Since Holmberg's study the proportion of women in the *Riksdag* has greatly increased, and they are drawn more from the middle class than from among manual workers.

Examination of the occupational titles of Members of Parliament reveals a group well represented there but not among the population as a whole: the appointed officials or office-holders in political parties, trade unions, business associations or other interest groups. Analysis of members of the Swedish Second Chamber by party (see table 4.8) showed this group to be present, perhaps not surprisingly, in large numbers in the Social Democratic Party, although there are also significant numbers in the other three parties. The same table shows the predominance of upper-class occupations in the Moderate Unity Party (conservatives) and the People's Party (liberals). It also illustrates the heavily agricultural representation in the Centre Party and, rather more surprisingly, the Moderates. The marked representation of professional 'organization men' in the Swedish *Riksdag* confirms the trend towards political professionalization noted at the beginning of our discussion of political recruitment.

In Britain or the USA it is generally assumed that to become a legis-

TABLE 4.8: SWEDEN: CLASS COMPOSITION OF SECOND CHAMBER REPRESENTATIVES, 1968–9, BY PARTY

| Social strata | Parties[1] SD (%) | CP (%) | FP (%) | M (%) | % totals | No. |
|---|---|---|---|---|---|---|
| Upper class | 24 | 23 | 45 | 42 | 30 | 83 |
| Middle class | 28 | 9 | 35 | 10 | 24 | 66 |
| Farmer class | 2 | 56 | 8 | 32 | 16 | 43 |
| Working class | 12 | – | 4 | 3 | 7 | 19 |
| Organization professionals[2] | 34 | 12 | 8 | 13 | 23 | 63 |
| Totals: % | 100 | 100 | 100 | 100 | 100 | |
| No. | 136 | 43 | 49 | 38 | | 274 |

[1] SD = Social Democrats; CP = Centre Party; FP = People's Party (Liberals); M = Moderates (Conservatives).
[2] The category of organization professionals comprises state and local councillors and party officials in appointed positions, together with appointed officials of trade unions, business associations and other interest groups. These individuals have been included in the upper- and middle-class categories in table 4.7.

*Source*: Holmberg, 1974, pp. 272–7.

lator is to take up a career. Turnover of MPs in Britain varies in relation to the interval between elections, but if we exclude the abnormal elections of 1945, 1951 and October 1974, between 14 and 28 per cent of MPs will be new to their task at the start of each Parliament (Mellors, 1978: calculation based on his table 2.1). Polsby (1968) shows that the percentage of new members in the House of Representatives declined from 50 per cent in the period 1800–50 to between 10 and 19 per cent in the 1950s and 1960s (quoted by Blondel, 1973, p.87). Comparable figures for Sweden are 16 per cent (1973) to 18 per cent (1976) (*Allmänna valen*, 1973, p.14, and 1976, p.16). Swedish levels of turnover have not varied greatly in recent decades, but in Denmark turnover of *Folketing* members has been very significantly higher: 35 per cent in 1971 and 42 per cent in 1973. The latter was, of course, a 'landslide' year, but turnover remained high following subsequent elections, at 21 per cent in 1975 and 33 per cent in 1977. In consequence, the median seniority of *Folketing* members at the start of a Parliament, which had been over six years in the 1960s, fell to two or three years in the 1970s. While facilitating innovativeness and flexibility of policy and permitting an increased number of individuals access to the parliamentary elite, this will also have significantly lowered the average levels of experience, expertise and effectiveness among *Folketing* members (cf. Putnam, 1976, pp. 66–7). The comparable level of median seniority for Norway and Sweden in the 1970s was about seven years.

Experience in local government is often a significant stage in a political career in Scandinavia. In Norway there is a marked tendency for parties to use a seat in the *Storting* to reward a career of steady representative achievement at the local level, and many *Stortingsmen* bring with them many years' experience in local government or as journalists on local papers. While this ensures that they are well attuned to the requirements of the localities they represent, it also tends to reinforce party conformity and to diminish political initiative. In Denmark experience in local politics figures a little less prominently in politicians' careers: the Social Democrats have prohibited *Folketing* members from holding joint office as either mayors (*borgmestre*) or party secretaries since 1969, although an amendment to the rule made it operate only prospectively so as to allow Erhard Jakobsen (then the Social Democrats' chief electoral asset, although he broke away to form the Centre Democrats in 1973) to continue to combine the careers of *Folketing* member and mayor of Gladsaxe. In 1980 the prohibition on dual office-holding was extended to prevent party members being elected to both the *Folketing* and the European Parliament or to both the *Folketing* and a local (*kommune*) or county (*amt*) council (Rules of the Social Democratic Party, para. 5).

CHAPTER FIVE

# Consensualism and Policy-Making in Scandinavia

It is now time to pick up the themes of conflict intensity and conflict resolution — relating to the second and third dimensions in our original scheme — and then to draw some threads together. No politician worth his salt, it may be argued, voluntarily seeks consensus: consensus has to be forced upon him, and it would be naive to suppose otherwise. There is a good deal of force in this argument, and it is no part of the present survey to contend that politicians in Scandinavia are somehow differently constituted from politicians anywhere else in the world. As an American historian of Sweden put it, referring to the confused period of minority government that followed the breakthrough of the parliamentary principle in that country in 1918–21, 'The politics of compromise was forced by the electoral situation, not by the fact that the Swedes loved compromise' (Scott, 1977, p. 476). During the period 1921–32, when no party was within sight of a majority in the *Riksdag*, the centre of gravity of decision-making shifted to the specialized parliamentary standing committees, supplemented by the commissions of inquiry whose reports were circulated to interested authorities, public and private, for open comment under the *remiss* procedure. Later in the 1930s, when the Social Democrats were consolidating their dominance, the complaint was that Parliament was being turned into a 'Royal Transport Company' for the carrying of government Bills. Similarly, Kalevi Sorsa, the Chairman of the Finnish Social Democratic Party and currently Prime Minister, expressed disapproval before the 1979 elections in his country of commissions of inquiry based upon the principle of PR. The grounds were that such commissions produce solutions to problems which contravene the principles of parliamentary government by failing to present the voters with clear-cut alternatives. Their end result, he argued, is commonly a degree of over-unification and an unpalatable 'ideological porridge'.

Preliminarily it may be said that the conflict is quite severe in the industrial sector in Denmark, Finland and Iceland but markedly less intense in this sector in Norway and Sweden. In the Danish case it frequently falls to Parliament to pick up the pieces (Schwerin, 1980). This process is materially assisted by the comparatively low intensity of conflict between the generally dominant Social Democratic Party and the allies which it seeks in the centre of the political spectrum and among the long-established parties in the system. (In this context the Conservative People's Party is regarded not as one of the centrist parties but certainly as long-established.) So the concertation of policy is more apparent in practice here at the parliamentary than at the corporate level, although mechanisms for conflict resolution exist at the corporate level, as has been seen in chapter 1. In Finland the intensity of conflict at the parliamentary level is also high, so that Parliament there is unable to resolve conflict as conclusively as in Denmark. Consequently, the authority of the President has had to be invoked on occasion in order to settle disputes. At the same time, the growth of concertative mechanisms may be noted since 1966, involving both the parliamentary and the corporate sectors. Iceland occupies a mid-position, in that the intensity of conflicts in the corporate sector is mediated by parliamentary coalitions with a degree of success that lies somewhere between the Danish and the Finnish. If the focus in much of what follows is on the management of economic policy, it is because this has been, and continues to be, a central political preoccupation throughout the region.

Denmark, Finland and Iceland all perennially experience the same type of parliamentary situation as Sweden in the 1921–32 era: the concertation of policy is forced upon their political elites because no single party finds itself within striking distance of a majority. Norway and Sweden have been in a different case for most of the period since the 1930s, with the Labour and Social Democratic Parties generally in a position to mould the course of events according to their will until the mid-1960s (Norway) or the mid-1970s (Sweden). Denmark and Finland, however, as has been shown earlier, have extreme multi-party systems in terms of the number of parties represented in their legislatures. The Social Democrats in Denmark regularly come closer to a majority position than any other party in these three countries, but suffer multiple frustrations because they as regularly fail to achieve it. The four-party basic structure in Iceland presents a simpler aspect, but the Independence Party, as the leading group in terms of numbers, has difficulty in achieving much more than a third of the total poll and furthermore in February 1980 split at the parliamentary level. In consequence, a peculiar condition now obtains in which a secessionist Independent, Gunnar Thoroddsen, is Prime Minister of a Progressive-People's Alliance Cabinet, with two fellow secessionists holding office also, while his party as such is in opposition.

The political agenda in Denmark is dominated by the problems raised by the management of the economy — not that there is anything peculiar about that in the conditions of world recession that have prevailed for most of the past decade, but Denmark has been more often in economic crisis than out of it for most of the past three decades. Large balance of payments deficits, high rates of unemployment and persistent inflationary pressures have combined to make the task of managing the economy peculiarly difficult. The early development of mechanisms for the containment of industrial conflict in Denmark was noted in chapter 1, but the fact is that the severity of economic pressures have combined with the comparatively high fragmentation of union structures — unions being predominantly organized along craft lines — to bring about frequent failures of the machinery to resolve deadlocks.

It may be useful at this point to document the incidence of industrial disputes in the advanced industrial countries of Scandinavia in a wider comparative context (see table 5.1), bearing in mind that the usual difficulties in the way of data standardization make this a rough and ready guide.

## DENMARK

The figures given for Denmark in the table are bound to be on the low side, not least because of the outbreak of a general strike in March 1973. This strike, it may be noted in passing, owed much to the imposition on employers by legislation of the charge for increased welfare benefits, hitherto a subject for collective bargaining; this imposition in turn was made possible by a rare period of majority for the combined parties of the left. Discussions between both sides of the labour market were promised for the future before any such enactment was repeated (Elvander, 1974a, p. 421). It may be further noted that in the decade 1960—9 Denmark came thirteenth out of a list of eighteen countries in a similar league table (and her figures then covered manufacturing only), Finland tenth, Norway fifth and Sweden, again, second to Switzerland.

TABLE 5.1: AVERAGE NUMBER OF WORKING DAYS LOST THROUGH INDUSTRIAL DISPUTES,[1] SELECTED COUNTRIES, 1969–78

| Country | Working days lost per 1000 employees[2] | Rank order |
|---|---|---|
| Denmark[3] | 575 | 10(+) |
| Finland | 1143 | 14 |
| Norway | 79 | 4 |
| Sweden[4] | 42 | 2 |
| Australia[5] | 1242 | 15 |
| Belgium | 467 | 8 |
| Canada | 1929 | 18 |
| France | 297 | 7 |
| German Federal Republic | 90 | 5 |
| India | 1379 | 17 |
| Ireland | 991 | 13 |
| Italy | 1938 | 19 |
| Japan | 231 | 6 |
| Netherlands | 75 | 3 |
| New Zealand | 525 | 9 |
| Spain | 928 | 12 |
| Switzerland | – (negligible, under 5) | 1 |
| UK | 897 | 11 |
| USA[6] | 1282 | 16(–) |

[1] In the mining, manufacturing, construction and transport industries.
[2] Figures for 1978 provisional.
[3] Figures to 1974 relate only to manufacturing; later ones include construction and transport.
[4] Figures to 1971 relate to *all* sectors of employment.
[5] Gas and electricity included, not transport.
[6] Gas, electricity and water included.

*Source*: Based on *Employment Gazette*, vol. 88 (London, HMSO, 1980), table 1.

Strikes in Denmark are, of course, most apt to occur upon the expiry of a collective bargaining agreement: these agreements exercise a restraining effect while in force. But the parliamentary channel of representation repeatedly has to try to sort out the difficulties experienced in the corporate channel. A number of points are worth making briefly in this connection.

First, competitive out-bidding by the political parties may have the effect of *compounding* the problems in the labour market. This effect was particularly marked in the 1960s in respect of welfare reforms: the 1968–71 Agrarian Liberal/Radical/Conservative coalition under Baunsgaard, for example, pushed up social security expenditure sharply. As a consequence, direct tax levels also rose steeply to levels, in the 1970s, well above those prevailing in Norway and Sweden in terms of a percentage of state revenues. Quite clearly, the main beneficiary of this type of pernicious competitive policy-making among the political elites was the protest party of Mogens Glistrup, the Progress Party, in the 1973 elections and subsequently.

Second, and more important in the present context of analysing the consensual elements in the states under review, the frequent perception of circumstances of economic crisis puts a premium upon results-orientated endeavour on the part of the parties in the system. The running in this direction during the period from 1975 onwards has generally been made by the Social Democrats under Anker Jørgensen: except for the curious interlude of their short-lived 1978–9 coalition with the Agrarian Liberals, they have successfully sought support for package deals of legislation from the parties in the centre of the political spectrum while holding office on a minority, single-party basis. Jørgensen has used the long summer recesses of the *Folketing* to conduct negotiations with potential allies in a relaxed atmosphere and on a bilateral basis, so that conflict between these potential allies can be kept to a minimum. In this way the 'September Compromise', or, perhaps more accurately, the 'September Package Deal' (*September Forliget*), of 1975 was put together with the assistance of the Radicals, the Christian People's Party, the Centre Democrats and the Agrarian Liberals, thus providing a parliamentary basis of 121 out of 179 members in support of the government programme of economic regulation in the ensuing session. Similarly in August 1976, when the Liberals withdrew their full support, the Conservatives were induced to lend a measure of assistance, and the smaller parties which had been numerically superfluous in 1975 became essential to ensure a majority for the programmatic but not governmental coalition. Again in August 1977 a fresh agreement was reached, this time between the four 'old parties' – the Radicals, the Liberals and the Conservatives as well, of course, as the Social Democrats. This, with the backing of 107 members, ensured the passage of some thirty Bills on energy saving, employment, the encouragement of commerce and the adjustment of taxation. This went some way towards forestalling moves by the non-socialist parties towards a concerted opposition to the government, something which is far from being a normal and expected occurrence in Scandinavian political life.

The point at issue here is that, as the elections of 1977 and 1979 in Denmark showed, the parties which are prepared to co-operate in seeking constructive solutions to the country's difficulties have tended to be those most appreciated by the country's voters. Consequently, there has been a slow and steady recession of the parliamentary turmoil induced by the protest election of 1973. A stress on the pragmatic, moderate and co-operative character of Danish political life forms a *leitmotif* of John Fitzmaurice's (1981) book on the country, and at the parliamentary level this thesis has convincing weight. Of course, the cobbling together of ad hoc majorities for economic packages raises the question of whether coherence can be maintained in the pursuit of regulatory goals. Despite a large budgetary deficit, inflationary pressures and the impact of the wider recession, the signs were that a more favourable trend in the balance of payments would at any rate have been secured in 1980 had it not been for the second stiff rise in oil prices during the decade towards the end of the previous year.

A third and final point may be made on this particular topic. The pursuit of an incomes policy has been a persistent preoccupation of successive Danish governments over most of the past three decades, and it has created perennial difficulties in particular for Social Democratic administrations. The connection between the pursuit of this objective and the reduction of the chronic deficits in the balance of payments is clear, and the end has been sought in conjunction with temporary price freezes, profit and divided limitations, cuts in public expenditure, etc. Legislative packages have commonly been imposed after the failure of mediation attempts in the collective bargaining field. Sometimes the legislation is in line with the wishes of the trade union movement, as represented by LO; more often there is a deviation. This imposes a strain upon Social Democratic–LO relations and provides ammunition for the radical left minorities in the labour movement, already distanced from the generally dominant party on matters of foreign and security policy. Thus the large General Workers' Union, for example, broke with its traditional loyalty in 1974 to support *all* the parties of the left in proportion to their parliamentary strengths.

This kind of difficulty was highlighted by the coalition which the Social Democrats entered into with the Agrarian Liberals in 1978. This particular combination was regarded with grave misgivings by LO leaders and viewed almost as treasonable to the ideals of the labour movement by many of the rank and file in the labour movement. The original party mandate to Jørgensen had been to try to include the Radicals in the government as well, so that they might fulfil their traditional brokerage role. But the Liberals feared that the Radicals might extract too high a price for acting as brokers, and their presence in a coalition could have created difficulties with the Social Democratic left wing because of their neutralist leanings and their opposition to nuclear power. In the event the Social Democratic Minister of Labour, Svend Auken, made it clear that he would serve in the coalition only if expressly asked to do so by the leader of LO. Once again, the March 1979 round of collective bargaining was marked by the breakdown of mediation attempts between LO and the employers' organization *Dansk Arbejdsgiverforening* and a government-imposed solution. This was reached after negotiations lasting over a week between representatives of the two governing parties, meeting in a specially established Labour Market Committee, and won LO consent to what was essentially a continuation of pre-existing agreements for a further two years, along with measures favouring the least well paid. This brought to an end a number of strikes and followed the first ever demonstration of civil servants in front of the *Folketing*. But the coalition broke up within the year, with the Liberals pressing vainly for an immediate wage and price freeze. After the subsequent elections the Social Democrats reverted to the more traditional tactic of seeking support from the parties of the centre. Another string of strikes in spring 1981 cast doubt on the viability of the 1979 package of incomes policy – the labour troubles included a three-month lock-out in the newspaper industry – but the imposition by law of a mediation proposal twice rejected by the labour side concluded the conflict. It is difficult to avoid the conclusion that many of the solutions reached through the parliamentary channel stick because both sides in the labour market are weary of deadlock. Similarly, some of the solutions reached through the parliamentary channel stick because of the absence of a viable majority against them. But the Social Democrats have the knowledge that they represent at the worst the least undesirable ally in government for the large majority in the labour movement, and for long stretches their relations with the union wing – from which, of course, Jørgensen himself originates – are much more fraternal than this reflection would imply.

To sum up the foregoing in terms of the third dimension of consensualism as earlier defined – the extent to which concertation is sought in the shaping of public policy – the argument is that parliamentary conventions and considerations of party interest combine to promote it. Parties which, like the Progress Party and the parties of the radical left, prefer to preserve iconoclastic integrity or ideological purity, find it hard to make headway. For the rest, despite numerous conflicts and much friction, a sharp sense of a common, overriding interest in concertation, induced by a recurrent atmosphere of economic crisis, is manifest. In the British adversarial system a similar sense leads, on occasion, to the suspension of partisan rivalry – in connection, on the whole, with the Ulster problem, for example, and in respect of race relations legislation. But, of course, the structure of the system means that only during a period such as 1974–9 could accommodations in the field of economic policy management become even remotely conceivable.

## FINLAND

The second of the three Scandinavian states with a permanent parliamentary majority-hunting problem, Finland, presents a more complex and difficult pattern to unravel in terms of an analysis of the elements of consensualism. Attention will be concentrated in what follows on a few salient points in respect of developments over the past decade and a half. The main theme may be stated at the outset: some decline in Sartori's *polarized* pluralism in the country during this period. But the growth of consensus has been fragile. The position of Finland in table 5.1 reflects the continuation of a long history of strife in the labour market. She has had the worst record of any Scandinavian state in this respect over the most recent period, having been in much the same bad case as Denmark over the preceding decade.

At the parliamentary level, to begin with, the 1970s saw no fewer than ten governments in Finland, including three Civil Service caretaker administrations, a stop-gap Social Democratic minority regime and a National Emergency Administration drummed together in a day by an irate President – scarcely *prima facie* evidence, one would think, for a low level of intensity of political conflict. Again, with such questions as farm incomes (reflecting the fact that nearly one-fifth of the total workforce still works on the land) regularly producing deadlock between the two core coalition groups, the Social Democrats and Centre Party, and on more than one occasion bringing about the collapse of a government, there would seem to be little evidence of any predisposition to reduce political conflicts by accommodation and compromise. Nevertheless, from the second half of the 1960s the interaction of three factors contributed to a significant increase in inter-elite consensus and the emergence of a new policy-making style.

The first of these factors has already been noted briefly in chapter 1: the reincorporation of the broad left in government in the wake of their electoral majority in 1966, the Communists after an absence of eighteen years and the Social Democrats (the largest single party in the system) after an absence of eight years. This left-wing participation in government has since been repeated on several occasions. So, despite a continuation in the traditionally high levels of governmental instability, there has been much stability in the basic party composition of coalitions: governments have been not minimal-winning but grand coalitions of the centre-left. The Koivisto administration of 1968–70, for example, had the support of 165 of the 200 *Eduskunta* members: the coalition from 1979, again under Koivisto, could count on 122 parliamentary delegates. At the same time, however, the Conservatives have acquired the unenviable status of 'untouchables' and, although currently the second largest party, have not participated in government since 1966.

Precisely how well integrated with the politico-economic structures the People's Democratic League is remains something of an open question, but the Communist-based organization has clearly come a long way down the co-operative road since 1966. Thus in 1969 the Communists removed the commitment to revolution from their programme, and their frequent participation in government has involved stimulation to the mixed economy in the face of world depression. One powerful motive behind this participation has been the desire to fight unemployment, with its particularly severe impact upon the young. Thus in 1977–8 the majority wing of the party supported a series of 'stimulation packages' which involved, among other things, cutting the social security charges on employers, together with reducing the investment tax. At the same time, this majority wing (currently eighteen Communist and six non-Communist members of the People's Democratic League) has accepted the Eurocommunist label while not distancing itself from the Communist Party of the Soviet Union in the manner of the Italian Communist Party. During the 1979 election campaign the party's desire to return to office as part of a centre-left arrangement was so manifest that the party secretary and Minister of Labour, Arvo Aalto, spoke in terms of a Finnish version of the 'historic compromise' (Arter, 1979b), and President Kekkonen was moved to comment that the extensive public debate about the composition of the post-election government was premature and contrary to the best traditions of parliamentary democracy. The hard-line Stalinist opposition (currently eleven strong, under the now extra-parliamentary leadership of Sinisalo), which broke ranks after the Soviet invasion of Czechoslovakia, has maintained a fierce opposition to all these co-operative tendencies.

The Communists have not been easy partners in government. Their three Ministers resigned from the Karjalainen administration in February 1971 in protest against relaxations to a wage freeze; they stayed out of Sorsa's ensuing majority coalition and made modest gains at the polls in 1975 from their position in opposition; in May 1976 their Ministers were allowed the unprecedented liberty of publicly disowning the Cabinet's plan to raise the sales tax; and they left the government again early in 1977. Nevertheless, they have been continuously in office since the creation of Sorsa's second centre-left coalition later that same year. Possibly this helps to account for the evidence of a declining popular support for more socialism in Finland. A Gallup Poll in November 1978 showed that 18 per cent of citizens wanted the country to move in a more socialist direction; a year later the proportion was 16 per cent. In 1979, too, 46 per cent of the supporters of the radical left did *not* want a more socialist society (Pesonen and Sänkiaho, 1979, p. 41). There is, in short, overwhelming support for the mixed economy.

The corollary of increasing Communist participation in government has, however, been the exclusion of the strong and growing Conservative Party from office: both Communists and Social Democrats have repeatedly refused to co-operate with it in government. The Centre Party, too, has not wished formally to associate with the Conservatives, partly for tactical reasons and partly for fear of losing its purported identity as a party neither socialist nor bourgeois. Informally, things have been different. The Conservatives have not in general used the powers at their disposal to block major economic legislation. Under the terms of the Constitution a two-thirds majority is required for tax increases designed to be in force longer than a year and a five-sixths majority for the passage of urgent legislation within the lifetime of a single Parliament. These qualified majorities, which were originally designed to safeguard the position of the Swedish-speaking minority, have consistently enhanced the position of the parliamentary opposition in relation to the government, and they have come under constant attack from the parties of the left. But the Conservatives gave a Centre minority government the support it needed for the passage of the 1976 budget — which included subsidies for agricultural marketing — and they followed basically the same line over the disputed 1977–8 'stimulation packages'. In 1980, moreover, for the first time ever, the government presented the main principles of the budget for parliamentary debate six months before the submission of the main Finance Bill in the autumn. In order to preserve party identity, the Conservatives have repeatedly followed the tactic of voting against the principle of proposed economic legislation while not obstructing it in practice. To date, their sole obvious reward for this forebearance — and also for abandoning their opposition to Kekkonen in the presidential elections of the late 1960s — has been their recognition as a responsible party of the moderate right by the formidable head of state.

The second factor, and the one with the most direct bearing on the emergence of a new policy-making style in recent Finnish politics, has been the heightening of inter-elite consensus in the corporate channel (Helander, 1977). The watershed here was the Liinamaa I Stabilization Agreement (so called after the name of the official mediator) of March 1968. This has been followed by a number of similar arrangements and the generation of what became known as the 'spirit of Korpilampi' (after the name of the hotel near Helsinki where the 1977 concertation of policy took place). Common to all these endeavours, which have met with varying success — the 'spirit of Korpilampi' can hardly be said to be as powerful as the 'spirit of Saltsjöbaden' — has been the association of representatives of both sides of the labour market with government representatives and senior officials in the search for comprehensive package deals. At the heart of all these has been the pursuit of an incomes policy, with price regulation, social reform (e.g. pensions in the 1973 version), rent control and so on forming components of the package at various times. In the process much new machinery for economic regulation has been created (e.g. a Board of Information on Applying Incomes Policy), and the labour market organizations have won representations on a host of administrative committees (e.g. in the education sector). And in June 1980, for example, representatives of the government, the Bank of Finland and peak interest-group organizations met to discuss the forthcoming budget and another incomes policy agreement.

The origins of this general trend can be traced to the devaluation of the Finnish mark and subsequently inflationary pressures in autumn 1967, coupled, of course, with the arrival in power of a centre-left coalition. However, the acute ideological splintering of the union movement has ensured that the level of industrial militancy has remained high. The majority wing of the Communists has veered between regarding incomes policy as a bait to induce workers to enter the capitalist trap and supporting measures directed against inflation and unemployment. The minority wing has remained inflexibly opposed to all concertative endeavours. Since 1966, moreover, the peak labour federation, SAK, has been unable to sign agreements binding on its members — employers negotiate separately with the appropriate union — and it has also lost the power to veto strike action by constituent unions. Contractual agreements have never been enforceable on individual members of unions in Finland, so wildcat strikes continue to be common.

In addition to these difficulties, the main farming interest organization, MTK (*Maataloustouttajain Keskusliitto*, the Confederation of Agricultural Producers), has contributed much to the repeated Cabinet crises over the level of farm incomes and to the limitation of stabilization agreements in the 1970s to guideline principles only, as far as the agricultural sector is concerned. The collapse of the Karjalainen government in 1971, after deadlock on farm incomes between MTK and SAK, led to MTK's following French precedent and arranging for 700 tractors to drown a speech given by the incoming Social Democratic Prime Minister. Similarly, in March 1980 MTK largely got its way by threatening to withhold supplies to the abattoirs and to halt collection of milk and eggs.

In short, the emergence of a new policy-making style has certainly not been accompanied by any marked depoliticization of the Finnish political system. It has also been criticized on the grounds of reducing the status of Parliament. Perhaps more significantly, it is little favoured by Mauno Koivisto, Governor of the Bank of Finland throughout the 1970s, later Prime Minister and the eventual winner in the presidential stakes when Kekkonen retired. In Koivisto's view, the primacy given to incomes policy has meant that wage increases have been largely unrelated to industrial productivity, while increased provision has been made for subsidizing the economically inactive through increased welfare expenditure.

The difficulty in Finnish circumstances of reconciling conflicts at both the parliamentary and the corporate level has brought into play the third new element in the situation since the late 1960s, namely, the central role played by the President as mediator and consensus-builder. The roots of his authority were traced in an earlier context (see chapter 4); the consolidation of his authority was marked by the passage in January 1973 of an Enabling Act extending his term of office for a further four years without recourse to the popular elections prescribed by the Constitution. This measure had the support of all the major parties, including the Conservatives, and of a total of 170 out of the 200 members of the *Eduskunta*. A similarly proportioned majority subsequently entrenched him in power in the 1978 presidential elections.

One or two illustrations may be given of Kekkonen's active role in policy-making. In 1972, for example, he desired to secure a majority government in order to underwrite the free-trade agreement which had been negotiated with the EEC. This involved resolving a protracted controversy over a pensions reform. When the Centre Party proved the stumbling-block in the way of a settlement, the President took the unprecedented step of playing an unheralded visit to their party executive meeting, at which he stated that failure to co-operate would be likely to prejudice their prospects of office. This worked. It may be noted in passing that the President had been able to enlist the help of interest-group leaders in working towards a solution of the pensions crisis, having two years earlier reponded to their request for aid in salvaging the incomes policy system. Again, in 1975 he used his authority to shape a five-party coalition to fight rising unemployment, bringing an ex-Centre Party provincial governor back into the political mainstream in order to resolve a deadlock between the prospective core coalition partners. Not only were all five party leaders invited to the presidential palace for discussions after it had been widely assumed that the Civil Service caretaker Cabinet would carry on, but the mass media were also invited to witness the proceedings. Many other examples of presidential intervention could be cited: suffice it to say here that Kekkonen came to be regarded as the arbiter of last resort when deadlock was reached and unhesitatingly used the prestige gained from his conduct of foreign affairs to steer politicians towards solutions regarded by himself as being in the national interest within the very broad limits set by the parliamentary situation.

In summary, the growth of consultative mechanisms in the corporate sector in Finland has a fragile infrastructure and an uncertain future. The full reincorporation of the radical left into political life, which facilated that growth, has entailed to date a threat to consensus on the first dimension because of an evident desire to exlude the Conservatives from office. The principle of fair play is one factor behind recent increases in the Conservative vote. What effect would a continuing increase in that vote have upon the more concertative style of policy-making that has emerged in recent years? Looking at the Finnish political scene in broad perspective, the system may be said to have become, on balance, slightly more consensual as a result of the operation of the three new factors outlined above. But the balance is a precarious one. A diet of 'ideological porridge' appears inescapable, anyway in the foreseeable future.

## ICELAND

As in Finland, the concertation of policy is forced upon Icelandic elites because of the lack of a single-party majority. But a measure of co-operation is necessary because in Iceland labour-market conflicts are frequent, and a major cause of these is the state of the economy. The oil price rises of the 1970s had a severe effect upon general price levels, especially as supplies were brought from the USSR on unfavourable terms; the general indexation of wages and prices has been a force working in the same direction; and full employment in a primary economy has produced a tendency to seek leap-frogging increases of wages above the automatic adjustment levels. These were among the factors which caused the currency to lose more than fifteen times its base value between 1967 and 1980 and induced a rate of inflation which was running at between 50 and 60 per cent for much of the latter part of the 1970s. Each of the major parties, moreover, has affiliations with the labour movement; collective bargaining is based upon agreements between individual unions and employers, with the umbrella Icelandic Federation of Labour having only such residual powers as are agreed by the member unions; and the machinery for regulating conflict in this sector (legally binding agreements, a Labour Court for the interpretation of disputes, etc.) has functioned creakily and intermittently under the severe economic pressures. So here again it has often fallen to the parliamentary parties to seek concerted action in order to resolve deadlocks, although in this case, unlike that of Finland, there has been no pattern of presidential intervention to pull the chestnuts out of the fire.

More coalitions have disintegrated over economic policy than from any other cause in the years since full independence (1944): even so, the rate of turnover has not been nearly as high as in Finland, as table 5.2 makes clear. Each of the four major parties in the system has collaborated in government with each of the others at one time or another, although since 1947 the right-of-centre Independence Party has never been in office together with the radical leftist People's Alliance. These two occupy opposite ends of the political spectrum on matters of foreign and security policy, as well as on domestic economic policy.

Thus the People's Alliance opposes both membership of NATO and the US base at Keflavik; the Progressives oppose the second but not the first; and the Social Democrats unite with the Independence Party in supporting both. So each party at either end of the spectrum has held office at different times with one or other, or both, of the parties in the middle. With four-fifths of the electorate regarding membership of NATO as important for the country's security, the People's Alliance has never held the premiership nor the Ministry for Foreign Affairs. Its strand of fiercely independent nationalism — it has, for example, no organizational links with Moscow — did, however, make it a natural choice for the Ministry of Fisheries when in coalition during the Cod Wars (1956–8 and 1974–8).

A few illustrations may be given of the nature of inter-party conflict over the management of economic policy. The Progressives, in government in 1958, brought in an imports surcharge and asked the union to defer their subsequent demand for compensation for the rising cost of living. When the unions proved unwilling, the Social Democrats and the People's Alliance, who were also in the government, published their own plan for subsidies to counter rising costs, and the Cabinet fell. In 1979 a similarly constituted coalition saw the People's Alliance minuting open disagreement with the proposals of its partners to set ceilings for wage increases and to cut some welfare benefits as inflationary pressures remained high. The Progressives in the same government sought to put through a ban on strikes for the second half of the year: in the spring there had been a lengthy seaman's strike, a strike by dairymen and another by civil servants when the rank and file rejected a salary agreement which had been negotiated between the government and the relevant union. Neither the Social Democrats nor the People's Alliance would support legislation to ban strike action, and in October the Social Democrats withdrew from the coalition and eventually precipitated the first mid-winter election in the country's history.

To sum up, various parliamentary combinations have sought, as in Denmark, to remedy the intense conflict in the labour market through the concertation of package deals. These package deals have derived legitimacy from being backed by a parliamentary majority which, under PR, reflects a majority in the country at large. Coalitions at the parliamentary level, moreover, have tended to produce mirror-image coalitions at interest-organization and local-government levels (Grimsson, 1977, *passim*). The parties of the left, as one might expect, have been readier than the non-socialist parties to envisage price freezes, increases in direct

TABLE 5.2: NORDIC GOVERNMENTS 1945–82: PRIME MINISTERS AND PARTY COMPOSITION

| Year | Denmark | Finland | Iceland | Norway | Sweden |
|---|---|---|---|---|---|
| 1945 | V. Buhl (*Soc. Dem.*) National unity coalition<br>K. Kristensen *Liberal* minority | J. K. Paasikivi National unity coalition | Olafur Thors *Independence*/ *Progressive*/ People's Alliance | E. Gerhardsen (A) National unity coalition<br>E. Gerhardsen *Lab.* majority | Per Albin Hansson (*Soc. Dem.*) National unity coalition<br>Per Albin Hansson *Soc. Dem.* |
| 1946 | | M. Pekkala Left–Centre | | | T. Erlander *Soc. Dem.* |
| 1947 | H. Hedtoft *Soc. Dem.* minority | | Stefan Stefansson *Soc. Dem.*/Progressive/ Independence | | |
| 1948 | | K. A. Fagerholm *Soc. Dem.* minority | | | |
| 1949 | | | Olafur Thors *Independence* minority | | |
| 1950 | E. Eriksen *Lib.*–Con. minority coalition | U. K. Kekkonen Centre, later Centre–Soc. Dem., then Centre | Steingrimur Steinthorsson *Progressive*/Independence | | |
| 1951 | | | | O. Torp *Lab.* majority | |
| 1953 | H. Hedtoft *Soc. Dem.* minority | S. Tuomioja Non-party | Olafur Thors *Independence*/Progressive | | T. Erlander *Soc. Dem.*–Agr. coalition |

Table 5.2 continued

| Year | Denmark | Finland | Iceland | Norway | Sweden |
|---|---|---|---|---|---|
| 1954 | | R. Törngren<br>Centre–Soc. Dem.<br>U. K. Kekkonen<br>Centre–Soc. Dem. | | | |
| 1955 | H. C. Hansen<br>*Soc. Dem.* minority | | | | |
| 1956 | | K. A. Fagerholm<br>Soc. Dem.–Centre | Hermann Jonasson<br>*Progressive*/Soc. Dem./<br>PA | E. Gerhardsen<br>*Lab.* majority | |
| 1957 | H. C. Hansen<br>*Soc. Dem.*/RV/<br>Justice majority<br>coalition | V. J. Sukselainen<br>Centre, later<br>Centre–Left<br>R. von Fieandt<br>Non-party | | | T. Erlander<br>*Soc. Dem.* |
| 1958 | | R. Kuuskoski<br>Non-party<br>K. A. Fagerholm<br>Soc. Dem.–Centre–Right | Emil Jonsson<br>*Soc. Dem.* minority | | |
| 1959 | | V. J. Sukselainen<br>Centre minority | Olafur Thors<br>*Independence*/Soc. Dem. | | |

Table 5.2 continued

| Year | Denmark | Finland | Iceland | Norway | Sweden |
|---|---|---|---|---|---|
| 1960 | V. Kampmann *Soc. Dem.*/RV/Justice majority coalition  V. Kampmann *Soc. Dem.*–RV majority coalition | | | | |
| 1961 | | M. Miettunen Centre minority | | E. Gerhardsen *Lab.* minority | |
| 1962 | J. O. Krag *Soc. Dem.*–RV majority coalition | A. Karjalainen Centre–Right | | | |
| 1963 | | R. Lehto Non-party | | J. Lyng (*Cons.*) Non-soc. minority coalition  E. Gerhardsen *Lab.* minority | |
| 1964 | J. O. Krag *Soc. Dem.* minority | J. Virolainen Centre–Right | Bjarni Benediktsson *Independence*/Soc. Dem. | | |
| 1965 | | | | P. Borten (*Cp*) Non-socialist majority coalition | |
| 1966 | | R. Paasio Left–Centre | | | |

Table 5.2 continued

| Year | Denmark | Finland | Iceland | Norway | Sweden |
|---|---|---|---|---|---|
| 1968 | H. Baunsgaard Con./V/RV majority coalition | M. Koivisto Left—Centre | | | |
| 1969 | | | | | O. Palme *Soc. Dem.* |
| 1970 | | T. Aura Non-party<br>A. Karjalainen Centre—Left | Johan Hafstein *Independence*/Soc. Dem. | | |
| 1971 | J. O. Krag *Soc. Dem.* minority | T. Aura Non-party | Olafur Johannesson *Progressive*/Lib. Left/ People's Alliance | T. Bratteli *Lab.* minority | |
| 1972 | A. Jørgensen *Soc. Dem.* minority | R. Paasio Soc. Dem. minority<br>K. Sorsa Soc. Dem.—Centre | | L. Korvald *Kr.F.*/Lib./Centre minority coalition | |
| 1973 | P. Hartling *Lib.* minority | | | T. Bratteli *Lab.* minority | |
| 1974 | | | Geir Hallgrimsson *Independence*/Progressive | | |

Table 5.2 continued

| Year | Denmark | Finland | Iceland | Norway | Sweden |
|---|---|---|---|---|---|
| 1975 | A. Jørgensen Soc. Dem. minority | K. Liinamaa Non-party M. Miettunen Centre –Left, then Centre coalition | | | |
| 1976 | | | | O. Nordli Lab. minority | T. Fälldin C/Fp./M majority coalition |
| 1977 | | K. Sorsa (Soc.) Left–Centre | | | |
| 1978 | A. Jørgensen Soc. Dem.–Lib. minority coalition | | Olafur Johannesson Progressive/Soc. Dem./PA | | O. Ullsten Fp. minority |
| 1979 | A. Jørgensen Soc. Dem. minority | M. Koivisto (Soc.) Centre–Left | Benedikt Gröndal Soc. Dem. minority | | T. Fälldin C/Fp./M majority coalition |
| 1981 | | | | Gro Harlem Brundtland Lab. minority Kåre Willoch Con. minority | T. Fälldin (C) Centre/Liberal minority |

*Table 5.2 continued*

The table shows the name of the Prime Minister of each government against the year of formation of the government, and is followed by the party composition of the government, with the Prime Minister's party underlined. Party abbreviations are as follows:

| | | | |
|---|---|---|---|
| *Denmark* | Soc. Dem. | Social Democrats | Socialdemokratiet |
| | RV | Radical Liberals | Det radikale Venstre |
| | Justice | Justice Party | Danmarks Retsforbund |
| | Lib. | Agrarian Liberals | Venstre, Danmarks liberale parti |
| | Con. | Conservatives | Det konservative folkeparti |
| *Finland* | Soc. | Finnish People's Democratic League | Suomen Kansan Demokraattinen Liitto |
| | Left | Social Democrats | Suomen Sosialidemokraattinen Puolue |
| | Agr. Centre | Agrarian, later Centre Party | Keskustapuolue |
| | Right | Coalition Party | Kansallinen Kokoomus |
| *Iceland* | PA | People's Alliance | Alþýðubandalagið |
| | Soc. Dem. | Social Democrats | Alþýðuflokkurinn |
| | Prog. | Progressive Party | Framsóknarflokkurinn |
| | Independence | Independence Party | Sjálfstæðisflokkurinn |
| *Norway* | A / Lab. | Labour Party | Det norske Arbeiderparti |
| | Lib. | Liberals (The Left) | Venstre |
| | Cp | Centre Party | Senterpartiet |
| | Kr.F. | Christian People's Party | Kristelig Folkeparti |
| | Cons | Conservatives (The Right) | Høyre |
| *Sweden* | Soc. Dem. | Social Democrats | Sveriges socialdemokratiska arbetareparti |
| | Agr. C | Agrarian, later Centre Party | Centerpartiet |
| | Fp | Liberals | Folkpartiet |
| | M. | Conservatives | Moderata samlingspartiet |

The term *coalition* here refers to a cabinet composed of two or more parties. The national unity coalitions of 1945 were cabinets comprising representatives from all the main parties, formed in the very uncertain circumstances of the time. *Majority* indicates that the cabinet had a parliamentary majority composed of the party or parties represented in the cabinet. *Minority* indicates that the party or parties represented in the cabinet had no such majority, instead obtaining support from one or more of the parliamentary groups not represented in the cabinet.

taxation, subsidies and untaxed food as elements in their packages. The atmosphere of economic crisis has been even more acute than in Denmark, at least over the past decade and a half, and the intensity of inter-party conflict has also been higher. In part this greater intensity of conflict owes something to the fact that the Social Democratic party does not occupy the same key strategic point in the system, nor does it command as wide a measure of cross-party support in the electorate for the initiation of package deals, as does its Danish counterpart; in part also it derives from the comparative strength of a radical left party which is much more reluctant than the other parties in the system to attempt the pursuit of an incomes policy.

This last point should not be exaggerated, however. For one thing, the device of minuting opposition while in government has enabled the People's Alliance to keep its own following happy at times while preserving co-operation over part of the field. More significantly, the party has in fact participated in a good many package deals. Thus, to take a recent example, in 1980 it helped to bring about wage settlements that were marginally below the level of a mediation offer accepted by the Labour Federation as a norm, in exchange for improvements in pensions and settlements for the most poorly paid that were slightly higher than average. In the Grøndal coalition, for the first time ever, it holds the Ministry of Finance and is participating in continuing collective efforts to make the economy 'inflation-resistant' by coupling index-linking (including, for example, bank loans and deposits) with adjustments to the currency exchange rate and the rejection of wage increases over and above those springing from the operation of indexation.

## NORWAY AND SWEDEN

Turning now to Norway and Sweden, the traditional picture of these two political systems may first be briefly sketched to provide a background for an analysis of the changes that have been taking place in both countries since the 1960s. That picture is one of a low intensity of conflict, together with highly effective machinery for conflict resolution. The predominant style of policy-making is seen as concertative and deliberative, and the level of inter-elite agreement is high.

One of the underlying causes of the emergence of this picture has been the structure of the party systems, which has facilitated stable, single-party government for long periods of time. The dominant Labour and Social Democratic parties have, moreover, cultivated a strong cross-class appeal, in competition with that of the non-socialist parties, for the growing tertiary sector vote, and they have in general been strongly in favour of the retention of a mixed economy. The parties of the radical left have been weak and have usually been prepared to sustain the moderate left in power for fear of worse befalling (there was a brief exception to this rule in Norway in 1963). The farmers' parties, again, have been smaller and less strategically placed than those, for example, in Finland, and they have also declined more speedily in terms of their rural base. Consequently, the conflict of producer and consumer interests has not been as salient as in Finland.

All these factors have contributed to the smooth running of concertative mechanisms in the two political systems. Thus Norwegian experience prompted Stein Rokkan to evolve the concept of a corporate channel of representation playing a crucial role in the formulation of economic policy (Rokkan, 1966): the debt owed to his analysis by the present survey is clear enough. Rokkan saw corporatism in the Norwegian system as implicit, latent and unofficial (ibid., p. 113) but concluded that many years of uneventful bargaining around a table were likely to have lasting effects. A later, extended analysis of the Norwegian system along the same lines alluded to the need for a more competitive political process to counter the 'excesses' of corporate pluralism (Kvavik, 1976, p. 164). Shortly afterwards appeared a study of 'consensual unified elites' in Norway, largely conducted in terms of an update of the 'end of ideology' argument in a post-industrial society (Higley *et al.*, 1976): in the closing sections of this study some consideration is given to the threats to system maintenance that arose out of political developments in the 1970s.

In both Norway and Sweden, as table 5.2 shows, the incidence of strikes in the industrial sector has been low. All groups except those on the numerically weak radical left have been in favour of stable and centralized procedures for wage-bargaining. In Norway successive governments have pursued limited forms of incomes policy (Elvander, 1974a, pp. 422–5). In Sweden, on the other hand, the tradition had developed of *voluntary* collective agreements between both sides of industry and without state intervention. Recession in the 1970s, however, began to draw Swedish governments into the bargaining process through such devices as background adjustments to the tax system. Recession in the 1980s has both badly affected the strike figures for Sweden and made the collective bargaining machinery there much more difficult to operate (this point will be taken up again later).

In Sweden especially, commissions of inquiry are used extensively for the concertation of views in advance of reforms. The comparatively small size of Ministries and the decentralized nature of the administrative system make the recourse to such commissions essential to the shaping of most legislative projects. The tradition of including opposition MPs on these bodies became firmly established during the era of minority parliamentarism in the 1920s and persisted during the long period of Social Democratic ascendency. This both helped to reconcile the opposition parties to their long spell out of office by giving them a share in the making of public policy and also did something to promote continuities of policy when a change of regime occurred. Commissions of inquiry also play a crucial role in policy formulation in Finland, it may be added, because administrative structures follow the Swedish pattern – which helps to explain Sorsa's stricture on them (see p. 160). In Denmark and Norway concertation in the formulation of legislative projects takes place more in departmental advisory committees, although in Denmark, for example, almost a third of the government's Bills in the 1972–4 period were considered in commissions of inquiry with external actors on them (Damgaard and Eliasson, 1980, p. 108).

As Richard Chapman has observed 'every problem and every decision in public administration is peculiar. There is no one, obvious, accepted "governmental process" to which all specific cases conform' (Chapman, 1968, p. 8). Nevertheless, the weight attaching to commissions of inquiry, particularly in the Swedish case, has contributed to a dominant policy-making style that is extraordinarily deliberative, rationalistic, open (in the sense that all interested parties are consulted in advance of a decision) and consensual (the agreement of all is sought) – the epithets are taken from Anton's survey of the phenomenon (1969, p. 94). Representatives of interest groups are frequently to be found serving on these commissions, as well as MPs from the opposition parties, as already mentioned. The significance of opposition representatives is clearly going to increase when a minority government is in office (as in Sweden in 1981 and in Finland intermittently). Again, in such circumstances parliamentary committees become another important arena for brokerage. MPs serving on commissions of inquiry can, moreover, draw upon the expertise acquired through their work on specialist parliamentary committees to buttress an argument in the face of interest-group and Civil Service representatives. Commissions deliberate in secret, which helps to reduce partisan pressures, and they publish lengthy and detailed reports. These are then circulated 'on *remiss*' to all interested public agencies and private organizations for open-minuted comment. At the end of this process the Bill which is presented to Parliament contains a conscientious summary of what has gone before and may well run to several hundred pages in length.

All of the factors enumerated above helped to make major political confrontations rare events in both Norway and Sweden during the period of majority rule by the Labour and Social Democratic parties. When the Labour Party in Norway had a clear majority in Parliament, its enactments commanded a wide measure of cross-party assent. It was rather as if a prolonged period of 'Butskellism' prevailed, but the centre ground was left of centre by British and American standards. The consensus included, for example, a period of strict economic planning in the interests of post-war national reconstruction. Agreement here was aided by the camaraderie between political leaders that stemmed from the common experience of wartime exile in London. The consensus also included a nationalization programme (e.g. chemicals, aluminium manufacture) which, though modest by British standards, was extensive by those of Scandinavia and which resulted, by 1977, in a tenth of total sales in Norway being accounted for by state-owned companies (Elvander, 1979a, p. 33). Much of this programme, however, was devised in the same spirit of pragmatic nationalism as earlier non-socialist ventures in the same direction had been.

In Sweden two major political confrontations can be discerned in the post-war period up to the 1970s. One arose in 1944 in connection with the adoption by the Social Democrats of a radical party programme envisaging measures of nationalization: when this showed signs of becoming a political liability, it was quietly shelved. The second major conflict, much more spectacular, centred on what might at first be thought to be the rather uninspiring issue of supplementary pensions schemes. At the heart of the controversy was a plan which had originated among the unions and had eventually been sponsored by the Social Democratic Party. It involved guaranteeing all workers, blue-collar and white-collar alike, a pension equivalent to well over half their wages during the most productive years of their working life. So the 1956—60 period saw the collapse of the Social Democratic—Agrarian coalition, a referendum on the issue of pensions and a quite exceptional mid-term election. The intensity of the conflict owed something to the fact that the reform entailed giving the state a great and growing share of the capital market through the use of pension funds. In Norway, by way of contrast, the incoming non-socialist coalition of 1965—71 took over and passed a pensions reform along similar lines, which had been introduced by the preceding Labour administration.

A first look was taken in chapter 1 at the readiness of the Swedish Social Democrats and labour unions to work with an overwhelmingly large private productive sector of the economy, characterized, it may be added, by a high degree of concentration of individual ownership. The extent of consensus about economic structures can be seen from a scrutiny of labour market policy. LO's strategy, evolved by Gösta Rehn within the research department, was to promote industrial efficiency by encouraging labour mobility from low-profit sectors to growth areas. To this end large and growing sums of money were devoted to retraining schemes, financial incentives to move, the provision of new housing stock, etc. The administration of the policy was vested in a Labour Market Board; its members, drawn from both sides of industry and from other interest organizations (e.g. agricultural ones), outnumbered the state representatives, who held 'the chairmanship and deputy chairmanship. But since the Board was granted considerable discretionary powers, the chairmanship was held by a staunch supporter of the Social Democratic Party. The consistent aim of the labour movement was to promote a general levelling-up of wage rates.

Again, the tripartite non-socialist coalition which came to power in Sweden under Fälldin in 1976 sustained and greatly expanded labour market expenditure, particularly on training schemes, in order to keep employment figures up at a time of recession. So keenly was this line pursued, indeed, that workers were increasingly being paid to stay where they were (sometimes receiving training without producing anything) or else to move to places producing unwanted products, and all the while the already swollen public sector of employment (service, local government, etc.) was taking up more and more of the manpower slack. This basic continuity of policy was, of course, popular with the unions and helped to establish a favourable climate for appeals for wage restraint in successive rounds of collective bargaining. The same was true of the efforts made by non-socialist administrations to pick up the pieces when recession hit the long-established basic industries — shipbuilding, iron and steel and, to a lesser extent, forest products. Not only was extensive state aid given to the declining sectors, but also a large programme of state take-overs was implemented.

There is, then, plenty of evidence to support the proposition that both Norway and Sweden have been characterized by high and persistent levels of consensus on both the second and the third dimensions. Equally, however, there is evidence to support the proposition that levels of political conflict have been rising during the past decade and that the traditional picture of these two political systems now stands in need of some revision. A useful framework for analysing recent developments is provided by the study of political cleavage lines in both countries that was carried out by Petersson and Valen (1979), in which a close kinship was discovered between both systems.

The general balance of the votes cast for socialists and non-socialists is strikingly similar in each case, and that balance is a fine one. The main areas of political dispute centre on socio-economic differences, as one would expect from the nature of the party structure. More specifically, the polar opposites in both systems include, notably, governmental versus private control of the economy; industrial growth and centralization versus environmental protection and decentralization; conservatives versus liberals on cultural and moral questions. Conflict along each of these axes, it may be added, has intensified in each country during the past decade. At the same time, a tendency for the lines of division to cross-cut one another has introduced elements of indeterminacy into the fundamental left—right bipolar cleavage (a closer look at one aspect of the Swedish case is taken in Elder, 1979a).

The cleavage on the general issue of public versus private control of the economy may first be considered. The process of polarization has been less marked in this respect in Norway than in Sweden, but it is still evident. Thus the Labour Party, with the support of the radical left, put a majority of parliamentary and local politicians on to the governing boards of the commercial banks in 1978 in the name of the extension of democratic principle. This measure met with solid opposition from all the non-socialist parties, which objected to the fact that the shareholders were being put into a minority position as well as to the costly financial compensation involved in what was seen as a doctrinaire exercise. Similarly, the non-socialist parties have opposed changes in the balance of representation on company boards in favour of the workforce. Currently there is likely to be a majority in the *Storting* in favour of cutting the dominance of the nationalized Statoil company in the exploitation of North Sea oil reserves and of giving private firms a larger share. On questions of this type there is not much evidence for the continued existence of Lijphart's 'coalescent elite behaviour', and policy reversals of the kind familiar in adversary political systems are in prospect.

In Sweden controversy on the axis of public versus private control of the economy has centred on 'worker fund' schemes. The original impulse here came from the powerful Metalworkers' Union in 1971: the intention was to earmark 'surplus profits' for funding in pursuit of an egalitarian wages policy. Rudolf Meidner, the LO economist, then drew up a detailed plan which was enthusiastically endorsed by the LO Congress in 1976. Briefly, a percentage of profits made by firms was to be used for share purchases through union-administered funds. Thus besides the original motive there was now an explicit intention to counteract private concentrations of power and ownership and to effect a decisive, if gradual, shift in industrial power relationships in favour of the unions. All the non-socialist parties united in opposition to the Meidner plan at the 1976 elections. The issue helped them to victory, for the Social Democrats, unlike LO, wanted time for reflection before committing themselves, and the labour movement entered the fray on a note of disunity. Since then both wings have taken pains to concert action and a joint Social Democratic–LO scheme was evolved in spring 1981, which was submitted to the scrutiny of the respective Congresses. With the deepening of the recession, the emphasis has shifted to the provision of capital resources for industrial investment. But the allocation of one-fifth of all profits in excess of 15–20 per cent forms a part of the latest scheme, and the new proviso that increased supplementary pensions charges would help to speed up the process of share purchase can be viewed as a radicalization of the original Meidner plan. All the non-socialist parties are strongly opposed to the latest scheme; all have brought out their own alternatives.

The course of this controversy in Sweden to date prompts a wider reflection. The emergence of highly charged political issues is apt to show up the limitations of concertative mechanisms. The Social Democratic government of the day set up a commission of inquiry into worker funds in 1975, with the support of the Liberals. At the time (1973–6) a most peculiar parliamentary situation prevailed: the socialist and non-socialist parties were tied in the *Riksdag* at 175 members apiece. Minor matters were settled by the simple expedient of drawing lots: on major issues – such as the pursuit of wage restraint – the government was obliged to shop around for support. The emergence of the Meidner plan immediately polarized opinion on the matter of worker funds. The commission of inquiry soldiered on for six years with three different chairmen – Mehr, Larsson, Öhman – but eventually, in spring 1981, recognized that no agreement was possible and presented a report merely setting out alternatives with the supporting arguments for them.

It should be stressed that the terms of reference and the composition of commissions of inquiry are settled by the government of the day and are subject to wide variation at governmental discretion. Interest-group representatives, for example, are usually excluded from Swedish commissions on taxation matters. Such matters are thrashed out between party representatives, and the Social Democrats and LO naturally made most of the running during the years of Social Democratic ascendancy (Elvander, 1972). Interest groups get their say at the *remiss* stage, and their influence is then confined to technicalities.

A second axis of conflict marked by sharpening tensions during the past decade is that between the supporters of industrial growth and centralization and the supporters of environmental protection and decentralization. Here again, 'coalescent elite behaviour' has not been much in evidence. The nuclear power controversy in Sweden can be assigned to this category. Essentially, it ranged Social Democrats, Moderates and Liberals in the first-named camp against the Centre Party and Communist Left in the second. It contributed to the loss of power by the Social Democrats in 1976 and split the Fälldin I coalition government, composed of Centre Party, Moderates and Liberals, two years later. In December 1976 Fälldin set up an energy commission with a mixed all-party and expert membership to see if any measure of agreement could be reached on the issue. To the extent that any agreement was possible, it was an agreement to fudge matters. In February 1978 the commission finished work, presenting majority and minority reports along predictable party lines (Vedung, 1979, pp. 30—2). But it could be argued that at least the commission secured a respite for the hard-pressed government. In March 1980 the whole matter was, for the time being at least, taken off the political agenda by recourse to a referendum. The news of the Harrisburg incident in the USA sent tremors through those parties which favoured the continuation of the Swedish nuclear power programme, and the Social Democrats found general support when they suggested that the people should be asked to decide the issue. It had proved too divisive for the established parties and for the usual concertative mechanisms to handle. (The referendum, it may be added, enabled the reactor-building programme to go ahead on a 58.2 per cent vote for the combined 'yes' alternatives.)

The great debate over the question of whether Norway should enter the Common Market may also be assigned, at least in part, to the same general category. This conflict was certainly one of high intensity, and, interestingly, it provided an example of an ad hoc cause group which both deviated from the prevailing corporate pluralist mould and exercised a major influence over the course of events. This was the People's Movement against the Common Market, whose long campaign had much to do with the 53.5 per cent 'no' vote which settled the issue at the September 1972 referendum (the participation figure, incidentally, was 79.2 per cent, as compared with 74.3 per cent in the Swedish nuclear power referendum). Here also one could argue that the issue proved too divisive for the established parties to handle. Certainly, it debilitated the Labour Party for some years and ranged the Centre Party and the Christian People's Party in alliance with the radical left against the Conservatives and the larger part of the Labour Party (Allen, 1979). The line-up here bore some resemblance to that which was brought about in Sweden by the nuclear power controversy. But in neither instance did a permanent realignment of the party system occur, although the Norwegian Liberals were particularly hard-hit and fragmented into two minuscule groupings.

The third and final line of cleavage in the Norwegian and Swedish political systems, it may be recalled, is that between conservatives and liberals on cultural and moral questions. This particular divide has greater salience in Norway, where the conservatives are more numerous and politically more influential, but it is still a lively source of conflict and debate in both countries. In Sweden it has perhaps the greater propensity to divide parties internally. In Norway disagreement over the matter of abortion law reform prevented the formation of a non-socialist coalition government after Labour's defeat at the polls in the September 1981 elections. Neither the Christian People's Party nor the Liberals could resolve their differences with the Conservatives on this question, for the differences were on a matter of principle. Confusingly, of course, the Liberal stance was conservative in this connection, and the Conservative stance was liberal. In the event a Conservative minority administration took office with the prospect of support from the other non-socialist parties on every issue save this one. Debates about temperance legislation, it may be said in this general context, also tend to produce intense conflicts of principle.

The past decade has seen a heightening of conflict intensity on each of the three lines of cleavage charted in the Petersson—Valen survey of the Norwegian and Swedish political systems. Furthermore, the deepening recession has made the machinery for conflict resolution in the industrial sector harder for non-socialist governments in Sweden to manage. In Norway, of course, the prosperity caused by oil revenues has provided a cushion against trouble, and in any case Labour held office from 1973 to 1981.

In Sweden the oil price rises of 1979 complicated matters immensely for the Fälldin II tripartite non-socialist coalition. The indexation of wages and salaries for tax purposes against inflation, which had been put through by the Fälldin I government, was unpopular with the unions because it widened differentials. Little or no room for manoeuvre now existed for the coalition to provide anything in the way of a *quid pro quo* for the workforce in return for wage restraint. The unemployment figures showed an upward trend, and cuts in public expenditure were felt to be inescapable.

At this point reference should be made to another finding of the Petersson—Valen survey: the existence of a large majority in the electorates of both Norway and Sweden in favour of the reduction of taxes on low incomes and of further equalization of incomes and conditions of work. Early in 1981 the Fälldin coalition came up with a proposal for tax reform which owed much to Moderate wishes for the encouragement of incentive and contained little or nothing to benefit those in low-income brackets. The redistributive effects of tax policies generate more intense conflict when times are hard, and the Centre Party leadership in particular faced difficulties in getting the package accepted by its rank and file. In April 1981 the coalition disintegrated on the issue. The Centre Party and the Liberals came to an accommodation with the Social Democrats to postpone a general tax reform until after the 1982 elections and then to fund it out of increased employers' contributions or a 'production factor tax' (this last was an old Social Democratic idea). The Moderates withdrew from the coalition in high dudgeon but did not seek to overthrow the minority government of Centre Party and Liberals that remained: the Social Democrats were riding high in the public opinion polls.

At first sight, perhaps, this episode appears to provide an illustration of the working of the old injunction from American political life 'If you can't beat 'em, join 'em.' But matters are not quite so simple. This is in part an example of conflict over socio-economic issues cross-cutting the socialist/non-socialist cleavage between governmental versus private control of the economy. A strong element of indeterminacy has re-entered the political scene. For one thing, the course of events will make it harder for the Social Democrats to attack the centre parties at forthcoming elections. By the same token, it will keep open the possibility of polarization over the 'worker fund' issue. A markedly egalitarian majority sentiment is not necessarily convertible into a majority in favour of the radical reform of socio-economic structures.

How far the 'worker fund' scheme in fact poses a threat to the continuation of the mixed economy in Sweden remains, however, something of an open question — to revert to a leading theme in Marquis W. Childs's (1980) reflections upon recent Swedish political developments. Certainly, Olof Palme is at pains to point out that no such threat exists, but it would certainly be no exaggeration to say that in connection with the issue a certain lack of clarity is currently discernible within the labour movement as a whole. Perhaps consensus will yet prevail and the voters will not be called upon to make a choice, but on the whole consensualism in both Norway and Sweden has receded in the last decade, and the voters have had more choices to make than for a long time past. Meanwhile it should be said that in Denmark the 'worker fund' issue has polarized opinion along the socialist/non-socialist line of cleavage. But the advocates of reform have not been able to win a parliamentary majority for it, and the matter was shelved again in 1981 for this reason.

This chapter may conclude with some necessarily brief observations, at a more general level, designed to answer the question 'So what?' raised in chapter 1 in connection with our three-dimensional scheme for the analysis of consensualism in a liberal democratic state.

The lack of consensualism on the second dimension may threaten consensus on the first (and most critical) dimension. This would occur if a party were to become so firmly convinced of the importance and rightness of its cause that it sought to deny its opponents the chance of a period in power.

A contrast, sometimes explicit and sometimes implicit, is drawn in the foregoing analysis between adversary and consensual systems in terms of our second and third dimensions. Adversary systems are, of course, consensual in some degree on both dimensions: they may even be consensual in high degree in some respects on both. For example, the concertation of policy (the third dimension) occurs in the British system when both the main contending parties recognize that there is some transcendent national advantage to be gained from resolving their differences over a particular issue. It has happened, for example, in connection with race relations legislation and again, to some degree, at least, with the problem of Northern Ireland. But such concertation is exceptional in this kind of system: for example, the shaping of economic policy is much less concertative in Britain than in Scandinavia.

On the second dimension too an adversarial system *may* be much more consensual than at first appears. One thinks here of the degree of ideological unity between the great American parties, in some respects so great as to give rise to the danger that grievances may be denied access to the system and categories of social groups alienated. But, of course, the differences between parties can be sharp, for example on the dimension of governmental versus private power.

Again, the policy gap between parties may be based on ideology or on conflicts of socio-economic interest in varying degrees and combinations. On the whole interests are more susceptible to concertation on the third dimension than are ideological differences. They *may* involve zero-sum-type conflict, as so often with producer/consumer conflicts in Finland, but in general they can be settled by horse-trading, which may be regarded as a form of concertation. Ideological conflicts tend to be more refractory, involving as they do matters of principle and values.

Finally, except in the extreme situation outlined in the first point of this short résumé, the matter of choosing between an adversary and a consensual system may be regarded in terms of cost-benefit analysis, so to speak. The costs of adversary politics *tend* to be higher because of policy reversals; on the other hand, the articulation of issues tends to be less satisfactory under a consensual system in terms of voter choice. So it might be suggested that at the time of writing Britain scores low in terms of consensualism on both the second and the third dimensions and as far as the long-established parties are concerned. The German Federal Republic has scored high on these dimensions in this same respect since Bad Godesberg and the introduction of concertation on economic policy (characteristically, by law) under the Grand Coalition, but there are reservations in other respects. France would seem to score low on both these dimensions at the parliamentary level, high on the third in the corporate channel because of the planning mechanisms, but the statist tradition reduces the policy gap somewhat on the second dimension and the imperfectly balanced weight of the participants has hitherto made concertation in the corporate channel less satisfactory than it might appear. In the USA the score must be high on both dimensions, despite the presence of an adversary system — with, however, some reservations about, for example, group alienation and industrial conflict.

CHAPTER SIX

# Regional Co-operation and International Roles

> Traditionally, each Nordic country is accustomed
> to taking the others into account in its decisions.
>
> *President Urho Kekkonen, Speech at the Swedish*
> *Institute of International Affairs, 8 May 1978*

This chapter has a dual mandate: to examine the nature of regional cooperation between the five Nordic states and to consider the role of Scandinavia as an international actor. The first section considers whether the consensualism of the respective national policy arenas has found parallel expression at the regional level. Has the undoubted sense of regional affinity, in short, been translated into a high degree of political integration in terms of *de jure* machinery for joint policy-making? There follows an examination of the part that the Scandinavian states play on the world stage and, in particular, of the question of whether the region performs a distinctive role in international affairs. Notwithstanding an historic sense of identity and the realization of extensive cross-national harmonization in certain legislative areas, it is argued that political integration has advanced less in northern than in western Europe, despite the greater socio-cultural diversity of the latter and its record of recent military conflict. Thus there is no elected regional Parliament or commitment to a united federal state of Scandinavia. Even so, through such means as détente initiatives and Third World development aid programmes, together with wholehearted support for the work of the United Nations, the Nordic countries have been engaged in a search for moral power — partly for its own sake but also, more important, in order to make a contribution towards enhancing global security and stablizing international relations.

Before enlarging upon these propositions, three facets of regional consensus warrant initial identification. First, there has been *consensus that within the context of differential security demands and commitments, the Nordic nations should weigh the implications of their individual actions for the collective interests of the region and the maintainance of the so-called Nordic Balance*, i.e. a strongly armed and neutral Sweden, flanked on one side by Finland, linked through treaty to the Soviet Union, and, on the other, by the two NATO members, Norway and Denmark. In the post-war era the Nordic states have found themselves situated in an exposed position on the strategic frontier between East and West, defending two focal points: the North Cape and the Baltic Straits. None has been more vulnerable than Finland, the only pluralist democracy within the Soviet sphere of military influence, obliged by an agreement of 1948 to prevent any attack on the Soviet Union through her territory. With the Germans specifically mentioned as potential aggressors, it has been of paramount importance both to Finnish and to Nordic security to ensure that the spectre of renewed German militarism remains permanently banished. It is in this light that Norway's repeated refusal to allow West German combat troops to take part in NATO exercises on her soil must be viewed.

Sensitivity to, and sympathy for, the differential security demands of fellow states in the region has involved acceptance of the need to maintain national control over the management of foreign and defence policy — the area of what Nils Ørvik has described as 'high politics' (Nils Ørvik, 1974). Thus it has been conventional to preclude matters of foreign and defence policy from the agenda of the Nordic Council which was founded in 1952. As S. V. Anderson has noted, 'while there is no limitation on topics which the Council may consider, fundamental differences in foreign policy among the member nations have led to the selective exclusion of that subject from the Council agenda . . . . with rare exceptions, proposals touching on extra-Scandinavian political and military topics simply have not been introduced' (Anderson, 1967, p. 103). The Finns, in fact, gave formal expression to this restriction, stating in 1955, the year before their accession, that if the Council, contrary to established practice, should proceed to consider questions of national defence or issues involving the taking of positions in the conflict of interests between the Great Powers they would abstain on these matters. Indeed, when early in 1981 an apparently forgetful Finnish Prime Minister suggested a special annual sitting of the Nordic Council to debate foreign and defence questions, the proposal was vetoed by his own Foreign Secretary! There is a sense, of course, in which the notion of the Nordic Balance is less a consciously evolved design than an '*ex post facto* rationalization' of national policies (Ulstein, 1971). Yet the fact remains that the concept has come to symbolize a spirit of accommodation and the custom, as Kekkonen put it, of each Nordic country taking the others into account in its decisions.

The Nordic Balance, to be sure, has not escaped the tremor of events. The Finns, for example, have been particularly concerned of late about Norway's decision to store heavy US Marine brigade equipment on its territory. Indeed, this issue (its wider implications together with a range of contemporary foreign policy — though not, of course, security policy — questions) have been the subject of some interesting exchanges in the Nordic Council. At its annual spring session in Reykjavik in 1980 support for President Kekkonen's proposal of a nuclear-free Nordic area (unquestionably an attempt to change the Nordic Balance) from the Swedish Left-Communists was followed by criticism from the Finnish radical left of Norway's decision to accept US arms depots on her soil. This prompted a delegate of the Norwegian Conservatives to counter that he was singularly unsurprised that Russia's special friends should seek to defend her foreign policy. He flatly denied, moreover, that there was any aggressive intent behind Norway's agreement to store arms. Interestingly, when the retiring President of the Council, Palme, quoted with approval the statement of H. C. Hansen, the Danish Foreign Minister at the 1956 session, that 'foreign policy and defence questions are not part of the Council's competence' — a view supported by the then Finnish Prime Minister, Urho Kekkonen — it was, in fact, widely contested. Jørgensen, the Danish Prime Minister, then proceeded to announce that by invading Afghanistan, the USSR has become responsible for casting doubt upon the viability of détente, but he added that the Nordic states would continue to do their best to work for peace. The Nordic group of nations, in short, have been far from immune from internal tensions and friction on such matters of 'high politics'. What does need emphasis, however, is that outside the security policy arena, a second facet of consensus has been apparent — *overwhelming consensus in favour of preserving the appearance of regional unity wherever possible and conversely a propensity to avoid partial solutions when differences have seemed intractable*. Act together or not at all: this has seemed to be the operational maxim of Nordic cooperation. Thus in the 1950s a proposed Nordic Customs Union did not materialize without the reluctant Norway, while Finland's withdrawal in 1970 from a fresh attempt at a Customs Union, Nordek, did not presage the formation of a more limited Scandek, despite the Danish Prime Minister's avowed preference for such an outcome. Toivo Miljan has depicted this approach as 'consensualism of the lowest common denominator': when consensus is not possible for internal reasons, 'then collectively either no decision is made or the matter is kept alive and under discussion without positions being taken which could lead to conflict' (Miljan, 1977, p. 101).

Finally, beyond the regional arena there has been evidence of a third facet of consensus: *consensus that although they are small nations, the Nordic countries can play an active and not simply a reactive role in world affairs, directed towards the consolidation of international peace and stability*. It was no surprise perhaps that in 1981 former Swedish Prime Minister and Social Democratic leader, Olof Palme, headed an Independent Commission on Security and Disarmament with a worldwide composition, including the Soviet Union, as well as acting as the United Nations' official mediator in the war between Iran and Iraq. It is no surprise either that the peace movement is particularly strong in Scandinavia. When at the end of 1980 the veteran Swedish pacifist Alva Myrdal proposed that the neutral European states, including Sweden and Finland, should take the initiative in establishing a nuclear-free zone in Europe, the regional reponse at the sub-national level was so encouraging that the Norwegian Labour Party came out in favour despite Norway's NATO membership! Earlier the same year a peace petition organized by Nordic women was signed by half a million people in next to no time.

## REGIONAL CO-OPERATION IN SOCIAL AND ECONOMIC POLICY

To argue that a high degree of political integration in Scandinavia has been neither achieved nor desired is not to deny that there has been considerable progress in the regional co-operation and harmonization of legislation, particularly in the field of social policy. Attempts at broad-gauge economic planning however, have thus far proved abortive.

In 1947 a proposed Customs Union involving Denmark, Norway and Sweden produced twelve years of fitful and ultimately fruitless talks, even if the formation of Uniscan in 1949, with its multilateral co-ordination of economic policies, did point the way towards regional membership of EFTA ten years later (see table 6.1). Finland joined

TABLE 6.1: REGIONAL CO-OPERATION AND ACTIVE
NEUTRALITY: A CHRONOLOGY OF POST-WAR EVENTS

| | |
|---|---|
| 1945 | Denmark and Norway join United Nations as Charter Members |
| 1946 | Sweden becomes a member of the United Nations |
| 1947 | Proposed Customs Union between Denmark, Norway and Sweden |
| 1947 | Fenno-Soviet Commercial Agreement; Finland refuses Marshall Aid |
| 1948 | Fenno-Soviet Treaty of Friendship, Co-operation and Mutual Assistance |
| 1948 | Swedish proposal for a Scandinavian Defence Union |
| 1949 | Denmark and Norway join NATO |
| 1949 | Formation of Uniscan |
| 1949 | Norwegian note to Soviet Union: no foreign troops on her soil in peacetime |
| 1952 | Formation of the Nordic Council |
| 1953 | Denmark follows Norway in precluding foreign troops in peacetime |
| 1954 | Common Labour Market Treaty |
| 1955 | Russians return the Porkkala naval base near Helsinki to the Finns |
| 1956 | Finland becomes a member of the United Nations and the Nordic Council |
| 1957 | Denmark and Norway refuse to accept the stationing or stockpiling of tactical NATO atomic devices on their territories |
| 1959 | Foundation of the European Free Trade Association |
| 1961 | Finland makes special FinnEfta agreement with European Free Trade Association |
| 1963 | Finnish President Kekkonen proposes a Nordic nuclear-free zone |
| 1968 | Danish initiative on a Nordic Customs Union (Nordek) |
| 1970 | Finns reject Nordek but stage Strategic Arms Limitation Talks |
| 1971 | Amendment of the Statute of the Nordic Council to provide for a Council of Ministers |
| 1972 | Referendums on membership of the EEC: Danes 64% in favour, Norwegians 53.5% against |
| 1972 (July) | Sweden signs Free Trade Agreement with EEC |
| 1973 (April) | Norway signs Free Trade Agreement with EEC |
| 1973 | Finland's Free Trade Agreement with the EEC ratified followed by a Comecon agreement |
| 1974 | Nordic Convention on the Protection of the Environment |
| 1975 | Conference on European Security and Co-operation held in Helsinki |
| 1975 | Creation of a Budget Committee in the Nordic Council |

| | |
|---|---|
| 1976 | Establishment of the Nordic Investment Bank |
| 1978 | Kekkonen renews appeal for a Nordic nuclear-free zone |
| 1979 | Danish People's Movement Against the EEC polls 20.9% of vote and 4 seats in the European Parliament following first direct elections |
| 1980 | Sweden offers to host a European Disarmament Conference |
| 1981 | Olof Palme, former Swedish Prime Minister, acts as official United Nations mediator in war between Iran and Iraq |

the latter by special agreement two years thereafter, in 1961. The Finnish position was extremely delicate. Required to pay a war indemnity to the Soviet Union largely in terms of heavy goods and machinery, Finland had signed a Commercial Agreement giving the USSR 'most-favoured nation' status. Indeed, it may be, as Max Jakobson has claimed, that Finland saved herself from Communism 'by saying "No" to the Marshall Plan' (Jakobson, 1968, p. 60), although it is noteworthy that Finland benefited indirectly from Marshall Aid especially where financial help from Sweden was concerned.

The formation of the Nordic Council produced an early dividend for regional co-operation in the form of the Common Labour Treaty. In the last few years this has enabled skilled Danish workers, for example, and particularly welders, to respond to a growing demand in a Norwegian economy buoyed by the discovery of North Sea oil. Earlier, and as a consequence of the rationalization of her agriculture that took place in the 1960s in particular, there was a considerable exodus of Finns, especially from the rural central and northern districts, to Sweden, where many nonetheless found the acquisition of the new language and industrial skills a difficult business. Twice as many Finns (something in the order of between 250,000 and 300,000) moved to Sweden between 1946 and the early 1970s as those who lost their lives in the 1939—44 wars against the Soviet Union. Although recently an increasing number of Finns have been returning from Sweden, there remains much validity in George Maude's cryptic comment that 'for Finland, a small country with a large-scale capital-intensive industry geared to export, for many years the greatest importance of Nordic co-operation was the opportunity it afforded to export Finns' (Maude, 1976, p. 111).

In the late 1960s renewed Scandinavian interest in a Customs Union was prompted by the failure of Britain's and Denmark's second application for membership of the European Economic Community.

Denmark's proposal for a Nordic Customs Union (Nordek), however, viewed unenthusiastically by the Swedes, was finally rejected by the Finns in 1970. Denmark proceeded to join the EEC in 1973, a referendum the previous year showing 64 per cent of the active electorate in favour, while the Norwegians decided to remain out, the corresponding referendum producing 53 per cent of voters against. Sweden signed a free-trade agreement with the EEC in July 1972; Norway followed suit in April 1973; and Finland ratified her free-trade arrangement the same year. She later entered into a commercial agreement with the Comecon countries, the first Western European market-economy state so to do.

The 1970s saw a move away from comprehensive economic plans like Nordek towards sectoral solutions which would allow for regional co-operation without antagonizing major domestic groups (Wiklund and Sundelius, 1979, p. 105). Thus in 1972 Olof Palme mooted the idea of a Nordic Action Programme on industrial and environmental policy, and this bore fruit with the establishment of a Nordic Investment Bank in 1976 and the holding of a large convention concerned with the protection of the environment two years later. Admittedly, all has not been plain sailing: the Norwegians, in particular, were incensed when the Investment Bank made funds available to improve the port facilities of Gothenburg. Yet regional harmonization has been extended beyond the passport union, the co-ordination of the major civil and criminal codes and early co-operation in the fields of education, health and social security to incorporate such new policy areas as tourism and women's rights. It needs emphasis, too, that EFTA remains important in facilitating access to regional markets. This can be exemplified by reference to the structure of Norway's exports to Sweden. The bulk of Norway's total exports are in the form of electrometals, chemicals, fish and ores (i.e. raw materials and semi-fabricates). A significantly higher proportion of her exports to Sweden, however, comprise advanced engineering machinery and manufactured products which take advantage of the elimination of internal tariffs on industrial goods. Norway, in fact, currently produces car parts (aluminium bumpers and so forth) for use in Swedish Volvo and Saab cars.

*The limits of regional consensus in the economic sphere*

While *historically* there is clearly much truth in Etzioni's assertion that northern Europe has been economically too weak to form a cohesive and distinctive unit, the size of the market *per se* (20–25 million was mentioned in the Nordek context) has been less important in the post-war period than fundamental intra-regional contradictions relating to considerations of national production and exportation (Etzioni, 1965, p. 221). The protracted negotiations over the proposed Nordic Customs Union in the late 1940s, for example, were dogged on the one hand by Danish and Norwegian concern about the impact of industrial competition from Sweden; on the other, Norway and Sweden were fearful of an influx of cheap Danish agricultural commodities. Iceland, for her part, has remained largely outside collective approaches to regional economic planning because of the monolithic structure of her productive base, which has been grounded primarily on fish exports and is too weak to survive integration with the other Nordic countries. In the Finnish case the transition from an agrarian to a large-scale capital-intensive economy in the post-war era has coincided with external political constraints on regional co-operation in the economic sphere. In the more recent past, the contrasting responses of the Norwegians and the Danes at the 1972 referendums on Common Market application illustrate well the nature of intra-regional conflicts of economic interest.

It must be allowed that the discovery of North Sea oil tended to work against the pro-market lobby in Norway, for with the average voter more affluent than ever before, the case for adhering to the EEC and the dire predictions concerning national unemployment in the event of her not doing so were less easy to sustain. Yet the decisive factor in the Norwegian case was that the primary sector of farmers, smallholders and fishermen, operating in generally adverse climatic and topographical conditions and afraid of the impact of the Common Agricultural Policy, united to oppose membership. It is a fair bet that much of the large agricultural sector in Finland (just under 20 per cent of the economically active labour force was employed on the land in the early 1970s) would have reacted in a similar manner had political conditions permitted an application for full EEC membership. As it was, the Norwegian case was particularly interesting because, with a clever twist, the anti-marketeers argued that the Norwegians would also be deciding the future of the Nordic area. It was claimed that a 'no' majority would improve the chances of a similar result in Denmark and thereby open the way for a revival of Nordek. The date of the referendum, 25 September, 1972 thus became 'a chance for the Nordic countries' (Allen, 1979, p. 150).

That the Danes did not opt to take their chance, but rather voted by a 64 per cent majority to accede to the EEC was not least the consequence of the concern of a traditionally efficient primary sector to expand into potentially large West European markets. True, there was almost an element of historic predetermination about the Danish result, for the Danish agriculturalists had long clung tenaciously to Britain's coat-tails. In the inter-war years, for example, the highly modernized larger farmers in the Agrarian Liberals, *Venstre*, were the only ones in Scandinavia to eschew membership of the Green Internationals which met in Prague. They had, in fact, nothing to gain from joining an organization of agricultural exporting countries wishing to penetrate precisely the British market, which Denmark virtually monopolized. Yet it was essentially a concern to progress *beyond* the British market into Western Europe which prompted the Danes to see the Nordek proposal that they initiated not as a long-term alternative to the EEC but simply as a stop-gap expedient for furthering her re-application to join the latter when the opportunity arose again. Indeed, it is important to note that whereas the two-thirds of her farm produce which Denmark exported experienced inevitable price fluctuations on the world market, the machinery of the EEC's Common Agricultural Policy offered Danish agriculture the enticing bait of increased stability and security (Fredriksen, 1973, pp. 15–26). Danish agriculture, it cannot be doubted, would have entered the EEC without Britain, and in 1963 de Gaulle offered Denmark entry without the UK. That a 1961 *Folketing* resolution, 'No entry without the UK', was adhered to, despite dissatisfaction from *Venstre* and the Conservatives, reflected the wider feeling that to ignore it would have been altogether too divisive and would risk, for example, arousing historic anti-German feeling in the labour movement. Significantly, however, in the late 1960s almost two-fifths of Danish MPs and an even higher proportion of Agrarian Liberals favoured seeking affiliation with the EEC *even if* Britain were unsuccessful in her attempts to join (Bonham, 1969, p. 152).

When de Gaulle resigned in April 1969, the way into the EEC opened up again, and by 1973 Denmark, along with Britain and Ireland, took her place as a full Community member. In short, if it was primarily, though not exclusively, economic interests which dictated Norway's decision to stay out of the EEC, it was economic considerations, albeit of a different kind, which weighed the balance in favour of Denmark's joining. Not that membership was unconditional or entered into in a spirit of unfettered enthusiasm. As John Fitzmaurice has noted: 'support for entry was essentially contingent upon obtaining economic benefits' (Fitzmaurice, 1980, p. 7). Clearly, there exists a good deal of elite satisfaction with the results to date, for no less than 109 delegates supported a motion before the *Folketing* in November 1980 on Denmark's remaining in the EEC and NATO, with only sixteen against and five abstentions.

*Consensus, co-operation and political integration*

Caught uneasily in the middle of the emerging polarization of post-war Europe, the possibility of political integration among the Nordic states foundered on the centrifugal forces of the security system built up in the region in the late 1940s. Initially, the omens were by no means inauspicious. Reaffirming their faith in collective security as the best defence against a future international conflagration, Denmark and Norway joined the United Nations as Charter members in 1945, and Sweden followed suit a year later. Moreover, Sweden, with strong Danish support, mooted a region-specific Scandinavian Defence Union in January 1948 which would have remained neutral in the event of war but would have come to the aid of any member nation attacked by a third state. As an attempt at political integration in the Nordic area, the Defence Union needs emphasis.

In taking the initiative in its organization, Sweden clearly wished to retain her practice of neutrality, which dated back to the post-Napoleonic era, albeit in this case through the maintenance of a collective military strength that would be adequate to act as a deterrent to possible invasion in times of crisis. Thus a fundamental feature of the Scandinavian Defence Union was the way in which its members would have remained neutral and independent of either formal or informal linkages with the world powers. To be fair, there was more to the Swedish calculus than mere history and tradition, for, as noted earlier, there has been a long-standing willingness on the part of member states in the region to accommodate, if at all possible, the interests of the others – the spirit later embodied in the concept of the Nordic Balance. In this instance motivating Sweden's insistence on continued Scandinavian neutrality, as Hancock has observed, was the concern that regional military alliance with the West might induce the Soviet Union to move against Finland. Like the Norwegians and Danes, the Finns had expressed initial interest in the Scandinavian Defence Union (Hancock, 1972, p. 246).

Stalin's menace, the Communist coup in Czechoslovakia in February 1948 and the coming of the Cold War sounded the death-knell for the Scandinavian Defence Union. With the Russians queering their pitch, the Finns were obliged to bow out, and in April 1948 they signed a Treaty of Friendship, Co-operation and Mutual Assistance with the

Soviet Union, which has been the cornerstone of Finnish foreign policy ever since. The Norwegians for their part, seeing the Cold War questioning the United Nations and the likely efficacy of global peace-keeping machinery, as well as rendering any Scandinavian Defence Union vulnerable without military assistance from the West, backed out of the Defence Union talks, and consultations finally collapsed in January 1949 in the face of the nascent NATO organization. The ultimate Western orientation of the Norwegians was not without its own logic: the Labour government in exile during the war was based in Britain; the nation's export trade and its vital mercantile marine depended heavily on the Western economy; Norway had strong links, through late nineteenth-century emigration, with the United States; and, not least, the ruling post-war Labour Party was strongly anti-Communist. Yet Norway, like Denmark and Iceland, had put her faith in the United Nations and joined NATO only reluctantly. Indeed, when Norway opted for NATO, the Danes initially sought a bilateral pact with Sweden, but the Swedes eschewed such an arrangement. The Scandinavian Defence Union and the possibility of political integration within the region, in sum, fell victim to the emergence of a bipolarized East—West security system and the consequently differing defence needs of the individual Nordic states.

By the late 1940s the Scandinavian security system which obtains to this day took shape. Denmark and Norway, both invaded by Nazi Germany during the Second World War, abandoned their former neutrality and in 1949 joined NATO. Norway's decision to join, incidentally, was to have damaging implications for the success of later schemes for comprehensive economic planning in the Nordic region. Nineteen years on, for example, when the Norwegian government agreed to enter into negotiations over Nordek, it did so only after the original proposals had been modified to ensure that the closer economic cooperation envisaged would not deleteriously affect her security policy interests. Mindful of the need to preserve the Nordic Balance, however, Norway has consistently refused to allow the stationing of NATO troops or nuclear weapons on her soil in peacetime. In a similar spirit, although Denmark accepted a joint NATO command with West Germany in Jutland in 1961, it was to function only during exercises and in wartime. Sweden, which narrowly escaped Nazi invasion, has retained a policy of armed neutrality. The practice of compulsory military service which is common to all the states in the region, a high level of defence spending and an elaborate nexus of underground harbours, etc. have combined to produce a picture of neutrality coupled with a high state of military readiness. Finnish neutrality, set within the confines of the 1948 Treaty but assiduously developed by Presidents Paasikivi and Kekkonen, has largely withstood foreign jibes about Finlandization, i.e. the increasing and insidious Russian penetration of Finland's internal affairs. To be sure, a number of crises in their mutual relations between 1958 and 1961 served as a reminder of the vulnerability of Finland's geographical position. Indeed, although the Finns' achievement in consolidating their cause in the post-war period has been considerable, there remains more than an element of truth in the renowned rejoinder of Paasikivi, on being asked what he did all day: 'I sit, read and ponder over how to keep this nation independent. . . . one mistake might well prove fatal' (Lehtinen, 1980, p. 83).

In Finland, as in all the Scandinavian countries except Iceland, over the last two decades there has been a solid consensus over existing foreign and defence policy alignments and the rejection of regional political integration. Thus in Sweden foreign policy is largely above the party system, and most foreign policy questions, though initiated by the Cabinet, are discussed on a cross-party basis in the *Riksdag*'s Advisory Council on Foreign Affairs. Finnish foreign policy management is exclusively a presidential preserve, although it is a measure of the widespread endorsement of the official handling of affairs, particularly with the Kremlin, that throughout the 1970s *all* the major parties backed Kekkonen's re-election as head of state (Arter, 1981). In both Denmark and Norway, despite the dramatic rise in the number of political parties in the last decade, there has not been a corresponding proliferation in attitudes towards foreign policy. In the former, as Ib Faurby has noted, the broad inter-elite consensus has included all but the Progress Party, and even this has supported Danish membership of NATO (Faurby, 1979, pp. 168—9). Only in Iceland, in fact, has the nation's NATO commitment been vigorously challenged over the years. In the none too distant past, for example, the current President, Vigdís Finnbogadóttir, was identified with the movement to expel the Americans from the Keflavik air base. This demand, though widely promoted by the radical left during general elections, has never prevailed in practice. The stern reality that the Keflavik base exists to provide airborne detection against Soviet submarines approaching Iceland and North America from the Kola peninsula is simply accepted by the centre-right as a fact of life.

As to elite attitudes towards regional political integration: in a study of 102 parliamentarians drawn from Denmark, Norway and Sweden in 1967, less than half favoured some kind of supranational arrangement for the region, while support for the idea that the Nordic Council should make recommendations on security policy was as low as 30 per cent in Denmark and Norway and 17 per cent in Sweden (Bonham, 1969). True, recent informal evidence suggests fairly widespread sympathy for a proposed Nordic nuclear-free zone, although just how far the general picture has changed is difficult to estimate.

If significant political *integration* in the region has not proved possible, measures of political *co-operation* have been achieved. Most notably, the Nordic Council was created, following a Danish initiative in 1952, to serve as an organ for consultation in matters involving joint action by member countries. Initially, the Council involved Denmark, Norway, Sweden and Iceland, but with the relaxation in Soviet attitudes following Khrushchev's accession to power and the early renewal of the 1948 Treaty (this also brought the return to Finland of the Porkkala naval base near Helsinki), Finland was able to join in 1956. The Council now comprises 78 representatives drawn from all five national Parliaments in the region, nominated on a party basis and organized these days on largely cross-national party lines. Although its discussions are wide-ranging, the Nordic Council's sole remit is to make suggestions to the governments of the five nations; in turn, it is informed by them of action taken on the Council's recommendations. Occasionally, Nordic leaders have launched important initiatives at meetings of the Council: in the late 1960s the Danish Prime Minister mooted his Nordek proposal in a plenary session. In the main, however, the Nordic Council has functioned as a valuable agency of communication and socialization, debating issues of concern to the region as a whole, while frequently pressing for the co-ordination of legislation. At the twenty-ninth session of the Nordic Council in Copenhagen in 1981, for example, it was determined by the narrowest majority (twenty-nine votes to twenty-eight) to produce proposals tightening up the laws relating to so-called 'violent pornography'. The original initiative on the matter had come the previous year in Reykjavik from the female delegates of the Nordic centre parties. It was also decided that the Nordic Council of Ministers — founded in the early 1970s — should come up with a definite proposal concerning the fate of the common Nordic television satellite, Nordsat. Incidentally, particularly enthusiastic about Nordsat was the representative of the Faeroe Islands, who clearly saw in the scheme an opportunity to provide the area with a basic television service.

The importance of the Nordic Council, with its Council of Ministers, should not be underestimated. True, the entrenched national perspectives of the region's political elites, particularly in the respective national bureaucracies, have contributed to weakening efforts at political solutions. But in recent years the machinery of joint decision-making and collective policy co-ordination at the regional level has become increasingly institutionalized. The Nordic Council of Ministers, for example, in creating an arena for formal and regularized ministerial co-operation, has lent enhanced political direction to proceedings. In support there are currently fifteen Permanent Committees of High Officials, together with over a hundred other ad hoc but permanent bodies. Over and above the Council of Ministers, the main initiating element in the regional policy process comprises the officials in the secretariat of the Nordic Council. These officials instigate proposals for recommendation by the Nordic Council and, with their predominantly regional perspective, have (potentially at least) considerable policy impact, particularly in their ability to liaise with political leaders.

Lately the Nordic Council, for long the solitary institution of Nordic collaboration, has emphasized its central scrutinizing and controlling function. In 1975 it established a Budget Committee, which meets twice a year with representatives from the Council of Ministers to discuss the total amount of the common Nordic budget and priorities between the different sectors. However, with the implementation of Nordic policy still carried out at the national level, it is clear that the national officials, especially the high-ranking officials assisting the Ministers, remain the crucial deliberators. For them, moreover, as Bengt Sundelius has observed in a recent study of the collective management of transnationalism in the region, domestic objectives and aspirations have been paramount (Sundelius, 1980, pp. 219–29). To be fair, this calculation of national rather than regional interest is hardly peculiar to Scandinavia, although against the backdrop of extensive socio-cultural affinity it is perhaps rather more surprising. On the other hand, it may be this very cultural homogeneity and consequent concern to preserve the essential elements of national identity that has created 'reluctant Nordics' in the region (Miljan, 1977, p. 284).

It is also conceivable that history, and more particularly the spectre of 'intra-Scandinavian "imperialism" ' has haunted regional co-operative ventures. Pursuing this line, Nils Ørvik has pointed to the fact that the two 'ex-imperialist' nations have promoted far more initiatives than the 'ex-colonies'. Sweden instigated the Scandinavian Defence Union in the late 1940s and throughout has been the most vigorous supporter of the Nordic Council. Denmark took the lead in the proposed Nordic Customs Union in 1947, the Nordic Council (to counter the failure of the Defence Union), as well as Nordek in the late 1960s. By comparison, the 'ex-colonies' have been passive. Finland has been hamstrung by a natural desire not to jeopardize amicable relations with the Soviet Union: the 'Scandinavianization' of her commercial and trade relations via FinnEfta in 1961, for example, was achieved with the explicit consent of the Kremlin. Norway, however, resisted the proposed Scandinavian Defence Union in 1948, and significant sections of her political leadership also balked at the prospect of a Nordic Customs Union and even the Nordic Council.

Too much should not be made of 'colonial' mentality as a constraint upon post-war regional co-operation. Certainly, at the level of the man in the street, the Norwegians have been traditionally rather scathing about the older 'imperial power', Denmark, and none too complimentary either about the attributes of her more recent successor, Sweden. But Norwegian reluctance to engage in the original Nordic Customs Union, for example, is to be explained in terms not of popular prejudice but rather of the real fear of a takeover by the then much stronger Swedish economy. Ironically, national roles have recently been reversed, with a tendency for the Norwegians nowadays to be courted by the Swedes on account of their North Sea oil: as an Oslo wit rather brutally put it, 'It is the ambition of every Norwegian to own a Volvo with a Swedish chauffeur!'

In one obvious and important sense, of course, Ørvik is right: the slate of Scandinavian history cannot be wiped clean, nor can the latent and engrained values stemming from the region's imperial past be totally expunged from the elite culture of the member nations. Yet if considerations of *realpolitik* underpinned the emergence of the Scandinavian security system, and if calculations of economic self-interest blighted comprehensive planning in the region, the spirit of regional affinity remains alive in the Nordic Balance, while the five Scandinavian nations have worked together remarkably harmoniously on the stage of international relations.

## SCANDINAVIA AS AN INTERNATIONAL ACTOR

In the post-war period there has emerged a broad regional consensus in support of the view that although small states unable to rely for the maintenance of their independence on either military or economic power, the Nordic nations can and should play an active rather than simply a reactive role on the world stage. President Kekkonen aptly encapsulated this distinctly Nordic approach to international relations when he stated in his speech at the Swedish Institute of International Affairs in May 1978 that 'Being small countries, we have become resigned to thinking that we are first and foremost objects of international politics. But the Nordic countries are also subjects and makers of policy in their own right.' The Nordic governments, Kekkonen continued, have both 'the right and the responsibility to attempt to influence the position of the region in the shifting currents of world politics'. To influence the position of the region on the international stage has involved in the Swedish and Finnish cases the pursuit of a policy of *active neutrality*. Throughout the region there has been a desire, and a concerted effort, to work towards the reduction of international tension.

In accordance with the orthodoxy of the respective governments in the region, Scandinavian security is likely to be enhanced by following a strategy designed to reinforce the international *status quo*. This has involved concentrating on two key areas: the East—West balance and the Third World. In the former case, the two neutral Scandinavian states have instigated attempts to limit the levels of arms at the disposal of the Soviet Union and the United States and have also been instrumental in initiating efforts to bring about a measure of detente between the super-powers. The Finns hosted the first Strategic Arms Limitation Talks (SALT) between the Russians and the Americans which commenced in 1970 — it had taken the two sides a year in Helsinki to negotiate over whether to negotiate! An extraordinary example of sleight of hand for a Finnish nation which clearly lies within the Soviet sphere of *military* influence, this was followed by the vigorous canvassing of diplomatic circles by a roving Finnish ambassador who helped to create a climate conducive to the organization of a Conference on European Security and Co-operation staged in Helsinki in 1975. In similar vein, the Swedes offered in March 1980 to hold a European Disarmament Conference (problems of disarmament were deliberately excluded from the Helsinki Final Act), a proposal initially mooted by the French at a special United Nations session on disarmament in May 1978.

As to Third World policy, the Scandinavian states have been concerned with the economic stablization — and as a consequence, it is hoped, the effective neutralization — of the Third World as an arena of great-power imperialism and conflict. Thus the Nordic governments have given active and consistent support to the notion of a New International Economic Order, the initiation of a North—South dialogue and the structural adjustment policies in the industralized nations that will be necessary if living conditions between the developed and less developed parts of the world are to be equalized. At their meeting in March 1980, for example, the Nordic Foreign Ministers placed great importance on the forthcoming global round of economic negotiations within the United Nations relating to raw materials, energy, trade and development. It is worth emphasizing that the generous development aid programmes of the Nordic governments are not only the product of inter-elite consensus but also have genuine support among the Scandinavian people, a fact that is both consonant with, and a reminder of, the strong missionary traditions of the region. Indeed, with an evangelical zeal well grounded in *realpolitik*, the Nordic countries have been engaged in a search for moral power and hence the force with which to influence post-war events in the direction of peace.

Concern to contribute towards the peaceful development of the world has not been incompatible with — indeed, at times has required — outspoken Scandinavian criticism of the domestic and foreign policies of regimes based on such things as apartheid, the violation of human rights and the suppression of the independence of other states. In the late 1960s Sweden was vociferous in her opposition to the Smith regime in Rhodesia, the Soviet invasion of Czechoslovakia and continuing United States involvement in Vietnam. More recently, all the Nordic states except Finland boycotted the 1980 Olympic Games in Moscow in protest against the Russian intervention in Afghanistan. For Greta Weiss and Norway, the boycott meant the probable loss of a rare gold medal on the track.

The Nordic search for moral authority has been mirrored in joint declarations on current issues of world politics, for these have combined a spirit of unashamed didacticism with a tone of slightly self-righteous indignation. The Nordic governments regret the delay in the implementation of the SALT 2 treaty; continue to uphold the unity, sovereignty and territorial integrity of Lebanon and to emphasize the role of the United Nations peace-keeping force in safeguarding peace both in Lebanon and in the whole Middle East; and maintain their support for decolonization in southern Africa, expressing satisfaction over developments in Zimbabwe and insisting that the illegal occupation of Namibia be ended. In addition to these specific stands, the Nordic governments have co-operated to promote the rights of indigenous peoples throughout the world and to proclaim the sanctity of human rights. They have given solid backing, for instance, to the United Nations' 1980 convention on the abolition of torture and the decision to set up a body to investigate the fate of missing and homeless persons and refugees. It is no surprise either that in the United Nations the Nordic nations frequently work and vote as a bloc, as well as boasting a number of senior officials, including the first Secretary-General Trygve Lie, the celebrated Secretary-General in the 1950s, Dag Hammarskjöld, and the UN High Commissioner for Refugees since 1978, Poul Hartling.

A decade ago the Nordic search for moral authority on the international stage involved minimal domestic cost; recently, however, economic recession has pointed up the rising costs and some evident contradictions in regional attitudes. Thus in Norway the import of Third World textiles has been tightly controlled in recent years, and, despite much criticism of South African apartheid, stricter immigration laws have been instituted. Recent legislation, for example, closed the door to further Turkish immigration. The door does not remain closed to all, however. Over Easter 1981 over a hundred Vietnamese refugees were rescued by Norwegian ships in the South China sea, taken to camps in Hong Kong and from there transported to Norway. Indeed, it is well known that Vietnamese refugees deliberately seek out Norwegian ships because Norway is one of the few countries willing to guarantee them sanctuary, houses and jobs. In Sweden there has been growing concern at the way in which the whole of the nation's traditional industrial base is being threatened by the New International Economic Order, not to mention its impact on the multinational companies that Sweden possesses abroad. Furthermore, the question of whether individual room for manoeuvre within existing alignments of the Scandinavian states has been enhanced by the high morality and visibility of their international role remains problematical. Certainly, it should not be forgotten that despite a vigorous desire to play an active part in settling their own destiny, the small Nordic nations are also, and inevitably, cast in a reactive role: the equilibrium of the strategic territory of northern Europe, in short, is inextricably linked to the actions of the super-powers.

In the Finnish case there is a constant, though never obsessional, awareness that the Bear remains very much next door. Solzhenitsyn's *Gulag Archipelago* failed to find a Finnish publisher (though an edition printed in Sweden was widely circulated), and a prison sentence awaited the nocturnal dauber of red paint on a statue of Lenin which the Soviet Union presented to the town of Kotka! Yet in return for observing a modicum of *autodiscipline*, Finnish neutrality is explicitly recognized by the Soviet Union, and the Treaty of Friendship, Co-operation and Mutual Assistance was extended in 1970 for a further twenty-year period. Indeed, when in July 1979 Marshall Ustinov, the Soviet Defence Minister, informally suggested to President Kekkonen that the armed forces of the two countries might hold joint exercises, Kekkonen was able to decline the invitation with impunity.

In contrast to the growing latitude of Finland's relations with the Soviet Union, Norway has apparently suffered some retrenchment in her traditionally independent position within the NATO alliance. This point, it is true, should not be exaggerated. Thus NATO's decision in the late 1970s to strengthen its northern flank was largely a response to the Soviet naval build-up on the Kola peninsula. Norway, moreover, has been embroiled with the Soviet Union over fishing problems, as well as over the prospective offshore oil reserves in the Barents Sea, where the maritime dividing line is still disputed. It should be stressed too that although Norway has not relaxed her policy of refusing to condone either nuclear weapons or foreign troops on her soil in peacetime, as noted above, the fact remains that in October 1980 the Labour government agreed, despite opposition from within its own ranks, to stockpile conventional American weapons – enough for between 6000 and 8000 marines – in the central Trøndelag district, but not in the sensitive northern territory close to the Soviet Union, as the United States and NATO originally intended. The issue was a divisive and controversial one, though with an average of four Russian planes intercepted every week over Norwegian airspace, there can be no doubt that the Soviet threat is felt to be real enough.

Sweden's policy of active neutrality has recently faced challenges on two counts: first, the increased arms build-up involving the super-powers and, second, her native economic difficulties. In the former context particular concern has been expressed at the possible violation of neutral Swedish airspace by great-power missiles equipped with nuclear warheads – NATO Cruise missiles, for example, or missiles of the Russian Delta class, able to reach targets in the United States without moving out of the Barents Sea. Admittedly, there has been little official Swedish support for the former Finnish President's suggestion of a Nordic nuclear weapon-free zone, which Kekkonen initially made in 1963 and revived fifteen years later. But in 1980 the Swedes did respond to Finland's proposed Disarmament Programme for Europe by offering to host a European Disarmament Conference when the time was ripe. On the domestic front economic pressures have forced the Swedes to make cuts in defence spending, which clearly weaken, albeit as yet only marginally, the regional equilibrium of northern Europe.

Invested with the vital role of defending the strategic Baltic Straits, Denmark like Norway, has undertaken to store heavy NATO equipment for American reinforcement units. However, economic problems have largely dictated that Denmark will not meet NATO's target of a 3 per cent rise in defence spending after allowing for inflation. Indeed, her Defence Minister was obliged to proceed on the basis of a zero-growth budget for 1981, a possible 10 per cent cut in personnel and 30 per cent in materials and the real fear that the defence of Sjaelland and Fyn will be reduced to an unacceptable level. It is, needless to say, of paramount importance to the stability of the whole Nordic region that Denmark should continue adequately to defend herself. Any reduction in her defence spending, leading to the prospect of a heightened West German naval presence to offset the increase in amphibious Warsaw Pact forces in the vital Baltic area, would unquestionably alarm the Russians. With specific reference to renewed German militarism incorporated into the Treaty of Friendship, Co-operation and Mutual Assistance, it would have serious implications for Finland too. The Nordic Balance, in short, is as tenuous as it is absolutely imperative.

*Regional co-operation and international activism in the 1980s*

The spirit of the Nordic Balance notwithstanding, the differential security demands and commitments of the immediate post-war years — and the primacy they gave to considerations of national sovereignty — have been fundamental bulwarks against political integration among the Nordic states. In short, no regional authority with binding legal powers over the entire Scandinavian territory has emerged, and, unlike the signatories to the Treaty of Rome, the five nations of the region are not committed to the creation of a federal union. The security interests of the Nordic nations have hardly facilitated the possibility of economic integration between them either. The lukewarm Swedish response to Nordek, for instance, reflected a perception that the economic opportunity costs of not joining were likely to prove smaller than the political costs of involvement in a protectionist bloc which included NATO members. The potential threat to the nation's neutral identity was simply too high a price to pay. In the Finnish case, as Miljan emphasizes, even the possibility of such calculations was ruled out by the dictates of Soviet security interests (Miljan, 1977, p. 281). To note the absence of region-specific machinery for *de jure* political and economic integration is not, of course, to deny the existence of a significant measure of practical co-operation between the Nordic states. Indeed, it might be argued that this constitutes a significant form of *de facto* political integration — backdoor integration by increments, one could almost say.

In this context Nils Andrén, in a seminal article in 1967, has posited an interesting variation on conventional thinking in the form of a cobweb theory of integration. Integration is here defined as a process of increasing mutual interdependence, and though the *individual* strands in the growing web of connections may be small, the *cumulative* effect can be great (Andrén, 1967). There is no doubt that the Nordic Council, via its Council of Ministers, standing committees and the wide range of topics discussed in its annual plenary sessions, has generated multiple strands in the cobweb. A few examples will illustrate the variety and diversity of ideas aired in the Nordic Council.

At the annual session in 1972, for instance, there was discussion of a modern textbook in comparative Nordic history to offset what some felt to be the unduly nationalist bias of a number of existing course books. The following year a decision was reached on co-operation between the ambulance services in the North Cape, while 1976 saw a draft convention on cross-border co-operation between local government authorities. Five years later came a convention proposing full social insurance cover for Nordic citizens everywhere in the region and a recommendation to the Nordic Council of Ministers for co-ordinating energy researches. In the same year, 1981, a convention was also concluded aiming to enable Nordic citizens to use their own languages in written or oral contacts with public authorities in other Nordic countries. In short, the cobweb of interdependence has expanded enormously in recent years.

At the same time it needs to be emphasized that more conventional integration theories have tended to identify areas of 'high' and 'low' spillover effects for integration, the latter defined, as in the bulk of this chapter, as a transfer of political loyalties to a new centre able to exercise political powers in its own right. Such approaches would undoubtedly call into question the significance of the Nordic Council's record of achievement for integration in the region. Take, for example, its standing committees. Of the five such committees in the Nordic Council, Economic Affairs would be the most important for integration but has been the least effective; the others (Cultural, Legal, Transport and Social Services) are concerned with 'low' areas; while defence and security policy, which would, of course, rank 'high' in their impact on integration, do not have committees at all. Yet if the real extent of regional integration must remain problematical, there can be no argument that in the harmonization and co-ordination of cross-national legislation, particularly in the social policy sphere, much has been achieved. Equally, there remain important challenges for the 1980s.

The expensive Nordsat project should provide a stern test of broad-gauge co-operation, requiring as it would, if approved, the complicated process of amending and standardizing national communications legislation. In fact in 1982 the Danes withdrew, so jeopardizing the entire Nordsat venture. Regional co-operation in the 1980s will also need to meet the challenge of finding a satisfactory resolution to the 'minorities' problem — not only the protection of the language, culture and livelihood of the Lapps (a hard core of whom were recently sufficiently incensed to hunger-strike in protest against a decision to build a hydroelectric power station across the Alta River in northern Norway), but also, as the national economy contracts, the problem of Finnish immigrants and the 'guestworker' Turkish population in Sweden. At a more general level altogether, there is clearly both room and need in the forthcoming decade to develop and strengthen mutual relations between some of the individual countries of the region. Multilateralism should supersede the present propensity for bilateralism. Put another way, although there is a close interchange of personnel and ideas involving, for example, Sweden and Denmark, the Finnish ambassador in Copenhagen has remarked that members of the Danish Cabinet are better acquainted with Warsaw and Tel Aviv than Helsinki — excepting, that is, the various conference places! (Väänänen, 1980, p. 115) Multilateralism also involves a continuing and important role for the network of Norden Societies created after the First World War, which have had as their primary aim the promotion of cultural exchanges and a better understanding between the Scandinavian states.

Finally, in the international arena the Scandinavians will remain in an exposed position in the bipolar security system, since its NATO members are many thousands of miles away from the friendly superpower, the United States, and all the nations in the region except Iceland, are too close to the Soviet Union for comfort. It is to be expected, therefore, that the Nordic states will continue to strive to lower the temperature of East–West relations; to mediate to prevent the possible escalation of localized conflict in the Third World; and to seek, through the United Nations welfare programmes, the moral power to influence world events in the direction of peace. It has long been abundantly plain to them that, in the words of a text on a crock-jug in a Stockholm shop, 'We cannot afford any other war than life itself!'

EPILOGUE

# Some Trends and Prospects

The voting trends evident at the Norwegian general election of September 1981 seem to indicate the continuation, albeit on a limited scale, of the volatility that characterized the Scandinavian electorate in the 1970s. The Conservatives won a resounding victory, advancing to claim almost 32 per cent of the vote, their highest share since 1924; the share of the governing Labour Party dipped to under 40 per cent for only the third time in its history; and there was a revival of the Progress Party, reflecting not only its anti-tax appeal but also, more sinister, its exploitation of the anxieties of an older generation of electors in the former Labour strongholds in the East End of Oslo where immigrant settlement is high. The swing to the Right in Norway clearly fed on a natural reaction to eight years of Labour government but was accentuated by the decline of the two main middle-ground parties, the Centre and the Christian People's parties.

These trends were replicated in some respects by the results of the December 1981 *Folketing* elections in Denmark. There the Social Democrat vote fell from 38 per cent to 33 per cent, only a little better than the heavy losses of 1973 and 1975. The main gainers were the Socialist People's Party on the left, who attained their strongest ever level of support and became one of the four largest parties in the *Folketing*. Important gains were also made at the non-socialist end of the spectrum, however: the Conservatives became the second-largest parliamentary group, while the Centre Democrats made even larger gains. At the same time the Progress Party was evinced less support than at any time since its formation, perhaps not surprising in the immediate aftermath of confirmation of Mogens Glistrup's conviction for tax fraud. The election showed winners on the left, centre-right and right but gave little direction to efforts to form a new government. The bourgeois parties indicated Henning Christophersen, the Liberal leader (and Foreign Minister in 1978–9) as a potential Prime Minister, but this possibility was blocked by its reliance on the involvement of the Progress Party. On the left, a combination of Socialist People's Party, Social Democrats and Radical Liberals could have had a bare majority. Lengthy negotiations to this end were led by the acting Prime Minister, Anker Jørgensen, but it proved impossible to persuade his two potential partners to agree with each other or with the economic programme which the Social Democrats regarded as essential to meet the country's problems. The negotiations helped to save the face of the Social Democrats following their electoral losses, however, and in the end they continued in office with an only slightly refurbished cabinet. The possibility of some cabinet seats at a later stage was held open to the Radical Liberals, but clearly the Jørgensen technique of governing with parliamentary support across the centre of the political spectrum, practised so skilfully during the 1970s, will prove more difficult in the 1980s.

Notwithstanding the Danish Centre Democratic gains, the steady erosion of the political centre is likely to constitute the most telling electoral trend affecting the Scandinavian region as a whole in the 1980s. The Swedish Centre, for example, boasting a quarter of the vote only a decade before, stood at a mere 10 per cent in the opinion polls in late 1981. Furthermore, an Environmental Party was formed in Autumn 1981 to challenge the Centre's record and credibility on 'green' issues, and it is significant too that the Christian Democrats, as yet unrepresented in the *Riksdag* but with the fastest growing youth movement of all the Swedish parties, rejected overtures from the Centre for an electoral alliance to fight the September 1982 general election. True, intermittently close co-operation between the middle-ground parties in the region has spawned ephemeral talk of a merger between the Liberals, the Centre and, in the Finnish case, the Swedish People's parties. Projecting ahead, however, it seems reasonable to assert that the inexorable decline in the size of the agricultural population will further undermine the basis of the historic divisions of the non-socialist camp into centre-aligned and right-wing groups. There are grounds, in sum, for being rather pessimistic about the future prospects of the Scandinavian centre.

The fragmentation of the bourgeois camp has meant, rather paradoxically, that whereas the non-socialists currently enjoy majority popular support across the region, nowhere have they been able to convert this support into cohesive governmental power. Thus the last non-socialist coalition in Denmark fell in 1971, and since then there has been intensified division among the non-socialist parties. The Centre rejected a coalition with the victorious Conservatives in Finland in 1979, and in Norway in September 1981 a three-party non-socialist government was ruled out by the intransigence of the Christian People's Party on abortion. In Sweden neither of the two broad non-socialist coalitions since 1976 managed to achieve two years in office. Moreover, relations between the bourgeois parties in Sweden were strained by the decision of the Fälldin Centre-Liberal administration to reduce VAT. The broad left opposed the proposal, and the strategically-placed Conservatives were keeping their options open. Fälldin threatened to resign in the event of a government defeat. Much then depended on the role of the Conservatives. Although as an opposition party they were well placed to avoid the electoral odour not infrequently associated with 'carrying the government can', they could not afford to oppose to the point of jeopardizing renewed non-socialist co-operation before the 1982 election. To fail to cement an agreement with the Centre and Liberals could leave the Conservatives as far out in the cold as their sister party in Finland.

It must be allowed that the logistics of the situation outlined above may well be largely abstract, for with public opinion polls in late 1981 putting support for the Social Democrats at 49.5 per cent, as compared with 43.5 per cent for the non-socialist parties, the Social Democrats appeared well-placed to renew their ascendancy of pre-1976 and put an end to what may come to be seen as an aberrational era of non-socialist instability. Indeed, with four administrations in six years, the period was reminiscent of the Weimar characteristics traditionally imputed to neighbouring Finland. Ironically, the collapse of non-socialist talks in Norway left Finland in the Autumn of 1981 as the only mainland Scandinavian state to boast a majority government.

The prevalence of stable minority governments in the region should elevate the role of Parliament and parliamentary standing committees in the policy process. In Sweden ad hoc legislative coalitions along Danish lines seemed inevitable while minority government continued. In Norway, however, the situation was rather different: when the Bruntland Labour administration presented its long-term programme in June 1981, prior to the September elections, the non-socialists countered with a joint response which was designed to form the basis of Conservative government for the next four years.

If Sweden seems poised to return to the pre-1976 pattern of socialist governments, Finland must adjust to the advent of a socialist head of state for the first time in her history, following the long-serving Urho Kekkonen's retirement through ill-health in the autumn of 1981. At the presidential elections early in 1982, the odds-on favourite, Mauno Koivisto, romped home far ahead of his two main bourgeois rivals and only six seats short of an absolute majority in the 301-seat electoral college. His success was assured when the non-Stalinist element in the radical leftist SKDL decided to support him at the first round of electoral-college voting. How will the status of the presidency be affected by a change of personnel at the top?

The answer is probably that while Koivisto's managerial style is likely to be different — lower-key and more informal — his overall position is unlikely to be significantly weaker than that of his illustrious predecessor. In the first place, Koivisto's unique image as a man above party politics, the charismatic figure aloof from the wheeling and dealing of intriguing elites, is likely to enhance the office of head of state, which is by convention non-partisan. Secondly, he will remain the embodiment of the prestigious Paasikivi—Kekkonen line of cordial, mutually advantageous Fenno-Soviet relations — a line over which there is overwhelming consensus. Finally, Koivisto will almost certainly need to play an active part in coalition-building. In light of his campaign commitment to maintaining the centre-left presidential *majorité* of his predecessor, the chances of a speedy governmental re-incorporation of the Conservatives after sixteen years in the wilderness do not seem bright. Above all, with Koivisto an ad hoc pragmatist rather than a doctrinal socialist, Finland will not experience a Mitterrand-style radicalization of policy-making to crush the precarious consensualism of the last decade and a half. It might be added as a post script that the extraordinary longevity of Kekkonen's term of office could well lead to constitutional amendments introducing a two-term, American-style limit to the number of terms that a single head of state may serve, as well as replacing the electoral college system by direct presidential elections.

On the eve of his enforced retirement President Kekkonen was doubtless gratified by the growing support for his long-standing proposal of a nuclear-weapon-free Nordic zone, the prospect of which prompted many young people to cycle and hike to a mass peace lobby in the Trøndelag in Norway during the summer of 1981. The Norwegian and Swedish Labour/Social Democratic parties were notably sympathetic to the idea, although the dominant orthodoxy outside the radical left has been that the establishment of such a zone should not involve any shifts in the Nordic Balance.

Any short section on trends and prospects in the region is necessarily selective, as space precludes consideration of a host of fascinating imponderables: for example, the cumulative impact of naturalized 'guestworkers' on Swedish voting behaviour, the fate of the 'worker fund' scheme in Sweden and Denmark, the future of the divided Finnish Communists, the resolution of the abortion issue in Norway, to name but a few. In keeping with the approach throughout this present volume, however, we must content ourselves with a few broad brush-strokes on the large but immensely challenging canvas of Scandinavian politics and government.

# Select Bibliography

*Note*: In Scandinavia the letters Æ or Ä, Ø or Ö and Å come at the end of the alphabet. For the convenience of English readers, Æ, Ä and Å have been placed with A, and Ø or Ö have been placed with O.

Aasland, Tertit (1974) *Fra landmannsorganisasjon til bondeparti. Politisk debatt og taktikk i Norsk landmansforbund 1896–1920*, Olso–Bergen–Tromsø: Universitetsforlaget.
*Administrationsudvalget af 1960* (1962) vol. 1, no. 301, Copenhagen.
Alanen, Aulis, J. (1976) *Santeri Alkio*, Porvoo: Söderström.
Alapuro, Risto (1976) 'On the Political Mobilization of the Agrarian Population in Finland: Problems and Hypotheses', *Scandinavian Political Studies*, vol. 11, pp. 51–77.
Allardt, Erik (1970) 'Types of Protest and Alienation'. In E. Allardt, and S. Rokkan (eds.) *Mass Politics*, New York: Free Press.
Allen, Hilary (1979) *Norway and Europe in the 1970s*, Oslo–Bergen–Tromsø: Universitetsforlaget.
*Allmänna Valen 1973* (1975) Del 3. *Riksdagsvalet. Specialundersökningar*, Stockholm: Sveriges Officiella Statistik, Statistiska Centralbyrån. Similar volume (1976).
Andersen, Per C. (1975) *Kristen Politik*, Odense: Universitetsforlag.
Anderson, S. V. (1967) *The Nordic Council*, Stockholm: Norstedt.
Andrén, N. (1964) *Government and Politics in the Nordic Countries*, Stockholm: Almqvist & Wiksell.
Andrén, Nils (1967) 'Nordic Integration – Aspects and Problems', *Co-operation and Conflict* vol. 2, pp. 1–25.
Andrén, N. (1968) *Modern Swedish Government*, 2nd edn., Stockholm: Almqvist & Wiksell.
Andrén, N. (1969) 'Scandinavia'. In S. Henig and J. Pinder (eds.) *European Political Parties*, London: PEP/Allen & Unwin.
Anton, T. J. (1969) 'Policy-Making and Political Culture in Sweden', *Scandinavian Political Studies*, vol. 4, pp. 88–102.

# Select Bibliography

Arter, David (1978a) *Bumpkin Against Bigwig. The Emergence of a Green Movement in Finnish Politics*, Tampere: Tampereen yliopisto.

Arter, David (1978) 'All-Party Government for Finland?', *Parliamentary Affairs*, vol. 31, no. 1, pp. 67–85.

Arter, David (1979a) 'The Finnish Centre Party: Profile of a "Hinge Group" ', *West European Politics*, vol. 2, no. 1, pp. 108–27.

Arter, David (1979b) 'The Finnish Election of 1979: The Empty-Handed "Winner"?', *Parliamentary Affairs*, vol. 32, no. 4, pp. 422–36.

Arter, David (1980a) 'The Finnish Christian League: Party or "Anti-Party"?', *Scandinavian Political Studies*, vol. 3 (n.s.), no. 2, pp. 143–62.

Arter, David (1980b) 'Social Democracy in a West European Outpost: The Case of the Finnish SDP', *Polity*, vol. 12, no. 3, pp. 363–87.

Arter, David (1981) 'Kekkonen's Finland: Enlightened Despotism or Consensual Democracy?', *West European Politics*, vol. 4, no. 3, pp. 219–34.

Bäck, P.-E. and Berglund, Sten (1978) *Det svenska partiväsendet*, Stockholm: Almqvist & Wiksell.

Bagehot W. (1949) *The English Constitution* (World's Classics ed.), London: Oxford University Press.

Berglund, Sten, and Lindström, Ulf (1978) *The Scandinavian Party System(s)*, Lund: Studentlitteratur.

Bjørnsen, M. K., and Hansen, E. (1972) *Facts about Denmark*, Copenhagen: Politikens Forlag.

Bloch, Kristian (1963) *Kongens Råd: Regjeringsarbeidet i Norge*, Oslo: Universitetsforlaget.

Blondel, J. (1973) *Comparative Legislatures*, Englewood Cliffs, NJ: Prentice-Hall.

Bonham, G. Matthew (1969) 'Scandinavian Parliamentarians: Attitudes toward Political Integration', *Co-operation and Conflict*, vol. 4, no. 3, pp. 149–61.

Bull, Edvard (1967) 'Industrial Workers and their Employers in Norway around 1900'. In Val R. Lorwin (ed.) *Labor and Working Conditions in Modern Europe*, New York: Macmillan.

Carlsson, Sten (1956) *Bondens politiska storhetstid 1867–1914. Bonden i svensk historia* III, Stockholm.

Castles, Francis (1975) 'Swedish Social Democracy: The Conditions of Success', *Political Quarterly*, vol. 46, no. 2, pp. 171–85.

Castles, Francis (1978) *The Social Democratic Image of Society: A Study of the Achievements and Origins of Scandinavian Social Democracy in Comparative Perspective*, London: Routledge & Kegan Paul.

Cerny, Karl H. (ed.) (1977) *Scandinavia at the Polls*, Washington, DC: American Enterprise Institute.

Chapman, R. A. (1968) *Decision-Making: A Case Study of the Decision to Raise the Bank Rate in September 1957*, London: Routledge & Kegan Paul.

Childs, M. W. (1948) *Sweden, the Middle Way*, New York: Penguin Books.

Childs, M. W. (1980) *Sweden: the Middle Way on Trial*, New Haven and London: Yale University Press.

Churchill, W. S. (1951) *The Second World War*, vol 4, *The Hinge of Fate*, London: Cassell.

*Constitutional Documents of Sweden* (1975), Stockholm: Swedish Riksdag publication.

Damgaard, E. (1975) 'The Political Role of Nonpolitical Bureaucrats in Denmark'. In Mattei Dogan (ed.) *The Mandarins of Western Europe*, New York: Wiley.

Damgaard, Erik (1977) *Folketinget under forandring*, Copenhagen: Samfundsvidenskabeligt Forlag.

Damgaard, E., and Eliassen, K. A. (1980) 'Reduction of Party Conflict through Corporate Participation in Danish Law-Making', *Scandinavian Political Studies* vol. 3 (n.s.), no. 2, pp. 105–21.

Derry, T. K. (1973) *A History of Modern Norway 1814–1972*, Oxford: Clarendon Press.

Duverger, Maurice (1964) *Political Parties. Their Organisation and Activity in the Modern State*, London: Methuen.

Duverger, Maurice (1980) 'A New Political System Model: Semi-Presidential Government', *European Journal of Political Research*, vol. 8, pp. 165–87.

Eckstein, H. (1966) *Division and Cohesion in Democracy: A Study of Norway*, Princeton, NJ: Princeton University Press.

Elder, Neil (1970) *Government in Sweden: The Executive at Work*, Oxford: Pergamon Press.

Elder, Neil (1975) 'The Scandinavian States'. In S. E. Finer (ed.) *Adversary Politics and Electoral Reform*, London: Wigram.

Elder, Neil, and Gooderham, Rolf (1978) 'The Centre Parties of Norway and Sweden', *Government and Opposition*, vol. 13, no. 2, pp. 218–35.

Elder, Neil (1979a) 'Bipolarity or Indeterminacy in a Multi-Party System?' *Hull Papers in Politics* no. 14.

Elder, Neil (1979b) 'The Functions of the Modern State'. In J. E. S. Hayward and R. N. Berki (eds.) *State and Society in Contemporary Europe*, Oxford: Martin Robertson.

Eliassen, Kjell A., and Pedersen, Mogens N. (1973) *The Professionalization of the Danish and Norwegian Legislatures*, Montreal: IPSA Ninth World Congress.

Elvander, N. (1969) *Intresseorganisationerna i dagens Sverige*, Lund: Gleerup.

Elvander, N. (1972) 'The Politics of Taxation in Sweden, 1945–70: A Study of the Functions of Parties and Organizations', *Scandinavian Political Studies*, vol. 7, pp. 63–82.

Elvander, N. (1974a) 'Collective Bargaining and Incomes Policy in the Nordic Countries: A Comparative Analysis', *British Journal of Industrial Relations*, vol. 12, no. 3, pp. 417–37.

Elvander, N. (1974b) 'The Role of the State in the Settlement of Labor Disputes in the Nordic Countries: A Comparative Analysis', *European Journal of Political Research*, vol. 2, pp. 363–83.

Elvander, N. (1974c) 'In Search of New Relationships: Parties, Unions and Salaried Employees' Associations in Sweden', *Industrial and Labor Relations Review*, vol. 28, no. 1, pp. 60–74.

Elvander, N. (1979a) 'Scandinavian Social Democracy: Its Strength and Weakness', *Acta Universitatis Upsaliensis* 39.

Elvander, N., et al. (1979b) *Sju socialdemokrater om löntagarfonderna*, Stockholm: Tidens Förlag.

*Employment Gazette* (1971, 1980), London: HMSO.

Etzioni, Amitai (1965) *Political Unification*, New York: Holt, Rinehart & Winston, Inc.

Faurby, Ib (1979) 'Party System and Foreign Policy in Denmark', *Cooperation and Conflict*, vol. 14, pp. 159–70.

Fitzmaurice, John (1979) 'The Danish Justice Party', Political Studies Association, Scandinavian Politics Group Conference Paper, Sheffield University.

Fitzmaurice, John (1980) 'The Influence of the Danish Anti-Market Movement on Danish Policy towards the European Community', Political Studies Association Scandinavian Politics Group, December Conference Paper, London.

Fitzmaurice, John (1981) *Politics in Denmark*, London: Hurst.

*Forretningsorden for Folketinget* (*Folketing* Standing Orders) (1975), Copenhagen.

Frears, John (1978) 'Legitimacy, Democracy and Consensus: A Presidential Analysis', *West European Politics*, vol. 1, no. 3, pp. 11–23.

Fredriksen, P. L. (1973) 'Danish Agriculture and European Integration'. In T. C. Archer (ed.) *Scandinavia and European Integration*, Aberdeen: University of Aberdeen Press.

Galnoor, Itzhak (ed.) (1977) *Government Secrecy in Democracies*, New York: Harper & Row.

Greenhill, Gaylon H. (1965) 'The Norwegian Agrarian Party: A Class Party?', *Social Science*, vol. 40, no. 4, pp. 214–19.

Griffiths, J. C. (1969) *Modern Iceland*, London: Pall Mall Press.

Grimsson, O. R. (1976) 'The Icelandic Power Structure 1800–2000', *Scandinavian Political Studies*, vol. 11, pp. 9–33.

Grimsson, O. R. (1977) 'The Icelandic Multilevel Coalition System', Háskoli Islands, *Félagsvísindadeild* no. 37.
Gustafsson, G., and Richardson, J. (1980) 'Post-Industrial Changes in Policy Style', *Scandinavian Political Studies*, vol. 3 (n.s.), no. 1, pp. 21–37.
Hancock, M. D. (1972) *Sweden: The Politics of Post-Industrial Change*, London: Holt, Rinehart & Winston.
Hartz, L. (1955) *The Liberal Tradition in America*, New York: Harcourt.
Heclo, H. (1974) *Modern Social Politics in Britain and Sweden*, New Haven and London: Yale University Press.
Heidar, Knut (1977) 'The Norwegian Labour Party: Social Democracy in a Periphery of Europe'. In W. E. Paterson and A. H. Thomas (eds.) *Social Democratic Parties in Western Europe*, London: Croom Helm.
Helander, Voitto (1975) *Kansanedustaja ja painostusryhmät: vuorovaikutus, legitiimiys ja vaikutus*. Turun yliopiston valtio-opin laitos. Tutkimuksia, sarja C, no. 28/75, p. 20.
Helander, Voitto (1976) *Kamari vai Kirjaamo? Eduskunnan suuri valiokunta Suomen lainsäädäntöjärjestelmän osana vuosina 1907–71*. Turku: Turku University Political Science Research Reports No. 32.
Helander, Voitto (1977) *Etutärjestöjen ja valtionsuhteiden kehityksen pääpiirteet toisen maailmansodan jälkeisessä Suomessa*, Helsingin yliopiston poliittisen historian laitoksen julkaisuja, 1.
Herlitz, N. (1969) *Elements of Nordic Public Law*, Stockholm: Norstedt.
Hernes, Gudmund (1973) 'Stortingets komitésystem og maktfordelingen i partigruppene', *Tidsskrift for samfunnsforskningen* vol. 14, pp. 1–29.
Higley, John, Brofoss, Karl Erik and Groholt, Knut (1975) 'Top Civil Servants and the National Budget in Norway'. In Mattei Dogan (ed.), *The Mandarins of Western Europe*, New York: Wiley.
Higley, J., Field, G. L., and Grøholt, K. (1976) *Elite Structure and Ideology*, Oslo: Universitetsforlaget; New York: Columbia University Press.
Himmelstrand, U. (1962) 'A Theoretical and Empirical Approach to Depoliticization and Political Involvement', *Acta Sociologica*, vol. 6 Copenhagen, pp. 83–110.
Himmelstrup, Jens, and Møller, Jens (eds.) (1958) *Danske Forfatningslove 1665–1953*, Copenhagen: J. H. Schultz Forlag.
Holmberg, Sören (1974), *Riksdagen representerar svenska folket. Empiriska studier i representativ demokrati*, Lund: Studentlitteratur.
Huntford, R. (1971) *The New Totalitarians*, London: Allen Lane the Penguin Press.
Huntington, S. P. (1968) *Political Order in Changing Societies*, London: Yale University Press.

Hvidt, Kristian (ed.) (1977) *Folketinget. Håndbog 1977*, Copenhagen: Schultz.
Ingham, G. K. (1974) *Strikes and Industrial Conflict, Britain and Scandinavia*, London: Macmillan.
Jakobson, Max (1968) *Finnish Neutrality*, London: Evelyn.
Jensen, Einar (1937) *Danish Agriculture: Its Economic Development*, Copenhagen: Schultz.
Johansen, Lars Nørby (1979) 'Denmark'. In Geoffrey Hand *et al.* (eds.) *European Electoral Systems Handbook*, London: Butterworth.
Johansson, S. (1966) *Politiska resurser*, Stockholm: Allmänna Förlaget.
Jonnergård, Gustaf (ed.) (1950) *Bröder, låtom oss enas! En krönika i ord och bild om bondeförbundet i svensk politik under fyra årtionden*, Halmstad.
Jörberg, Lennart (1973) 'The Industrial Revolution in the Nordic Countries'. In Carlo M. Cipolla (ed.) *The Emergence of Industrial Societies*, 11, London: Collins/Fontana.
Kalela, Jorma (1976) 'Right-Wing Radicalism in Finland during the Inter-War Period', *Scandinavian Journal of History*, vol. 1, pp. 105–24.
Kastari, P. (1970) 'The Constitutional Experience in the Nordic Countries', *Israel Law Review*, vol. 5, pp. 513–26.
Kauppinen, J. (1973) *Evankelioiva herätysliike*, Tampere: Kirkon tutkimuslaitos.
Kelsen, Hans (1967) *The Pure Theory of Law*, Berkeley: University of California Press.
Kirby, D. G. (1979) *Finland in the Twentieth Century*, London: Hurst.
Kornhauser, William (1959) *The Politics of Mass Society*, Glencoe, Ill.: Free Press.
Korpi, Walter (1971) 'Working Class Communism in Western Europe: Rational or Nonrational?' *American Sociological Review*, vol. 36, no. 6, pp. 971–84.
Korpi, W. (1978) *The Working Class in Welfare Capitalism: Work, Unions and Politics in Sweden*, London: Routlege & Kegan Paul.
Kristjánsson, Svanur (1978) *The Independence Party: Origins, Organization, Ideology and Electoral Basis*, University of Iceland, Conference paper.
Kristjánsson, Svanur (1979) 'The Electoral Basis of the Icelandic Independence Party, 1929–44', *Scandinavian Political Studies*, vol. 2 (n.s), no. 1, pp. 31–52.
Kuhnle, Stein (1975) *Patterns of Social and Political Mobilization: A Historical Analysis of the Nordic Countries*, London: Sage.
Kvavik, R. B. (1976) *Interest Groups in Norwegian Politics*, Oslo: Universitetsforlaget.

Laakso, M. (1979) 'The Maximum Distortion and the Problem of the First Divisor of Different PR Systems', *Scandinavian Political Studies*, vol. 2 (n.s.), no. 2, pp. 161–70.
Lægreid, Per and Olsen, Johann P. (1978) Byråkrati og beslutninger: en studie av norske departement. Olso: Universitetsforlaget.
Landén, Vincent (1978) *Sveriges Riksdag: The Swedish Parliament*, Stockholm: Administrative Office of the *Riksdag*.
Landström, Sten-Sture (1954) *Svenska ämbetsmans sociala ursprung*, Uppsala: Almqvist & Wiksell.
Larsson, H. A. (1980) *Partireformationen – från bondeförbundet till centerparti*, Lund: Gleerup.
Laulajainen, Pertti (1979) *Sosialidemokraatti vai Kommunisti*, Mikkeli: Itä-Suomen Instituutti.
Lees, John D., and Shaw, Malcolm (eds.) (1979) *Committees in Legislatures: A Comparative Analysis*, Oxford: Martin Robertson.
Lehtinen, Lasse (1980) *Virolainen: tasavallan isäntärenki*, Porvoo–Helsinki–Juva: WSOY.
Levine, D. (1978) 'Conservatism and Tradition in Danish Social Welfare Legislation, 1890–1933: A Comparative View', *Comparative Studies in Society and History*, vol. xx, pp. 54–69.
Lijphart, A. (ed.) (1969) *Politics in Europe*, Englewood Cliffs, NJ: Prentice-Hall.
Lijphart, A. (1975) *The Politics of Accomodation*, 2nd edn. (rev.), Berkeley–Los Angeles and London: University of California Press.
Lindbeck, A. (1975) *Swedish Economic Policy*, London: Macmillan.
Lindbeck, A. (1979) *Fondfrågan*, Stockholm: Albaidé.
Lindblad, I., Wahlbäck, K., and Wiklund, C. (1972) *Politik i Norden*, Stockholm: Aldus/Bonniers.
Lipset, S. M., and Rokkan, S. (eds.) (1967) *Voter Systems and Party Alignments*, New York: Free Press.
London, Gary (1975) *The End of an Opposition of Principle: The Case of the Finnish Socialist Workers' Party*, University of Helsinki, Institute of Political Science Research Reports No. 37.
Lundberg, Bengt (1979) *Jämlikhet? Socialdemokratin och jämlikhetsbegreppet*, Malmö-Lund.
Lund-Sørensen, A. (1970) 'Statssekretær – en god eller dårlig idé?' *Aarhuus Stiftstidende* 29 July.
Mackenzie, W. J. M. (1958) *Free Elections*, London: Allen & Unwin.
Madeley, John T. S. (1977) 'Scandinavian Christian Democracy: Throwback or Portent?', *European Journal of Political Research*, vol. 5, pp. 267–86.
Madeley, John T. S. (1979) 'Church and State, Religion and Political Community: The Case of Norway', paper at Political Studies Association, Scandinavian Politics Group Conference, London School of

Economics and Political Science.

Magnússon, S. A. (1977) *Northern Sphinx*, London: Hurst.

Marquard, Arne (ed.) (1979) *Folketingsårbog 1978–79*, Copenhagen: Schultz Forlag, for Folketingets Praesidium.

Martinussen, W. (1977) *The Distant Democracy. Social Inequality, Political Resources and Political Influence in Norway*, London: Wiley.

Matheson, D., and Sänkiaho, R., (1975) 'The Split in the Finnish Rural Party: Populism in Decline in Finland', *Scandinavian Political Studies* vol. 10, pp. 217–23.

Maude, George (1976) *The Finnish Dilemma*, London: Oxford University Press.

Meijer, H. (1969) 'Bureaucracy and Policy Formulation in Sweden', *Scandinavian Political Studies*, vol. 4, pp. 103–16.

Mellors, Colin (1978) *The British MP*, Farnborough: Saxon House.

Mezey, Michael L. (1979) *Comparative Legislatures*, Durham, N. Carolina: Duke University Press.

Miljan, Toivo (1977) *The Reluctant Europeans*, London: Hurst.

Miller, K. E. (1968) *Government and Politics in Denmark*, Boston: Houghton Mifflin.

Molin, B. (1966) 'Swedish Party Politics: A Case Study', *Scandinavian Political Studies*, vol. 1, pp. 45–58.

Molin, B., Månsson and Strömberg (1969) *Offentlig förvaltning. Stats – och kommunalförvaltningens struktur och funktioner*, Stockholm: Bonniers.

Monrad, J. H. (1970) *Et land bygges op. Venstre i 100 år*, vol. 2, Copenhagen.

Nordal, Jóhannes, and Kristinsson, Valdimar (eds.) (1975) *Iceland 874–1974*, Reykjavík: Central Bank of Iceland.

*Nordisk Kontakt* (periodical), Stockholm: Nordic Council.

Nousiainen, Jaakko (1968) 'Research on the Finnish Communism', *Scandinavian Political Studies*, vol. 3, pp. 243–52.

Nousiainen, Jaakko (1971) *The Finnish Political System*, Cambridge, Mass.: Harvard University Press.

Nousiainen, Jaakko (1977) 'Näkökohtia eduskunnan asemasta ja päätöksenteko-järjestelmästä,' *Politiikka* vol. 2, pp. 113–31.

Nuechterlein, D. E. (1961) *Iceland, Reluctant Ally*, Ithaca, NY: Cornell University Press.

Ørvik, N. (1967) 'Integration – For Whom, Against Whom?', *Co-operation and Conflict*, vol. 2, pp. 54–9.

Ørvik, Nils (1974) 'Nordic Co-operation and High Politics', *International Organization*, vol. 28, no. 1, pp. 61–88.

Panitch, L. (1976) *Social Democracy and Industrial Militancy*, Cambridge: Cambridge University Press.

Pedersen, M. N. (1967) 'Conflict and Consensus in the Danish Folketing,

1945–65', *Scandinavian Political Studies*, vol. 2, pp. 143–66.
Pedersen, Mogens N. (1969) *Lawyers in Politics: The Deviant Case of the Danish Folketing*, conference paper, University of Iowa.
Pedersen, Mogens N. (1976) *Political Development and Elite Transformation in Denmark*, London: Sage.
Pedersen, Mogens N. (1977) 'The Personal Circulation of a Legislature: The Danish Folketing 1849–1968. In William O. Aydelotte (ed.) *The History of Parliamentary Behavior*, Princeton, NJ: Princeton University Press.
Pesonen, P. (1968) *An Election in Finland*, New Haven and London: Yale University Press.
Pesonen, Pertti (1974) 'Finland: Party Support in a Fragmented System'. In R. Rose (ed.) *Electoral Behaviour: A Comparative Handbook*, New York: Free Press.
Pesonen, P., and Sänkiaho, R. (1979) *Kansalaiset ja kansanvalta*, Juva: Söderström.
Petersen, Niels (1973) 'Oversigt over centraladministrationens udvikling siden 1848'. In Jørgen Nue Møller (ed.) *Den offentlige forvaltning i Danmark*, Nyt fra samfundsvidenskaberne No. 33 (Copenhagen).
Petersson, O. (1977), *Valundersökningar Rapport 2, Väljärna och valet 1976* Stockholm: Statistiska centralbyrån.
Petersson, O., and Valen, H. (1979) 'Political Cleavages in Sweden and Norway', *Scandinavian Political Studies*, vol. 2 (n.s.), no. 4, pp. 313–31.
Polsby, N. W. (1968) 'The Institutionalization of the US House of Representatives', *American Political Science Review*, vol. 62, pp. 144–68.
Popperwell, Ronald G. (1972) *Norway*, New York and Washington: Praeger Publishers.
Puntila, L. A. (1975) *The Political History of Finland 1809–1966*, London: Heinemann.
Putnam, Robert D. (1976) *The Comparative Study of Political Elites*, Englewood Cliffs, NJ: Prentice-Hall.
Rantala, Onni (1967) 'The Political Regions of Finland', *Scandinavian Political Studies* vol. 2, pp. 117–40.
Rasila,Viljo (1966) 'Vuoden 1914 viljatulliasetus', *Historiallinen Arkisto*, vol. 60, pp. 278–400.
Rasmussen, Erik, and Skovmand, Roar (1955) *Det radikale Venstre 1905–1955*, Copenhagen.
Rohde, Peter P. (1973) 'The Communist Party of Norway'. In A. F. Upton (ed.) *The Communist Parties of Scandinavia and Finland*, London: Weidenfeld & Nicolson.
Rokkan, S. (1966) 'Norway: Numerical Democracy and Corporate Pluralism', in R. A. Dahl (ed.) *Political Oppositions in Western*

## Select Bibliography

*Democracies*, New Haven and London: Yale University Press.
Rokkan, S. (1968) 'Elections: Electoral Systems'. In D. L. Sills (ed.) *International Encyclopedia of the Social Sciences*, vol. 5, New York: Macmillan and Free Press.
Rose, R. (ed.) (1974) *Political Behaviour*, New York: Free Press; London: Collier-Macmillan.
Rose, R. (1979) 'Ungovernability: Is there Fire Behind the Smoke?' *Political Studies*, vol. 27, no. 3, pp. 351—70.
Rowat, D. C. (ed.) (1965) *The Ombudsman: Citizen's Defender*, London: Allen & Unwin.
Rudholm, Sten (1965) 'Sweden's Guardians of the Law: The Chancellor of Justice'. In D. C. Rowat (ed.) *The Ombudsman: Citizen's Defender*, London: Allen & Unwin.
Rustow, W. A. (1955) *The Politics of Compromise*, Princeton: Princeton University Press.
Salervo, Olavi (1976) 'Eduskunnan valiokuntalaitoksen kehittämisestä', *Politiikka*, vol. 2, pp. 105—18.
Särlvik, B. (1970) 'Voting Behaviour in Shifting "Election Winds" ' *Scandinavian Political Studies*, vol 5, pp. 241—83.
Särlvik, Bo (1974) 'Sweden: The Social Bases of the Parties in a Developmental Perspective'. In R. Rose, (ed.) *Electoral Behaviour: A Comparative Handbook*, New York: Free Press.
Sartori, Giovanni (1976) *Parties and Party Systems*, Cambridge: Cambridge University Press.
Scase, Richard (1977) 'Social Democracy in Sweden'. In W. E. Paterson and A. H. Thomas (eds.) *Social Democratic Parties in Western Europe*, London: Croom Helm.
Schwerin, D. S. (1980) 'Norwegian and Danish Incomes Policy and European Monetary Integration', *West European Politics*, vol. 3, no. 3, pp. 388—405.
Scott, F. R. (1977) *Sweden, the Nation's History*, Minneapolis: University of Minnesota Press.
Sharpe, L. J. (1978) 'Is There a Fiscal Crisis in West European Local Government?', Political Studies Association Annual Conference Paper.
Smith, Gordon (1976) *Politics in Western Europe*, London: Heinemann.
Smith, Gordon (1979) 'Western European Party Systems: on the Trail of a Typology', *West European Politics*, vol. 2, no. 1, pp. 128—44.
Sørensen, Magnus (ed.) (1968) *Folketinget 1968*, Copenhagen: Schultz.
SOU: Statens Offentliga Utredningar (Swedish State Papers)
    1958, 29:  research by Carl-Gunnar Janson on effects of changes to the electoral system
    1965, 54:  Författningsfrågan och det kommunala sambandet (Constitutional reform proposals and the local government connection)

1975, 41: Local Government Democracy

Sparring, Å. (1973) 'The Communist Party of Sweden'. In Upton, A. F. (ed.) *The Communist Parties of Scandinavia and Finland*, London: Weidenfeld & Nicolson.

Stacey, Frank (1978) *Ombudsmen Compared*, Oxford: Clarendon Press.

Steiner, Kurt (1972) *Politics in Austria*, Boston: Little, Brown.

Stjernqvist, Nils (1966) *Samhälle och riksdag*, vol. 4, *Riksdagens arbete och arbetsformer*, Stockholm: Almqvist & Wiksell.

*Stortinget 1969–73* (1972) Oslo: Universitetsforlaget.

*Stortinget 1977–81* (1978) Oslo: Universitetsforlaget.

Sundelius, Bengt (1980) 'Coping with Transnationalism in Northern Europe', *West European Politics*, vol. 3, no. 2, pp. 219–29.

Svalastoga, K. (1959) *Prestige, Class and Mobility*. Copenhagen.

Svensson, S. (1970) *Enkammarriksdag*, Stockholm: Almqvist and Wiskell.

*Svensk författningssamling* (1979) No. 932–6, Stockholm: Norstedt.

Tannahill, R. Neal (1978) *The Communist Parties of Western Europe*, London: Greenwood Press.

Thomas, Alastair H. (1973) *Parliamentary Parties in Denmark, 1945–1972*, Occasional Paper 13, Strathclyde University.

Thomas, Alastair H. (1975) 'Danish Social Democracy and the European Community', *Journal of Common Market Studies*, vol. 13, no. 4, pp. 454–68.

Thomas, Alastair H. (1977) 'Social Democracy in Denmark'. In W. E. Paterson and A. H. Thomas (eds.) *Social Democratic Parties in Western Europe*, London: Croom Helm.

Tilton, Timothy A. (1979) 'The Swedish Road to Socialism: Ernst Wigforss and the Ideological Foundations of Swedish Social Democracy', *American Political Science Review*, vol. 73, no. 4, pp. 505–20.

Tomasson, R. F. (1970) *Sweden: Prototype of Modern Society*, New York: Random House.

Torgersen, U. (1962) 'The Trend Towards Political Consensus: the Case of Norway', *Acta Sociologica*, vol. 6, pp. 159–72.

Törnudd, K. (1968) *The Electoral System of Finland*, London: Evelyn.

Torstendahl, Rolf (1969) 'Mellan nykonservatism och liberalism. Idébrytningar inom höger och bondepartierna 1918–1934', *Studia Historica Upsaliensia* No. 29.

Ulstein, E. (1971) *Nordic Security*, Adelphi Papers, No. 81, London: International Institute of Strategic Studies.

Väänanen, Yrjö (1980) Suomi pohjoismaisessa yhteisössä, In Juhani Suomi (ed.) *Näkökulmia Suomen turvallisuuspolitiikkaan 1980 – luvalla*, Helsinki: Otava.

Valen, H. and Katz, D. (1964) *Political Parties in Norway*, London: Tavistock.
Valen, H. and Rokkan, S. (1974) 'Conflict Structure and Mass Politics in a European Periphery'. In R. Rose (ed.) *Electoral Behaviour: A Comparative Handbook*, New York: Free Press.
Valen, Henry (1978) 'The Storting Election of 1977: Realignment or Return to Normalcy?' *Scandinavian Political Studies*, vol. 1 (n.s.), no. 2, pp. 83–107.
Vanhanen, Tatu (1978) 'Keskustapuolueen kannatuspohja vielä yksipuolinen', *Suomenmaa*, 24 April, p. 16.
Vedung, E. (1979), 'Kärnkraften och regeringen Fälldins fall', *Skrifter utgivna av statsvetenskapliga föreningen i Uppsala*, No. 85, Uppsala: Rabén & Sjögren.
Verney, D. V. (1957) *Parliamentary Reform in Sweden 1866–1921*, London: Oxford University Press.
Vilhjalmson, Thor (1973) 'Forholdet mellem embedsmænd og politikere i et lille samfund', *Nordisk Administrativt Tidsskrift*, vol. 54, nos. 3–4, pp. 161–99.
Vinde, Pierre (1971) *Swedish Government Administration: An Introduction*, Stockholm: Bokförlaget Prisma/The Swedish Institute.
Virolainen, Johannes (1965) *Pääministerinä Suomessa*, Helsinki: Kirjayhtymä.
Wennergren, Bertil (1971) 'Civic Information – Administrative Publicity', *Administration* (Dublin), vol. 19, no. 1, pp. 61–71.
Wiklund, C. and Sundelius, B. (1979) 'Nordic Cooperation in the 1970s: Trends and Patterns', *Scandinavian Political Studies*, vol. 2 (n.s.), no. 2, pp. 99–120.
Worre, Torben (1980) 'Class Politics and Class Voting in the Scandinavian Countries', *Scandinavian Political Studies*, vol. 3 (n.s.), no. 4, pp. 299–320.
Yearbook of Nordic Statistics 1980 (1981) Vol. 19, Stockholm: Nordic Council and Nordic Statistical Secretariat, and similar volumes for other years.

# Index

*Note*: In Scandinavia the letters Æ or Ä, Ø or Ö and Å come at the end of the alphabet. For the convenience of English readers, Æ, Ä and Å have been placed with A, and Ø or Ö have been placed with O.

abortion: 25, 67, 188, 217
accountability, 128–9, 138
Ådalen (Sweden) (1931), 16
administration, central, 110, 114
adversary politics: policy-making 190, 191; political systems, 185; in Britain, 166
Afghanistan, 194, 208
Agrarian Liberals, *see* Liberals
Agrarian parties, 17, 18–19, 30, 33, 38–42; co-operation between, 70–1; in Norway and Sweden, 181; *see also* Farmers' Parties; Centre Parties
Agrarian Party:
  Finland (*Maalaisliitto*), 40, 54, 55; emergence (1906), 17; support, 60; *see* Centre Party
  Norway, support, 41; *see* Centre Party
  Sweden (*Bondeförbund*), 40, 41
Agrarianism, decline of, 59, 69
agricultural co-operatives, 15
Agricultural Producers, Confederation of, (*Maataloustouttajain Keskusliitto*) (Finland), 170
airspace, Swedish, 210
Åland Islands, 1, 4, 14
Alkio, Santeri, 41
Alta/Kautokeino hydro scheme, 15, 213
alternation of power, 97
*Althing*, *see* Parliament (Iceland)

Alto, Arvo, Finnish Minister, 167
Anders Lange's Party, Norway, 90, 95, 97
Andrae, C. C. G., Danish mathematician, 144
anti-system parties (Sartori), 10–12, 13, 43, 97
apartheid and immigration, 209
arbitration, compulsory, 26
arms depots, US, in Norway, 194, 210; in Denmark, 211
Auken, Svend, Danish Minister of Labour, 165

Baltic Straits, 193
Barents Sea, 210
Baunsgaard, Hilmar, Danish Radical Liberal Prime Minister, 92, 163
Benelux countries, 2
bicameralism, 121; *see also* unicameralism, modified
Bills, documentation for, 128
blue-collar vote, *see* working-class
Brundtland, Dr Gro Harlem, Norwegian Labour Prime Minister, 20, 24, 217
Bryn, Olav, 66
*Bund der Landwirte*, Germany, 34
by-elections, obviated by PR, 149

Cabinet government, 106
Cabinets: caretaker, 108; in Finland, 55, 166, 171; size, 108

232

## Index

Cajander, A. K., Finnish Prime Minister (1937–9), 13
canvassing, electoral; no tradition of, 125
Carl XVI Gustaf, King of Sweden, 104
catch-all parties, 20
centre, political, eroded, 216
Centre Democrats (Denmark), 15, 83, 85, 95, 149, 152, 163, 215; MPs, 153
centre parties, 30, 91; Agrarian parties changed name to, 17, 69; and electoral system, 148
Centre Party:
 Finland (*Keskustapuolue, Centerpartiet*), 18, 54–5, 93, 166, 168, 171, 217; in government, 71; regional support, 72
 Norway (*Senterpartiet*), 18, 95, 154, 215; regional support, 72; against EEC membership, 74, 188
 Sweden (*Centerpartiet*), 18, 25, 91, 93, 98, 156, 216, 217; as catch-all party, 73; support for, 74–5; policies, 74; opposed to nuclear power, 187; in coalition, 187; tax reforms, 189; *see also* Fälldin, T.
Chancellor of Justice, 138–9
Chief Legal Officer (*rättschef*), 114
Christian Democratic Union:
 Sweden (*Kristen demokratisk Samling*), 67, 68, 216; West Germany, 30
Christian People's parties, 59, 67, 89
Christian People's Party:
 Denmark (*Kristelig Folkeparti*), 67, 152, 163; MPs, 153, 155
 Norway (*Kristelig Folkeparti*), 30, 31, 50, 64–6, 68, 89; support, 66; MPs, 154–5; and EEC, 188; and abortion, 217
Christian Workers' Party (Finland), 36, 65

Christophersen, Henning, Danish Liberal leader, 215
Church–State relations, 48, 65; *see also* Evangelical Lutheran Church
civic indifference, 96
civil servants, 115–17
Civil War, Finnish, 12, 41, 43
class party: Danish Liberals as, 73
class voting: decline of, 98; *see also* middle, working class
cleavages: political, 11, 33; social, 13; urban–rural, 17; cross-cutting, 36, 185; moral and cultural, 188
coalescent elite behaviour (Lijphart), 185, 187
coalition-building, 11, 25; pivotal parties, 18, 71; Finnish Centre Party as hinge group, 71 (*and see* Radical Liberals in Denmark); role of Finnish President in, 218
coalition governments: table, 174–9
 Denmark: of bourgeois parties, 73; Liberal–Radical–Conservative, 92, 163; Justice Party in, 89; Liberal–Conservative, 119; Social Democrat–Liberal, 163, 164; formation of, 165
 Finland, 60, 167, 168
 Iceland: Progressive-Social Democratic (1934–9), 54; Progressive–Independence, 91; Progressive–People's Alliance, 161; support for, 173
 Norway, 183–4, 188
 Sweden: Liberals and Social Democratic (1917–20), 50–1; Social Democratic–Agrarian, 183 (*and see* Red–Green alliance); non-socialist, 184, 189; Fälldin, T., 187
Coalition, in West Germany, 191
Coalition Party (Finland), *see* Conservatives, Finnish

## Index

coalitions: non-socialist, 64, 217;
  support relationships in
  legislature, 109, 217; liaison
  with party groups, 129–30;
  at local level, 150
Cod Wars, Iceland, 173
co-determination law, 24
collective bargaining, 21, 24; in
  Denmark, 162, 164; voluntary
  agreements, 181
Comecon, Finnish commercial
  agreement with, 198
Comintern, 9, 44, 45, 46
Commissions of Inquiry, 28, 128,
  182, 186–7
Common Labour Treaty, 197
Common Market, see European
  Economic Community;
  Danish parliamentary
  committee on, 134–5
Communist Left (Sweden)
  (*Vänsterpartiet
  kommunisterna*): opposition
  to nuclear power, 187
Communist Party:
  Denmark (*Danmarks
  kommunistiske Parti*), 46, 83;
  MPs, 153
  Finland (part of Finnish
  People's Democratic League),
  (*Suomen Kansan
  Demokraattinen Liitto*,
  SKDL), 13, 27, 33, 43, 44,
  59, 60, 84, 91, 97, 169, 218;
  proscribed in 1930, 12;
  legalised in 1944, 59; support,
  60, 61, 62; factions in, 167;
  in government, 167, 168
  Iceland, 43, 44, 53, 54
  Italy, 167
  Norway, in Socialist Electoral
  Alliance, 95
  Soviet Union, 167
  Sweden (*Sveriges
  kommunistiska Parti*), 46
community systems (Eckstein), 9
comprehensive state educational
  system, 22

concertation, 11, 98, 160; by
  Commissions of Inquiry, 182
confidence, vote of, 107
conflict: parliamentary, in Finland,
  160; corporate, in Iceland,
  160; of producer and
  consumer, 181; axes of, 185
conflict resolution, 11; in Norway
  and Sweden, 180; in industrial
  relations, 188
conscription, 202
consensual decision-making, in
  Sweden, 127; and policy,
  182
consensus, 51, 56, Ch. 5; in
  political society, 96;
  constitution as a force for,
  103; and open government,
  143; inter-elite, 167, 169,
  203, 208; in economic crisis,
  163, 184, 198; as concertation
  of public policy, 165–6; in
  Finland, 166–72; Finnish
  President's role, 170; receding
  in Norway and Sweden, 190;
  on foreign and defence policy,
  203; at Nordic regional level,
  192, 194; 'of the lowest
  common denominator', 195
consensus systems (Lijphart), 9
Conservative Parties, 17, 48, 91;
  see also Independence Party
  (Iceland)
Conservative Party, British, 30, 48
Conservative People's Party
  (Denmark) (*Det konservative
  Folkesparti*), 23, 33, 46–7,
  160, 163, 200, 215; MPs, 153
Conservatives:
  Finland (Coalition Party,
  *Kansallinen Kokoomus*), 13,
  23, 46, 47, 48, 54–5, 89, 168,
  169, 171, 217; occupational
  support, 60; regional support,
  61; excluded from government, 167, 218
  Norway (*Høyre*, the Right), 23,
  95, 154, 215; and EEC, 188;

and US arms depots, 194; in government, 217
Sweden (*Moderata Samlingspartiet*, Moderate Unity Party), 76, 156, 157, 217; changed name from *Högerpartiet* in 1969, 23; displaced as leading non-socialist party, 84; support for nuclear power, 187; in coalition, 187; tax reform proposals, 189
Constitutional People's Party (Finland), 85, 89, 94
Constitutions: change, 10; and consensual policy-making, 103; Danish, 101, 119; Finnish, 4, 102; amendment, 103; dispensation from, 102; Icelandic, 102, 103; Swedish reform of, 101; amendment, 104
Continuation War (Finland), 13
co-operation: between parties, 164, 204; regional, 205
co-operative: credit associations, Denmark, 42; farming, 37
corporate pluralism, 181, 187
corporate representation, 26, 181
Council of State, 106, 115
Customs Union, Nordic, 194, 195, 199, 206; *see also* Nordek
Czechoslovakia, 168, 201, 208

decentralization, 93, 110, 118; Swedish Centre Party, 76
decolonization, 208
defence: and security policy, 6; proposed Scandinavian Defence Pact (1948–9), 6, 7, 201, 202, 206; expenditure, 50, 202, 211
deference vote, not a feature of Scandinavian voting, 19
de Gaulle, Charles, 200
Depression, the Great, 51, 52, 54, 55
détente initiatives, Nordic, 192

diffusion of institutions: 64, 66–7; of Ombudsman, 142
directorates, 110, 112, 114
disarmament: security and, Independent Commission, 195; European Conference on, 207; proposed programme for Europe, 211
dissolution of Parliament, 126

economists, in civil service, 116
economy: and democracy, 24, 25; mixed, 21; modernization, 62; management, in Denmark, 161; package deals, 163–4; planning, Nordic, 202; public or private control of, 185; *see also* nationalization
Edén, Nils, Swedish Liberal, 50
*Eduskunta. See* Parliament
*Efri Deild*, *see* Parliament (Iceland)
egalitarianism, and agrarian radicalism, 19
Ehnrooth, Georg, 85
Eidsvoll, 101
Eldjarn, Professor Kristjan, 103
elections: interval between, 122; turnout, 122; results, 1969–81 (tables), 86–8; publication of results, 155; (1981), 215; electoral cartels prohibited in Norway, 146; electoral alliances, 147; *see also* suffrage reform
electoral systems, 143–51; proportional (PR), 12, 16, 17, 159; Norwegian, 45; thresholds, 89, 146; redistribution of seats, 146;
electoral volatility, 85–98
elite accommodation, 52, 56, 166
Employers' Federation: Danish, *Dansk Arbejdsgiverforening*, 165; Swedish, *Svenska arbetsgivareföreningen, SAF*, 21, 27
Enabling Act, 1973, (Finland), 170
environment: protection of, 18,

25, 80; Nordic Convention on Protection of (1974), 196
Environment Party (Sweden), 216
Erlander, Tage, Swedish Social Democratic Prime Minister, 79
Eurocommunism, 97, 167
European Economic Community (EEC), 91, 94; Danish membership of, 7, 95, 196, 197, 198, 200–1; possible Scandinavian membership, 83; free trade with Finland, 171; proposed Norwegian entry, 187, 199; Common Agricultural policy, 199–200; Britain and Ireland in, 200
European Free Trade Area (EFTA), 3, 195, 196, 198. *See also* Finn EFTA
European Parliament, 197
Evangelical Lutheran Church, 65, 67, 68
Evensen, Jens, Norwegian Trade Minister, 108
executive and parliament, 115
exports, 33, 37, 94, 96
extreme multi-party system, 13

factionalism, 91; in Finnish Labour Movement, 82; in Finnish Communist Party, 167; in union movement, 169
Faeroe Islands, 1, 14, 204
Fälldin, Thörbjorn, Swedish Prime Minister, 18, 76; non-socialist majority coalition, 194, 187; Centre–Liberal minority coalition, 189, 217; *see also* Centre Party (Sweden)
farm incomes, in Finland, 166
Farmers' Party:
 Denmark (*Bondepartiet*), 42
 Iceland (*Baendaflokkur*), 42
 Sweden (1915–21) (*Jordbrukarnas Riksförbund*), 41
Farmers' Union, Norwegian, 40
farmers, voting by, 98–9
Fascist parties, in Scandinavia, 53

federalism, not relevant, 120
Fenno–Soviet relations, 71–2, 91, 193, 206, 209, 218
Fenno–Soviet Treaty of Friendship, Co-operation and Mutual Assistance (1948), 196, 201–2, 203, 211; extended to 1995, 210
Finance Bill, in Finland, 169
Finance Committee, in *Althing*, 134; in *Eduskunta*, 135; in *Folketing*, 137
finance of political parties, 16
'Finlandization', defined, 94, 203
Finnbogadóttir, *see* Vigdis
FinnEFTA agreement, 196, 206
Finnish Christian League (*Suomen Kristillinen Liitto*), 67, 68
Finnish Party (*Suomalainen Puolue*), 35
Finnish People's Democratic League, *see* Communist Party
Folk High Schools, Denmark, 5, 15
*Folketing*, *see* Parliament
*Folkpartiet*, *see* Liberal Party
Foreign Affairs, Advisory Council on, in Swedish *Riksdag*, 203
fragmentation of party support, 89
Free Liberals (*Frisinnade Folkepartiet*), Sweden, 49
Freedom of the Press Act, 142

*Gemeinschaft/gesellschaft*, 41
George, Henry, American theorist, 30; single tax on land, 50
German Federal Republic, 19, 191
German minority in Denmark, 144
Glistrup, Mogens, Danish Progress Party leader, 90, 92, 93, 95, 96, 98, 163; panacea-peddling, 94; convicted, 215
Gothenburg, 198
governments: formation and influence of monarch on, 104; instability in Finland, 55; relation to non-government parties, 127; composition,

## Index

leadership and duration of in Scandinavia (table), 174–9; minority, single-party, 163
Grand Committee, Finnish, 121
Green International, 42, 200
Greenland, 1; and EEC, 14
Grundtvig, Bishop, 5; Grundtvigians, 65

Haakon VII, King of Norway, 102
Hammarskjöld, Dag, UN Secretary-General, 209
Hansen, H. C., Danish Foreign (later Prime) Minister, 194
Harpsund Democracy, 79
Harrisburg, nuclear accident, effect in Sweden, 187
Hartling, Poul, Danish Liberal Prime Minister, 73; small Cabinet, 108; UN High Commissioner for Refugees, 209
Haugians, Norway, 65
Hedtoft, Hans, Danish Prime Minister, 7, 174
Helsinki Conference on European Security and Co-operation (1975), 108, 207
House of Commons, UK, 123
House of Representatives, USA, 123, 157
Hurwitz, Professor Stephan, 141
hybrid presidential/parliamentary regime, 101

Iceland, union with Denmark, expired in 1944, 53
*IKL, see* Patriotic People's Movement
impeachment, 115
Imperial Preference, Britain's adoption of (1933), 42, 52
incomes policy, 21, 27, 28; in Denmark, 164; in Iceland, 180; indexation, 189
independence: of Finland (1917), 4; of Iceland, 4, 53
Independence Party (Iceland) (*Sjálfstaedisflokkurinn*), 19, 30, 33, 46, 53, 54, 64, 91, 161, 172, 173
industrial conflict, regulation of, 27, 160–2, 166; in Denmark, 161–3, 165; comparative figures for disputes (table), 162
industrial democracy: advocated by Swedish Centre Party, 76; by Social Democrats, 79
industrialization, 40, 58, 70, 91; weak impact in Ireland, 63
inflation, 94
integration, cobweb theory of (Andrén), 212; political 201, 204, 211, 212, defined, 212; regional, 198–9, 213
interest organizations: integration with administration, 110; contacts with legislators, 125; peak, 169; conflict of producer and consumer, 181; in Sweden, 184; on Swedish Commissions of Inquiry, 182, 187; *see also* Agricultural; Employers'; Farmers'; Labour; *LO*; *MTK*
interpellations, 128
Investment Bank, Nordic, 197–8

Jakobsen, Erhard, Danish Centre Democrat leader, 85, 158
Johnson, Gisle, 66
Jørgensen, Anker, Danish Prime Minister, 163, 165, 194, 216
Justice Party (*Retsforbundet*), Denmark; 30, 50; support for, 89; social origins of MPs, 153

Kalmar Union (1397–c. 1523), 3
*Kansallinen kokoomus, see* Conservatives (Finland)
Karjalainen, Ahti, Finnish Prime Minister, 168, 170
Kautsky, Karl, 38
Keflavik, US air base, 173, 203
Kekkonen, Urho, Finnish President (1956–81), 71, 72, 85, 94,

107, 167, 169, 171, 192, 194, 196, 197, 207, 210, 218
*Keskustapuolue, see* Centre Party
Khruschev, Nikita, 204
King's Bay, Spitzbergen, 107
Koivisto, Mauno, 23, 170; Prime Minister, 167; Finnish President (1982– ), 218
Kola peninsula, 203, 210
Korpilampi, spirit of, 169
Labour: migrant, 37; mobility in Sweden, 184; Turkish guest-workers, 209, 213
Labour Court, 26; in Iceland, 172
Labour Federation, Finnish (*SAJ*), (*SAK*), 170; Icelandic, 64, 172, 180
Labour Market Board, Sweden, 184
Labour-Market Committee, in *Folketing*, 165
labour movements, 45; *see also LO*
Labour Organization, the Central Finnish (*Suomen Ammattijärjestö*, SAJ), 56
Labour Party (Norwegian) (*Høyre*), 12, 37, 65, 76, 90, 95, 152, 185; policies, 79, 183; MPs, 154–5; parliamentary majority of, 183; and EEC, 188; 1981 election and, 215
Laestadians, 65
*Lagting, see* Parliament
land reform, 41
*Landstinget*, Danish Upper House before 1953, 47
Lange, Anders, 89–90, 98; *see also* Progress Party (Norway)
language: Danish influence on Norwegian, 3; Swedish used in Finland, 4; Icelandic, 5; Finnish, 71; Norwegian, as a political issue, 34
Lapps, 14–15, 213
Lapua Movement, 12, 55–6
Larsen, Aksel, Danish socialist, 83
Larsson, Allan, 186

lawyers, in civil service, 116
Lebanon, Nordic attitude to, 208
Left: broad, in Finland, 167
Communists, in Sweden (*Vänsterpartiet kommunisterna*), 91, 194
radical, in Finland, 168
Socialists, in Denmark, 83; MPs, 153
Socialists, Norway, MPs, 154
Social Democratic Party, in Sweden (*Sveriges socialdemokratiska vänsterparti*), 46
Left (*Venstre*), transformed into Liberal Parties, 29, 46–51; in Norway, 34, 42; *see also* Liberal Parties
legislatures: unicameralism, 119–22; plenary sessions, 122–30; parliamentary committees, 130–8; reactive (Mezey), 122; preparation of legislation, 125; types of Bill in Finland, 126; *see also* Parliament; interpellations; qualified majorities; questions
legitimacy of regime, 10
Lenin, V. I., 43, 210
Liberal Centre(Denmark)(*Liberalt Centrum*), 73
Liberal International, 18
Liberal parties: decline, 84, 91; Liberalism, 48; *see also* Free Liberals (Sweden); Progressive Parties in Finland and Iceland; Radical Liberal Party (Denmark)
Liberal Party:
Denmark (*Venstre, Danmarks liberale parti*) (Agrarian Liberals), 33, 39, 42, 90, 91, 163, 165, 200; in government, with Social Democrats (1978–9), 18; with Radical Liberals and Conservatives, 92, 163; in minority govern-

ment, 73, 108; change of name, 72–3; support, 73; MPs, 153; *see also* Agrarian parties; Hartling, Poul; Liberal Centre
Norway (*Venstre*), 65, 95; MPs, 154; and EEC, 188
Sweden (*Folkpartiet*), 46, 50, 84, 156, 157, 186, 216; in coalition with Centre and Moderate parties, 187; and nuclear power, 187; coalition with Centre Party, 217
Lie, Trygve, UN Secretary-General, 209
Liinamaa I Stabilization Agreement, 169
Lindgrén, Astrid, 92
local government, reform of, 118
LO (*Landsorganisationen*), national confederation of trade unions in Denmark, Norway, Sweden: and Swedish state share in capital market, 22; relations with Labour Cabinet in Norway, 113; relations with Social Democrats in Denmark, 164, 165; in Sweden, on labour mobility, 184; worker funds in Sweden, 186; *see also* Labour Federation; Labour Organization

majority government, in Finland, 217; qualified majorities, 168
Margrethe II, Danish Queen, 104
Marshall Aid, 196, 197
Marthinussen, Karl, Norwegian pastor, 67
Mehr, Hjalmar, 186
Meidner, Rudolf, 186; *see also* worker funds
middle class: voting, 38, 93, 98–9; and Liberal voting in Denmark, 73; recruited by Swedish Centre Party, 75; 'old' and 'new', 81, Social Democratic voting, 78–9, 81
Middle East, Nordic policy, 208
migration, inter-Nordic, 197
'ministerial socialism', 38
ministers: joint portfolios, 112; assistant, 112; staffs, 113
ministries, growth of, 111, 112; titles and responsibilities, 113; table, 111
minorities, ethnic and religious, 14; German, in Denmark, 144; Lapps, 14–15, 213; Swedish-speaking, in Finland, 168; Turkish guestworkers, 209
minority governments:
  Denmark, 127
  Finland, 55, 168
  Norway, by Conservative Party, 188; stable, 217
  Sweden, period of, 159; (1981) 182; minority coalition, 189
Mitterrand, François, French President, 218
MKL, *see* Agricultural Producers, Confederation of, in Finland
Moderate Unity Party, *see* Conservatives (Sweden)
modernization, 29, 33, 65
monarchy, 7, 104
moral dimension in politics, 65; and cultural cleavage, 168; and international authority as an object of Nordic policy, 208–9
MTK (*Maataloustouttajain keskusliitto*), farming organization in Finland, 170
multinational companies, Swedish, 209
Myrdal, Alva, Swedish Social Democrat, 80, 195

Namibia, Nordic attitude, 208–9
National Coalition Party, *see* Conservatives (Finland)
nationalization; 21, 23, 24, 82, 183
national question, the, 35; in Finland, 41; in Iceland, 48

National Socialists, Danish: low vote for, 53
National Unity Movement (*Nasjonal Samling*), Norway, 53
NATO (North Atlantic Treaty Organization), 6, 7, 83, 94; and Iceland, 91, 96, 173; Denmark and Norway, 193, 201, 202, 203, 210; Swedish attitude, 212; Nordic countries and, 213; *see also* defence expenditure
neutrality, 201, 202, 203; Swedish, armed, 6, 202; Icelandic, 63; active, 207, 210; Finnish, 210
New International Economic Order, 208, 209
Nielsen, L. Nordskov, 141
non-socialist parties, 98–9, 144; lack of unity, 32; in Denmark, 163; *see also* individual parties in table, 31
Nordek, proposed Nordic Customs Union, 195, 196, 198, 199, 200, 202, 204, 206, 211
Norden Societies, 6, 213
Nordic Balance, 7, 193, 194, 201, 202, 211, 218
Nordic Council, 2, 5, 7, 193, 196, 197, 204–6; Council of Ministers, 204–5, 212; Permanent Committee of High Officials, 205; Budget Committee, 205; committees, 213
Nordsat, Nordic television satellite, 204, 213
*Norsk Landmansforbund, see* Norwegian Farmers' Union
North Cape, 193
Norway, union with Sweden (1814–1905), 102
nuclear-free zone, Nordic, proposed, 194, 196, 197, 204, 210, 218; European, proposed, 195
nuclear power: referendum in Sweden, 18; Swedish Centre Party and, 25; as issue, 187
nuclear weapons and foreign troops excluded from Danish or Norwegian territory, 210
Nygaardsvold, Johan, Norwegian Prime Minister, 52

occupations of MPs, 151–8
*Odelsting, see* Parliament
Ohlin, Bertil, Swedish Liberal, 84
Öhman, Berndt, 186
oil: price rises, effects in Iceland, 172; in Sweden, 189; reserves, 185; North Sea, 197, 199, 206
Olaf V, King of Norway, 104
ombudsman, 110, 112, 138–42
open government, 110, 142
opposition: concerted, not normal in Scandinavia, 164; parliamentary, in Finland, 168
'organization men': professional politicians, 156–7
Ottedahl, Lars, 65
Oxford Group movement, 66

Paasikivi, J. K., 94; Paasikivi–Kekkonen line, 218; *see also* Fenno–Soviet relations
pacificism, 42; in Liberal parties, 50
Palme, Olof, 190; President of Nordic Council, 194; Social Democratic leader, 195; UN mediator, 195, 197
Parliament:
Denmark (*Folketing*), 119, 121, 123; turnover of members, 157; Labour Market Committee in, 165
Faeroe Islands (*Lagting*), 14
Finland (*Eduskunta*), 121 and *passim*
Iceland (*Althing*), 119, 120, 121; modified unicameralism, *Efri Deild, Nethri Deild*, 120; committees in, 134

## Index

Norway (*Storting*), 2, 102; modified unicameralism in, *Odelsting, Lagting*, 102, 120, 134; committees in, 131
Sweden (*Riksdag*), Second Chamber, 156; turnover of members, 157; no majority, 159
West Germany (*Bundestag*), 123
parliamentarism, 48, 65, 106
Parliamentary Commissioner for Administration, British, 139–40
parliamentary government, 11, 15, 48, 65, 101, 102, 106, 115
Parliaments: unicameral, 119–30; modified unicameralism, 120; fixed-term, 123; opening of sessions, 123; dissolution of, 126; questions in, 128; interpellations, 129; party groups, 129; presidium in, 129; turnover of members, 157
committees in: 130–8 development of, 130; in Swedish *Riksdag*, 130, 182; in Australia, 130; specialization in, 131; independent right of initiative, 131; in Norwegian *Storting*, 131; table of, 132–3; in Danish *Folketing*, 134; functions of, 135
occupational composition of, in Denmark, 152–3; in Norway, 152, 154–5; in Sweden, 155–7
participation in elections, 122, 151
parties: catch-all, 69–70, 73; factionalism, 49, 50, 83, 85; with low governing eligibility, 97; discipline, 129; youth organizations of, 151; in government (table), 174–9; non-socialist, in Norway, 185
party systems: Scandinavian bipartism, 29, 34, 49, 95;
tripartism (Duverger), 35; Scandinavian five-party, 29, 30, 31, 33, 48, 49; table, 31; multi-party, 16, 144; 'extreme multipartism' (Sartori), and Finland, 54; heightened multi-partism, 85; cleavage-dominant, 57; convergent, 56; frozen (Rokkan), 58; influence of electoral system on, 148; instability, 91; and stable one-party government, 180
Patriotic People's Movement (*Isänmaallinen Kansan Liike*, IKL), in Finland, 12, 13, 30, 56
Pekkala, Mauno, Finnish radical left Prime Minister, 13, 60
pensions, supplementary scheme, in Sweden, 183
People's Alliance, Iceland, 32, 85, 91, 96, 97, 172–3, 180; changed name from United Socialist Party, 63
People's Democratic League (Finland), 33–4, 167
People's Movement against the Common Market (Norway), 94, 188
People's Party (Sweden) *see* Liberal Party
People's Unity Party (Finland), 85, 89, 90, 149
Permanent Secretary (*Expeditionschef*), 114
Petersen, K. Helveg, Danish Minister, 135
Petri, Carl Axel, 108
polarized pluralism, 55, 166
policy formation, 114; style, in Sweden, 182
political culture: Finland, 62; and proportionality, 149–50
political mobilization, 36, 151
political polarization, 24
Popular Front Coalition (Iceland), 44

population, 1
populism, 89–90, 94
Porkkala naval base, 196, 204
presidency; powers of, 103, 106–7
  election, 149
Prime Ministers, powers of, 108–9;
  party and periods of office
  (table), 174–9
professionalization of politics, 151
Progress Party:
  Denmark (*Fremskridtspartiet*),
  12, 33, 73, 89–90, 97, 98,
  149, 163, 166, 215, 216; MPs,
  152–3; excluded from inter-
  elite consensus, 203; *see also*
  Glistrup, Mogens
  Norway, 89–90, 215
Progressive Party:
  Finland (liberals), *Kansallinen
  Edistypuolue*, 46, 50, 54, 55
  Iceland (*Framsóknarflokkur*),
  39, 40, 42, 53, 54, 73, 91;
  pivotal, 18; attitude on US
  base and NATO, 173
Prohibition: Norway (1919–26),
  48, 49, 65, 66, 71; referendum
  on, 105; in Sweden, 49
proportionality, influence on
  political culture, 149
*Proporz* principle, 150
public administration, 110

qualified majorities (Finland), 168
questions, parliamentary, 128
Quisling, Vidkun, 12, 53

race relations, in Britain, 166, 190
Radical Democrats (Finland), 44
radical left, 31, 43–6, 59, 61, 91,
  95, 96, 98; in Denmark, 83;
  in Iceland, 96; in Norway, 96;
  in Norway and Sweden, 185;
  parties of (table), 31
Radical Liberals (Denmark) (*Det
  radikale Venstre*), 20, 33, 42,
  50, 84, 91, 163, 165, 216; and
  EEC entry, 95; MPs, 153
radical right, 30, 89–90, 91, 93,
95, 98; parties of (table), 31
recession, 93; in Denmark, 164; in
  Sweden, 181
recruitment to politics, 151–8
Red–Green alliance, 12, 18, 20,
  52, 54, 56, 57, 70
referendum: Greenland's
  withdrawal from EEC, 14;
  turnout for, 16; on
  prohibition of alcohol in
  Sweden (1922), 49; and in
  Norway (1919), 50; on EEC
  membership, 83, 95, 105,
  199; Danish legislation on,
  104–5, 119; on legislation in
  Denmark, 121; on pensions in
  Sweden, 183
regional co-operation, Nordic, 195
Rehn, Gösta, 184
religiously based parties, 17, 67
*Remiss* procedure, 159, 182, 187
republicanism: 104; Finnish, 71;
  republics (Finland and
  Iceland), 7; *see also* presidency
retraining labour in Sweden, 184
Rhodesia, Smith regime opposed,
  208
Right (*Høyre*), *see* Conservatives
Right, as Conservative Parties, 29,
  46–51
Rösiö, P. J., 41
rural industries, 36
Rural Party (Finland), 62, 72, 85,
  89, 90, 93, 97
Rural Party (Sweden)
  (*Lantmannapartiet*), 34
rural proletariat, 37
Russian Empire, Finland in, 4, 43
Russian Revolution (1905), 145

Saab cars, 198
Saarinen, Finnish Communist, 13
*SAF, see* Employers' Federation
*SAJ, see* Labour Organization
*SAK, see* Labour Federation
Saltsjöbaden Agreement, 1938
  (Sweden), 26; spirit of, 169
Scandek, *see* Customs Union

# Index

Scandinavian Defence Union, 206
Secrecy Law, Swedish, 142
sectoral affiliation of MPs, 137–8
secularization, 66
Security and Disarmament,
  Independent Commission, 195
semi-presidential government, 105
seniority: of MPs, 157–8
*Senterpartiet, see* Centre Party
separation of powers, 101
September Package Deal
  (*Septemberforliget*), 163
Sinisalo, Taisto, 97, 168
*SKDL, see* Communist Party
Slesvig, 14; Slesvig-Holstein
  question, 144; Slesvig Party,
  Denmark, 149
Social class: and voting, 16, 17;
  *see also* middle class; working
  class
social democracy: 32, 36, 91;
  fissures in, 59; in Norway, 95;
  participationist strategy, 52
Social Democratic Opposition
  Party, Finnish, 84
Social Democratic Parties: 20, 27,
  35, 218; predominance in
  Scandinavia, 20–1, 51, 52,
  76, 180; electoral primacy,
  77; policies, 79; gradualism,
  79; fall in vote for, 80;
  distribution of support, 81;
  achievements, 82
Social Democratic Party
  Denmark (*Socialdemokratiet*),
  76, 90, 160, 163; formation,
  35; policies, 79; support, 81;
  and EEC entry, 95; MPs, 153,
  155; dual mandates
  prohibited, 158; dominance,
  160; government, 164;
  coalition formation, 165; and
  1981 election, 215, 216
  Finland, 12, 23, 44, 54–5, 76,
  166, 168; support, 60, 61,
  81–2; government, 167
  Iceland, 44, 53, 89, 96, 180; in
  government, 18; attitude to

US base and NATO, 173
  Norway (1921–27), 45; *see
  also* Labour Party (Norway)
  Sweden, 18, 76, 156, 157;
  displaced Liberals by 1914,
  37; support, 82; dominance,
  159; programme, 183; and
  private sector, 184; and
  worker funds, 186; and *LO*,
  186, 187; support for nuclear
  power, 187
West Germany (*SPD*): Erfurt
  programme (1891), 38; Bad
  Godesberg Programme, 79,
  191
Socialist Electoral Alliance
  (Norway), 83, 95
Socialist People's Party:
  Denmark, 83, 215, 216; against
  EEC entry, 95; MPs, 153
  Norway: against EEC, 83; in
  Socialist Electoral Alliance, 95
Socialist Workers' Party (Finland)
  (*Suomen sosialistinen
  Työväenpuolue*), 43, 44,
  54–6; banned in 1923, 12
social mobility, 156
Solzhenitsyn, Alexander, 209
Sorsa, Kalevi, Finnish Social
  Democrat Prime Minister, 23,
  159, 168, 182
Soviet Union, 16, 43, 45, 201; oil
  supplier to Iceland, 172; *see
  also* Fenno–Soviet relations
Spitzbergen, 107
Statoil, 185
*Statsråd*, 110
*Storting, see* Parliament (Norway)
Sträng, Gunnar, Swedish Finance
  Minister, 92
Strategic Arms Limitation Talks
  (SALT), 197, 207; SALT 2
  Treaty, 208
strikes, *see* industrial conflict
suffrage reform: universal, 38, 51,
  145; in Sweden, 46, 47
Svalbard, 107
Sverdrup, Jakob, 65

Svinhufvud, P. E., 56
Swedish People's Party (Finland), 4, 14, 30, 31, 84, 85, 89, 91, 216
Switzerland, 19

Tanner, Väinö, 55
tariff laws, Russian Empire, effect on Finnish economy, 43
taxation: reform of, 81, 189; of house owners, 83; as political issue, 91–2, 98; levels in Denmark, 163; sales, in Finland, 168
temperance, in Norway, 188; *see also* referendum
Third World: Nordic policy on, 192, 207–8; control of textile imports, 209
Thoroddsen, Gunnar, Icelandic Prime Minister, 161
Trade Union Confederation, *see LO*
Tranmael, Martin, 12, 45

Ulster, 166
Under-Secretary of State, 114
unemployment, 80, 94; in 1930s, 52; in Finland, 62; in Sweden, 189
unicameralism, modified, 120–1
Union, Metalworkers' (Sweden), 186
Union of Liberals and Leftists (Iceland), 85
unions: and labour movement, 20; small independent, 38; *see also* Labour Federation; labour movement; *LO*
United Left (*Det forenede Venstre*) (Denmark), 34
United Nations, 6, 201–2, global economic negotiations, 208; abolition of torture, 209; Nordic bloc voting, 209

United Socialist Party (Iceland), 43, 44, 53, 59; changed name to People's Alliance, 32, 63
USA: base, Keflavik (Iceland), 173; weapons stockpiles, in Norway, 194, 210; in Denmark, 211
Ustinov, Marshall, 210

Vennamo, Veikko, 72, 85, 90, 93, 94, 98
*Ventre, see* Liberals
*Verzuiling* ('pillarization'), 68
Vietnam, 208, 209
Vigdís Finnbogadóttir, Icelandic President, 103, 203
Virolainen, Johannes, 70
Volvo cars, 198, 206
voter: turnout, 10, 16; mobility, 20
voting: age lowered, 54; for personalities, 147

Warsaw Pact forces, in Baltic, 211
Weiss, Greta, Norwegian athlete, 208
Welfare: legislation, 22; reappraised, 80; high costs, 82; states, 91, 92; schemes, 110; benefits, 161, 163
Westerholm, Raino, 69
White-collar vote, *see* middle-class
Wikborg, Erling, 66
Winter War, Finland, 94
women, in Swedish *Riksdag*, 156
worker funds, 24; Sweden, 185, 186, 189–90; Denmark, 190
Workers' Councils, 45
Workers' Information Committee, Norwegian, 83
working class voting: 19, 35, 47, 98–9; Danish Liberals, 73; Swedish Centre Party, 75; Social Democratic, 77, 79, 80; conservatism, only in Iceland, 77; declining, 78; Danish Socialist People's Party, 83